THE COMPLETE BOOK OF

KITCHEN WISDOM

THE
COMPLETE
BOOK OF

KITCHEN
WISDOM

Frieda Arkin

Published in 1993 by

Galahad Books
A division of Budget Book Service, Inc.
386 Park Avenue South
New York, NY 10016

Galahad Books is a registered trademark of Budget Book Service, Inc.

Published by arrangement with Henry Holt & Company, Inc.

Library of Congress Catalog Card Number: 93-70578
ISBN: 0-88365-823-2

Designed by Hannah Lerner
Illustrations copyright © 1993 by Richard Gassmann

Printed in the United States of America

THE COMPLETE BOOK OF

KITCHEN WISDOM

ALMONDS: see NUTS

ANCHOVIES

If you find anchovies too salty for your taste, you can partially de-salt them by soaking in cool water for 10 minutes; remove and pat dry with a paper towel and then immerse them in olive oil again.

A thoroughly mashed anchovy or two added to any fish, chicken or meat sauce or gravy will really give a master touch.

Try mixing a few mashed anchovy fillets or 1 tablespoon of anchovy paste into 2 cups of ground veal mixture for patties.

APPETIZERS: see HORS D'OEUVRES

APPLES

See also *Pie.*

There are about 3 medium-sized apples to a pound.

3 pounds of apples will give you about 9 cups of slices, and 4 cups of applesauce.

More and more apples are coming to market coated with wax. This is unconscionable and no consumer should stand for it. You can hardly find a Granny Smith apple (one of the greatest in the world in my opinion) which hasn't been wax-dipped, and many Golden Delicious are now likewise being desecrated. Complain. Refuse to buy them.

For eating, buy Baldwin, Delicious, Golden Delicious, Granny Smith, McIntosh, Opalescent, Pippin, Stayman and Winesap apples. If the apples are red or yellow varieties, look for those which are green around the stem and flower ends—they're more tasty than the all red or completely golden ones.

Rub the cut surface of an apple with lemon juice to keep it from turning dark.

When you're making large quantities of peeled, cut apples, toss them in a mixture of 1 cup of cold water and 1 tablespoon of vinegar or lemon juice. Keeping the apples in this mixture until you're ready to use them will prevent them from discoloring.

For baking, the best apples are Rome Beauty, Jonathan and Northern Spy.

For pie, the best apples are Granny Smith, Gravenstein, Pippin, Greening and Northern Spy. McIntosh give a beautiful flavor to a pie but tend to become mushy during baking. If you prefer them, cut into thicker slices than you would the firmer varieties.

If you want baked apples that won't develop wrinkled skins, make a few short slits here and there in the apples before you set them in the oven, or use a potato peeler to pare a narrow band around the center of the apples.

For a treat, pour a little port wine over baked apples just before you take them from the oven.

APPLESAUCE

The best apples for applesauce are Baldwin, Cortland, Granny Smith, Gravenstein, Greening, Jonathan, McIntosh, Northern Spy and Golden Delicious. Some of these are more sour than others— taste the applesauce as it's cooking and if necessary add sugar or honey for sweetening. You don't usually need to increase tartness, unless you're using very sweet apples, but you can always add a little lemon juice to the sauce as it cooks.

If you like your applesauce to have a rosy pink color, wash and core red apples and cook them whole with their skins on. Purée them afterward, skins and all.

To make applesauce without cooking, simply drop pieces of peeled apple in the blender and add a little lemon juice. You can also add some sugar or honey if you like, or a touch of nutmeg or cinnamon.

APRICOTS

Apricots spoil rapidly once they're bruised. Be sure you handle them carefully when packing or unpacking them. Because they don't keep well—they quickly become mealy and tasteless—eat them within a couple of days of buying.

There are about 3 cups of dried apricots in 1 pound, which yields about 5 cups when cooked.

APRONS

The best apron is one that covers you to the neck. Also, big pockets are useful for that towel you're always wiping your hands on.

ARROWROOT: see THICKENERS

ARTICHOKES

Pick artichokes by weight, not size; the heavier, the better.

When you buy artichokes, choose firm, closed ones. Don't buy them if the leaves are loose, opened or yellowed; they're overmature, have little flavor, and are inclined to be woody.

There are two ways to avoid pricking your fingers when you handle artichokes: either wear rubber household gloves, or snip off the ends of the sharp pointed leaves with kitchen scissors.

It is not necessary to remove the choke of an artichoke before cooking, but if you want to, force open the center leaves from the top and cut out the fine leaves and the choke with a curved grapefruit knife.

Before you cook artichokes, let them stand for 1 hour in a large pot of cold water to which you've added 1 tablespoon of vinegar for every quart of water. This will prevent discoloration, and the flesh will be more succulent after cooking.

Don't cook artichokes in aluminum or iron pots; the artichokes will turn a grayish color.

Artichokes are much tastier if cooked in broth instead of water.

Add 1 thick slice of lemon for each artichoke when cooking in boiling water or any other liquid. Cover the pot and cook for 30 to 40 minutes.

An artichoke is done when the leaves come off easily with a slight pull.

You can remove the choke from an artichoke very easily after it has been cooked. Spread the top leaves apart gently, pull out the fine prickly leaves in the center and scoop out all the hairy choke with a spoon.

A nice way to serve cooked artichoke is to pour melted salted butter into the "cup" which is left after the choke is removed.

It's traditional to dip cooked artichoke leaves in melted butter, but you can use dozens of other dips: mayonnaise or sour cream mixtures, or other sauces you dream up.

For a perfect dish, dice cooked or canned artichoke hearts or bottoms into very small bits and add to an omelet.

ASPARAGUS

1 pound of asparagus will usually serve 3 people.

When you buy asparagus, choose spears with firm green stalks and hard-closed tips. Fresh asparagus have tightly closed tips. If the tips have begun to spread, the asparagus aren't fresh and have lost a lot of flavor. Avoid asparagus which is limp or yellowed.

Fresh young asparagus are delicious raw. Wash, and serve with a mayonnaise sauce. Or cut them up to use in salads.

Asparagus continues to age and toughen after it has been cut, so the sooner you cook it after buying, the better.

You can store asparagus in the refrigerator for a day or two, but no more. Before refrigerating, trim the stem ends slightly (you'll trim them further just before using) and wrap the cut ends in wet paper towels.

If you bend an asparagus stalk it will snap at the point where it becomes tender—just where you want it to.

It is possible to use much more of the asparagus spear than just the upper part that snaps off from the bottom, but you have to peel rather deeply to remove all the tough outer portion.

If asparagus stalks are thick, peel the lower portions up to the tenderer part with a potato peeler.

After you've prepared and are waiting to cook asparagus spears, stand them upright in the refrigerator in a small amount of cold water, covered with a plastic bag. You can also refresh limp asparagus in this way. Let it stand in the cold water for half an hour before cooking.

Asparagus can be cooked flat in a pan, but there's always the danger of overcooking the delicate tips. It's better to tie the spears together or wrap them in cheesecloth in bundles of 8 or 10, so that you can remove them easily from the water. Stand them in gently boiling water with the tips just above water level for about 12 minutes. You can invert a deep saucepan as a cover for the cooking asparagus. The tips will steam to softness while the tougher stems cook.

You can use a percolator coffeepot to cook asparagus vertically. Asparagus, like spaghetti, should be cooked *al dente.*

Open a can of asparagus from the bottom so that you can pull out the spears without breaking the tips.

You can cook frozen asparagus, and it can be delicious, but it will always be limp.

Before you serve asparagus, roll it quickly in a dishtowel to remove all the water, then serve with or without a sauce.

Parboil fresh asparagus tips and pat dry; then sauté lightly in butter and add to an omelet.

ASPICS AND GELATIN DISHES
Aspic is thickly jellied consommé.

To make aspic, use 1 tablespoon of gelatin for every 1¾ cups of liquid.

1 envelope of unflavored gelatin equals 1 tablespoonful.

Clarified stock for aspic must have every bit of fat removed.

For lining an aspic mold, use 1 tablespoon of gelatin for every 1½ cups of liquid.

Use a metal mold for aspic—it makes unmolding much easier. (To unmold partially immerse in very hot water for a few seconds.)

Rinse the inside of the mold with water or grease it very lightly with oil before you fill it with aspic. Either will make unmolding easier.

Here's how to line a mold with aspic: first, put the mold in the freezer. Then stir the liquid aspic over a bowl of cracked ice until it begins to get syrupy like the consistency of unbeaten egg white. Take the mold from the freezer and pour the syrupy aspic in to the top of the mold. Then turn the mold gently in the cracked ice so that all its outer surface gets evenly chilled. When you see that a layer of aspic has set (⅛ inch thick is enough) pour out the unset jelly. You can spoon out what you don't need from the center. Refrigerate the mold until the aspic lining has thoroughly set.

If you're in a hurry to fill it, put the lined mold in the freezer for 15 minutes. If you want a thicker layer of aspic at the bottom of the mold (this will be at the top when you've unmolded it), add a few more spoonfuls of syrupy aspic after the first layer has congealed, turning the mold to cover the bottom well, and return to the refrigerator until this too has set firmly.

If you refrigerate aspic to cool it for lining a mold (instead of setting it in cracked ice), remove frequently and stir, so that it thickens uniformly and not just on the surface.

Chill all solids thoroughly before setting in aspic. Then anchor each piece into the mold with a dab of thickened aspic, return the mold to the refrigerator and chill again thoroughly. This is a procedure which requires patience—build up the interior of the mold a little at a time, making sure that the aspic jelly remains at the right consistency and that you refrigerate each new addition until it's firm. (If you pour all the aspic jelly over the solids at one time, they'll float in it and won't stay in position.) If the jellied aspic thins, stir it over cracked ice again.

Fresh pineapple contains an enzyme which prevents gelatin from setting. If you want to use pineapple in a gelatin dish either use it canned or, for fresh pineapple, first parboil it for 5 minutes.

An aspic or gelatin dessert will set quickly if you put it in the freezer for about 25 minutes. Then remove and refrigerate. (You'd better use a timer for this so you won't forget it's in the freezer.)

If you're serving a gelatin dish as part of a buffet meal, make 2 or more small ones instead of 1 large dish. Keep the extras in the refrigerator, replacing as needed, so there'll always be a fresh firm one ready for serving.

Gelatin desserts will sparkle twice as much if served in glass dishes.

Try using a cup of yogurt in place of a cup of water in a gelatin dessert. It will be creamy and lightly tart, especially delicious with fruit. Dissolve the gelatin in whatever hot water you do use, then add yogurt without additional heating. Add the fruits last.

AVOCADO

An avocado is also called an alligator pear.

One medium-sized avocado, cubed, will give you about 1½ cups.

A ripe avocado is soft-fleshed under its leathery skin. Press the skin gently to test it. If it is for immediate use, don't get one whose skin is green and shiny—it should be well mottled with brown, or even all brown, as long as it doesn't feel mushy.

Dark or sunken spots, are usually a sign of decay.

Avocados don't ripen well in the refrigerator. If you have one that is too hard and green to use right away, it will ripen in a few days in the dark or in a brown paper bag in a warm place. Check it daily, though.

If you're buying an avocado for mashing, buy it a little riper than you ordinarily might. It should be very soft and its skin uniformly dark, not just dark in spots.

A good way to mash an avocado is to put it through a ricer. This gives it a uniform consistency.

The flesh of an avocado won't discolor if you pull the skin off by hand so as not to break the inner green surface. If you do cut into the surface, rub with lemon juice to keep it from darkening.

BACON

2 ounces of raw bacon will yield about ⅓ cup diced.

To freeze bacon, arrange the strips flat, slice by slice on waxed paper, then roll them up. Put them in a plastic bag, then in the freezer. To use, unroll and peel the slices off. There's no need to thaw bacon before you cook it.

Many dishes which call for bacon as an ingredient will taste much better if you parboil the bacon before cooking (simmer for about 5 minutes) to remove some of the strong smoky flavor and fat.

The best way to cook bacon is in a cold skillet, heated with a low flame. This will pull out more fat. (Pour the fat off from time to time.)

Bacon will lie flat in the cooking pan if you prick it thoroughly with a fork as it cooks. This also releases fat more quickly.

You can also cook bacon by baking it, especially if you have to make a lot at one time. Spread the slices on a rack over a shallow pan (to catch the fat) and cook it in the oven at 375° until it reaches the crispness you like. (It is not necessary to turn the bacon.)

Here's a way to have bacon cooked and ready when you want it. Fry the slices ahead of time, drain them, then wrap in waxed paper. Freeze in a plastic bag or other freezer container. When you want to use them—they thaw quickly—just place in a skillet and heat.

You won't have to use as much paper toweling to absorb fat from bacon strips if you put several thicknesses of newspaper under a sheet of paper toweling, and set bacon strips to drain on this.

You can also press cooked bacon, while it's still hot, between two paper towels or paper napkins to get rid of some unnecessary fat.

Don't pour bacon drippings down the drain as this will eventually clog it. Pour them into a coffee can with a plastic cover and when full, refrigerate or freeze to harden the fat, and discard with the garbage.

Bacon dices easily when frozen. Put several frozen slices on top of one another and then cut crosswise with a sharp knife or kitchen scissors.

For a delicious change, mix ⅓ cup of crumbled, crisp-cooked bacon into corn bread batter before you pour the batter in the baking pan.

A small amount of bacon fat is a tasty addition to corn bread or corn muffin batter.

BAGELS

An easy way to shape bagels from dough is to make a ball of dough just as you would when you make rolls. Then dip your index finger in flour and poke it through the middle of the ball. Whirl the dough around your finger until the opening is the size you want.

BAKING

See also *Energy Savers, Ovens.*

Save on fuel! Plan your meals so that when you're baking or roasting a main dish, you're also baking or roasting something else: a baked vegetable dish to be served with what you're roasting, or a cake or a pudding for dessert, or a dish to be served in the future which you can freeze.

In a top-of-stove baker you can bake a couple of potatoes or cook individual servings of frozen foods without having to heat a large oven. These economical bakers are made to fit over a burner, but be sure to get one with a snugly fitting top.

For proper circulation of heat in the oven, place cake or pie pans so they don't touch one another or the oven walls.

If you have to keep an oven-cooked dish warm but don't want it to become soggy, leave it in the oven and cover it with aluminum foil pierced in the middle to let out the steam.

With the possible exception of some breads, anything to be baked should be placed in a preheated oven.

BAKING POWDER

Baking powder keeps its potency for about a year and a half. Because it deteriorates with age, to test to see if it's still active, add ¼ teaspoon of baking powder to 1 tablespoon of water. If the baking powder bubbles, it's fresh enough to use.

Run a piece of Scotch tape across the top of an opened baking powder tin. Use this for leveling spoonfuls. (The cap will screw on over the tape.)

In most doughs and batters, use 1 teaspoon of baking powder to each cup of flour.

If you like an especially delicate crust on batter-fried foods, add from ½ to 1 teaspoon of baking powder to the frying batter.

If you find yourself without baking powder when you need it, 1 teaspoon of baking soda mixed with 2 teaspoons of cream of tartar can replace 1 tablespoon of baking powder for most uses.

BAKING SODA

Baking soda is affected by moisture in the air. Once you open a box, pour the contents into a jar with a tight screw cap. It will keep longer.

Like baking powder, baking soda's potency deteriorates with age. To test for freshness, add ¼ teaspoon of baking soda to 1 tablespoon of vinegar. If the baking soda bubbles, it's usable.

When using sour milk, sour cream or buttermilk in a recipe, or substituting any of them for sweet milk or cream, add ½ teaspoon of baking soda for each cup of liquid. Sift the soda with the dry ingredients. If the recipe calls for baking powder, deduct 1 teaspoon of baking powder, since baking soda mixed with the acid from sour milk, sour cream or buttermilk will produce leavening of its own.

15

Baking soda added to cake or cookie batters with sour milk or buttermilk in place of sweet milk gives a very tender product.

When using molasses in batter, use ¾ teaspoon of baking soda to each cup of molasses.

Don't use baking soda when cooking vegetables. It destroys vitamin C and also gives the vegetables a bitter taste.

BANANAS

One ripe medium-sized banana will give you ½ cup sliced and ⅓ cup mashed.

Buy bananas on the green side and let them ripen at home. They're one of the few fruits that improve after they've been picked green. The very yellow bananas in the stores have often been artificially ripened by gas. They don't taste as good as those that ripen naturally and slowly in your own kitchen.

There are about 3 bananas (unpeeled) to a pound.

Lemon juice will keep peeled bananas from darkening.

Storing and Freezing

Bananas *can* be stored in the refrigerator. The skins will darken, but the bananas themselves will stay firmer and fresher than if you keep them at room temperature.

Bananas can be frozen. Don't peel them. Pop them in the freezer until you want them. Then hold them under warm water for about 1 minute. They defrost quite quickly, but are best used when sliced into a fruit salad while they're still a little frozen.

Another way of freezing bananas is to mash them, add a little lemon juice to keep them white, and put in a covered container in the freezer (leave room for expansion). You can use them in baking any time you like.

You can also slice bananas, lay the slices out on a cookie sheet, and freeze. Store the frozen slices in a plastic bag. Use in banana pie, fruit salads, and for snacks.

Desserts and Other Delicacies

Fully ripe bananas—preferably those with brown spots on them—are the best to use for banana bread, milk shakes, etc. Such bananas are not only softer, but they also have more flavor.

You can put whole bananas, with their skins on, right on the grill the next time you have a cookout. Cook about 8 minutes, turning several times. They're wonderful.

To bake bananas, peel them, put them in a baking dish, brush with lime juice, and pour a little white wine mixed with honey over them. Dot with butter or margarine and bake at 400° F for 30 minutes, until they're lightly browned. Baste them now and then. What a dessert!

To make a banana layer cake, add an extra egg to regular white cake batter and 1½ cups of very ripe mashed banana. Also add ½ teaspoon of baking soda to the dry ingredients.

To make a lovely cake icing out of mashed bananas, add a little soft butter, lemon juice, cream, and some confectioners' sugar. Mix well.

You can also mash bananas into pancake batter to make banana fritters.

Here's a low calorie substitute for whipped cream that's thick and delicious: Whip an egg white until it's stiff, then whip in a ripe banana, one thick slice at a time. You don't even need to add sugar. A touch of vanilla extract, maybe, or some honey.

If you leave a banana in the freezer until it's semifrozen, it will have the consistency of sherbet. Peel it, put it in a dish, and, if your taste so inclines, dribble a little chocolate syrup over it when you serve it.

Quarter bananas lengthwise, sauté them in a little clarified butter and serve them as you would a vegetable course. Prepared this way, they also make an interesting garnish.

BARBECUING

Charcoal absorbs moisture readily. Store it in airtight plastic bags. It will ignite faster.

If rain forces you indoors, remember that most recipes for barbecuing chicken or meat on an outdoor spit are easily adapted to oven roasting. Cook in a low oven and baste often.

BASIL: see HERBS AND SPICES

BASTING
Pieces of suet or unrendered fat placed over a roasting bird or piece of meat automatically baste the bird or meat.

If you have the leafy ends of some celery stalks handy when you need to baste meat, chicken, or fish, use this "nature's brush" for your basting. You can then cut up the leaves and use them in gravy. A small bunch of parsley can be used for this, too. You won't have to wash a basting brush.

BATTER
See also *Blender, Cake, Pancakes.*

Batter containing flour will get thicker on standing. So if you mix a batter and don't use it right away, add a tiny bit of milk or water just before you're ready to use it, then beat it a little.

For frying, use olive oil instead of butter in batter if you like a good crisp coating.

Add ½ to 1 teaspoon of baking powder to a frying batter for an especially delicate crust. And a tablespoon of sherry or brandy never hurts, particularly for frying fish and seafood.

BEAN SPROUTS
If you're sprouting mung or other types of beans in a jar, remember that the sprouts increase to about five times the volume of the original beans. Be sure you choose a jar that will allow room for this.

BEANS
Stringbeans
As a cooked vegetable, 1 pound of green or yellow stringbeans will be enough for 4 people.

Treat wax (yellow) beans in the same way as green beans.

Not all stringbeans need stringing. Most beans on the market today are tender, stringless varieties, green or yellow, and only need trimming at each end before being washed and cooked.

If beans do have strings, the quickest way to string them is to snap off one end and pull it down the side of the bean, drawing the string with it. Then do the same with the other end of the bean, pulling the string down the other side.

Sauté stringbeans in a small amount of oil before you add liquid to them. The flavor is enormously improved and you also preserve vitamins because the overall cooking time is shortened.

When cooking stringbeans, the fewer beans in the pan the quicker they'll cook and the better they'll taste. If you cook more than a pound at a time, use 2 separate pans.

Lima Beans

1 pound of fresh lima beans will give 1¼ cups shelled. For a vegetable course, this makes 2 slightly scant servings.

Some fresh lima beans are hard to shell. Using scissors, cut a thin strip along the inner edge of the pod where the beans are attached. You can then remove the beans easily.

Put a whole onion in the pan in which you cook fresh lima beans. It will give a fine flavor to the beans, which then need little else but salt and butter.

Dried Beans

Like rice, dried beans and lentils expand greatly during cooking. 1 cup of small-sized dried beans or lentils will give about 2½ cups cooked; 1 cup of large-sized, about 2 cups cooked.

You needn't soak dried beans in cold water for hours to soften them. Instead, cover with boiling water and let stand for 1 hour before cooking.

Most lentils on the market today have softer coats than they used to and don't require lengthy soaking before cooking.

When cooking dried beans, simmer rather than boil, otherwise they're likely to foam up and overflow the pot. Also, too high heat breaks them up and makes them stick to the pot. When stirring, do it gently with a wooden spoon to avoid breaking the skins.

Dried beans cooked without salt become tender sooner.

When you buy a package of dried beans, be sure they are of uniform size. Small beans cook faster than large ones.

Also pick beans that are bright and uniform in color. If they show fading, they've been stored too long.

You can get rid of the gassiness produced by cooked dried beans if you soak them for 2 or 3 hours before cooking. Throw away the soaking water, cover with boiling water and cook for half an hour. Discard that water too. Cover with more boiling water and cook until the beans are done. The result is very tender and nongassy beans.

Canned Beans

Try adding some curry powder to canned baked beans.

Mash canned or baked beans, season them and make into croquettes. Dip the croquettes in egg, then crumbs, then deep-fat fry them.

BEEF

See also *Beef Cuts, Hamburger, Meats, Roasts, Steak, Stew, Tongue.*

Better-quality steaks are not very lean—they should be at least slightly marbled with fat. The redder the meat, the fresher (less aged) the steak. A steak is more tender and flavorful when it's aged—slightly purplish in color—and gives easily when you press it with your finger.

Instead of buying cube steak, it's generally cheaper to buy round steak and have your butcher cube it.

If you need several steaks, consider buying a rib roast and having your butcher cut it into steaks. This is much cheaper than buying rib steaks separately. (You can freeze what you don't use.)

When broiling a steak, make slashes about an inch apart on the fat surrounding the meat. This will keep the edges from curling.

Some cuts of meat are very lean and need larding before you roast or braise them to improve the flavor and keep the meat from becoming dry. To lard meat, cut salt pork into long, shoelacelike strips. Thread a long larding needle with a strip and push it through the meat. Pull the needle out the other side and cut the pork strip flush with the meat. Do this several times. (The number of strips depends on the size of the piece of meat.)

The tannin in tea is a good meat tenderizer. Cook tough cuts of meat in strong tea instead of water when you're making stews.

When you brown beef in fat for stew or for braising, keep it over the flame until the outside is *dark* brown: this seals in the juices and improves the flavor of both the meat and the gravy.

BEEF CUTS

It helps a lot, when you go to the butcher (or to a restaurant) to know the kinds and characteristics of steaks and other cuts of beef. Here they are, arranged alphabetically:

Arm steak: a steak cut from the chuck, requiring rather long, slow cooking.

Blade steak: same as arm steak.

Brisket: the chest portion of the beef, usually extending some distance back from the forelegs; flavorful but rather tough, used mainly for pot roasts and braising.

Butcher's steak, or butcher's tenderloin, or hanging tender: the muscle (pillar of the diaphragm) which hangs behind the diaphragm, between the left kidney and the filet mignon; one of the most flavorful (and rare—only 1 to an animal) cuts of beef. Traditionally, the butcher takes it home.

Châteaubriand steak: a very thick fillet of beef, exceedingly tender and juicy, cut laterally from the tenderloin.

Chicken steak: a small, very tender and flavorful steak cut from the shoulder blade.

21

Chuck steak: a cut of beef from the region of the shoulder, neck and upper back, slightly tough, used mainly for braising and stewing or for grinding into hamburger.

Club steak: a rib steak from the top portion of the tenderloin. The higher the rib (closer to the shoulder) the larger the steak; size depends on thickness of cut also, and may serve 1 or 2 people; very tender and juicy.

Cube steak: a beef cut, usually top round or top sirloin, which is tenderized by a "cubing" process involving pounding with a special mallet or being run through a cubing machine.

Delmonico steak: also called boneless sirloin, or shell steak; a tender cut from the tenderloin.

Entrecôte: same as Delmonico steak.

Eye round: the cut through the thickest (upper) part of the round steak.

Filet mignon: a thick, boneless and extremely tender cut of beef from the tail side of the tenderloin—not, however, the most flavorful of steaks.

Fillet: any steak served without the bone.

Flank steak: the triangular belly muscle from the underside of the flank of beef. When broiled, served rare and sliced thin (cut as horizontally as possible) you'll find this tender and juicy. It's sometimes called London broil. Flank steak is also served with a stuffing, rolled and baked. (There are 2 flank steaks to an animal.)

Flat bone (sometimes called double bone) sirloin: the portion of the sirloin just behind the pin bone.

Grillade: an individual serving of round steak, usually top round, and usually broiled.

Hanging tenderloin: same as butcher's steak.

London broil: same as flank steak. Also, a cut from the top round or top sirloin, quite thick. It should be at least 1½ inches thick, so the inside will be properly rare. (A London broil should always be cut in strips, close to the horizontal.)

Minute steak: a tender and juicy, very thin steak cut from the top round, which can be quickly sautéed, broiled or pan-broiled.

Pin bone steak: a steak cut from the front end of the sirloin.

Porterhouse steak: a steak cut from the thick (hind) end of the tenderloin, or short loin.

Rib steak: a steak cut from the rib portion (the part of the beef from which the standing rib roast or rolled rib roast is also taken); a club steak.

Round bone sirloin: see *sirloin.*

Round steak: meat from the thick central portion of the hind leg. This is divided into top round and bottom round. Bottom round is drier, and is generally used for making *sauerbraten* and for pickling.

Shell steak: same as Delmonico.

Short loin: same as tenderloin.

Sirloin: the portion of the beef between the tenderloin and the rump. Types of sirloin steak from front to back of the animal are: pin bone (next to the porterhouse of the tenderloin); flat bone (sometimes called double bone) sirloin; round bone sirloin (contains more meat and less bone by weight than other sirloins); wedge bone sirloin, the least tender of the sirloins, containing some tough gristle, but very flavorful.

Skirt steak: the diaphragm muscle, a little-known but delicious cut of beef, very tender and juicy if broiled or pan-fried quickly and served rare. (There are 2 to an animal.)

Steak Diane: a very thin piece of steak.

Steak tartare: very lean beef, minced and served raw.

Swiss steak: a steak (usually bottom round, sometimes lean chuck) into which seasoned flour has been thoroughly pounded before cooking.

T-bone steak: a cut from the center portion of the tenderloin, directly in front of the porterhouse.

Tenderloin: also known as short loin, the portion of the beef between the ribs and the sirloin. Steaks from the tenderloin are (from front to back) club steak, T-bone and porterhouse.

Tournedos: small fillets of beef cut from the tail side of the tenderloin (fillet) of beef.

Wedge bone sirloin: the hindmost end of the sirloin. See *sirloin.*

BEER

When boiling shrimp, try using beer for the cooking liquid. Season as you wish, but don't overcook. The flavor is marvelous—a little reminiscent of lobster.

Use beer in place of water or stock to make an excellent beef stew. This is what the Belgians do—it's called a *carbonnade*.

BEETS

2 pounds of fresh beets will serve 4 to 6 people.

Beet greens are really delightful in salad, especially young tender ones. If you're going to cook beets to serve as a vegetable course, cut off the greens and wash and chill them. Then shred them and mix with lettuce or other salad vegetables, to serve separately or the next day. Beet greens can also be cooked in a little liquid and served much like spinach. (I think they taste better than spinach.)

Instead of boiling beets, try baking them, like potatoes. Baked beets are twice as good as boiled ones. Scrub but don't peel them. Bake at 325° F for at least an hour or until the beets have totally shrunk away from the skin and the skin itself is thoroughly wrinkled. The flavor of baked beets is truly marvelous.

Cook beets with their skins on and greens attached, then plunge them into cold water. The skins will slip off easily. Retain the greens which are tender and delicious.

Beets cooked with their skins on will remain very red if you leave about 2 inches of stem. A little vinegar or cream of tartar added to the cooking water also keeps them from fading.

If adding beets to a mixed dish, put them in just before serving—they stain everything.

Beet stains on plastic or wooden bowls are difficult or impossible to remove. Remember this when preparing or storing beets.

BERRIES

You will need 4 cups of fresh berries to make a 9-inch pie.

Don't wash berries until you need them. Wet berries don't keep as long in the refrigerator as dry ones. But if you have washed berries and must store them, spread them on a towel to dry before you put them in the refrigerator.

Well-chilled berries are less likely to become mushy while being washed.

Berries are highly crushable. Don't let them stand for too long in tall narrow containers—the bottom ones will become mushy.

For an unusual dessert, freeze washed and drained berries in a flat serving dish, then at serving time remove from the freezer and pour cream over them. The cream will freeze slightly to the berries. The combination is wonderful.

Fresh berries that are frozen and then thawed release much of their juices. If you're going to make fruit sauce or jelly or jam, freeze the berries first; the result will be much richer.

If you're making a pie or pudding using frozen berries instead of fresh ones, use less liquid and a little more thickener because frozen berries are much juicier when thawed than fresh ones.

A great way to freeze berries for storage is to lay them out flat in plastic bags (you can sprinkle a little sugar over them if you like) and set the bags in the freezer. When you want to defrost some, break off a piece of the frozen sheet of berries. There's no need to defrost the whole package.

When you're serving berries as a dessert, try pouring wine over them instead of cream.

Blueberries

There are about 3½ cups of blueberries in 1 pound.

If you're making a blueberry pie with fresh berries, bake the crust first; then cook the berry filling on top of the stove, using only half the berries. When the filling is cooked, combine gently with the rest of the uncooked berries. Fill the baked pie crust and chill. You'll get the nicest blueberry pie ever.

Cranberries

1 pound of cranberries equals about 4 cups; it will also give you 4 cups of cranberry sauce.

Freeze cranberries before you grind or chop them, and you'll have less mess.

Keep a container of whole fresh cranberries in the freezer—
they last for months, and you can use them exactly as you would
fresh ones, without defrosting.

Add a few cut cranberries to hot or cold sauerkraut to give it
more zest.

Cranberries should be cooked only until they "pop"—about
5 minutes.

Raspberries

1 pound of fresh raspberries yields about 3½ cups.

Strawberries

When buying strawberries, look for ones whose caps are bright
green and well attached. Brown caps indicate aging fruit.

To give not-so-sweet strawberries a richer flavor, wash them
quickly in cool water, pat dry with a towel, remove the hulls, then
stand the berries, hulled side down, on a tray that has been
sprinkled with white granulated or light-brown sugar. Cover
lightly with paper towels and let stand at room temperature for
a few hours.

When you prepare strawberries for a pie, always wash and pat
them dry with a towel before removing the hulls otherwise water
will get into the berries, dilute their flavor and make them
mushy. Then set them to drain on layers of paper toweling. This
will get rid of the excess moisture and your pie won't be mushy.

BIRDS

See also *Chicken, Duck, Goose, Stuffing, Turkey.*

Since only young game birds are tender enough for roasting
(older ones should be stewed or braised) it's important to know
their age. Look at the spur on the inside of the foot: an old bird
is sharp-spurred; a young one has a rounded spur.

If possible, season poultry the day before cooking. The meat
will be much more flavorful. Be sure to remove the bird from
the refrigerator about an hour before you cook it.

Marinate older, tougher birds, using a warmed mixture of oil,
herbs and wine. Pour this over the bird and let stand 8 hours at

room temperature, or in the refrigerator for a day. In either case turn or baste often.

To truss a bird, tie the legs together at the ends of the drumsticks (you can use a pipe cleaner, twisting it around the drumstick ends). Spread the wings, then bend the second joints out and fold them under from the back—they'll remain in place, without tying, close to the body. Large birds that require long roasting should have their wings tied close to the body (use white string or dental floss) to keep the breast juicy.

If you thaw whole frozen birds before cooking, the flesh will be less stringy. Frozen parts such as legs and breasts can be sautéed without prior thawing, but keep them covered during the early part of cooking.

To cook a game bird in any way, always add a liberal amount of fat to it—wild fowl rarely have enough fat for essential flavor or self-basting during cooking. To roast, tie strips of fat or bacon around the bird, or add fat to the pan, turning the bird often while basting.

If you find while roasting a bird that the fat tends to burn, baste it with ¼ cup of water or stock.

The best way to lift a hot, cooked bird out of its pot is with your hands, wearing a clean pair of rubber household gloves. Get yourself a pair to keep in the kitchen solely for handling foods.

Use 1 or 2 wooden spoons rather than a fork to turn a bird in cooking so that you don't pierce the flesh and lose juices.

BISCUITS
See also *Baking Powder, Muffins.*

You'll turn out the best biscuits if you mix the dough only a short time—just long enough to moisten the ingredients.

Biscuit dough should be handled as little as possible to keep the fat from melting. Tenderness and flakiness depend on finely cut cold fat mixed with flour (this is also true of pie pastry).

Biscuits will be crisp on the outside and flaky in the center if you roll the dough about ¼ inch thick and fold it over once before cutting biscuits from it. They'll also split open easily and neatly when you're ready to butter them.

You can form biscuits quickly if you roll out the biscuit dough into a rectangle and use a knife dipped in flour to cut into squares for baking. (Who says biscuits have to be round?)

Baking powder biscuits get slightly smaller when they're baked, so you can set them rather close together on the baking sheet.

To reheat biscuits with very little trouble, cover a very heavy pot or a large skillet tightly and heat for 5 minutes over medium heat. Turn off the heat, put the biscuits in, cover again, and let stand for about 10 minutes.

Another way to reheat biscuits is to put them in a well-dampened paper bag, twist it closed and put it in a low (300°) oven.

Here's a quick way to make doughnuts: cut the centers from refrigerator biscuits, then drop the biscuits into hot fat, as you would doughnuts.

BLENDER

The blender is a very handy piece of kitchen equipment and it isn't very expensive. It's remarkable for the things it can do: puréeing, making smooth gravies and sauces, making foamy drinks, and much more.

When a recipe calls for forcing food through a sieve, try putting it in the blender instead.

You can make practically every kind of salad dressing in the blender. It's quick, nonmessy, and the emulsion (the even mixing of the oil and the vinegar or lemon juice) seems to hold longer. If you want to add small chunks of solids such as blue cheese to the dressing, add them after the dressing has been blendered.

The mayonnaise you make in a blender is more delicate and delicious, and much less expensive, than store-bought mayonnaise. Most cookbooks contain at least one mayonnaise recipe you can make in a blender.

When you make a cake, try blendering the granulated sugar slightly before adding it to the batter. This gives the cake a more delicate texture and the crumb will be more finely grained.

A blender is great for taking the lumps out of brown sugar.

If you blend granulated sugar for a short time, you'll get a very fine-grained (castor or super-fine) sugar. If you're out of confectioners' sugar, you can make a nearly perfect substitute by putting granulated sugar in the blender and grinding it until it becomes powdery. But be careful not to overdo it—the sugar may begin to caramelize.

Use the blender to fine-grind small amounts of nuts.

For grated orange or lemon peel, first peel the orange or lemon into thin strips with a potato peeler. Then drop the strips into the blender. Presto: grated peel.

You can make delicious hot soups by using up many cooked leftovers. Combine them with some stock or other liquid and necessary seasonings. Into the blender, and you have a great soup! Add sour cream (or yogurt) to the leftovers and stock in the blender, and you've got a great cold soup.

If you want to thicken a vegetable soup, pour a cup or more of the soup—including some of the vegetables or other solids—into the blender. Mix until it's well puréed. Once this is poured back into the soup, the soup will be tastily thickened without the addition of a single calorie.

Use the blender to grind up leftovers to make unusual sauces or gravies to go over vegetables, meat, fish, or chicken.

No need to grate the skin off your fingers every time you need some grated cheese. Dice the cheese into small pieces and drop these into the blender (if the pieces are too large they may get stuck in the blades). The drier the cheese, the finer it can be grated.

The blender does a nice job of grinding nutmeg and cloves. Set your blender at high speed and drop in half a nutmeg, then clamp on the lid. When you want ground cloves, you can drop in several at a time. The flavor is much better than that of ready-ground spices. You will probably end up with more than you need, so bottle it. It will always be fresher than store-bought.

Try substituting a different kind of flour for an equal amount of white flour in any bread, roll, or cookie recipe. With the blender, ½ cup or more of uncooked Wheatena, for example, can

29

be ground up quite fine, and it adds a marvelous nutty quality to a home-baked bread. Similarly, you can use almost any uncooked or dry cereal—oats, bran, any rice cereal, corn flakes, etc. For bread doughs, there are infinite variations. You can substitute for an equal amount of white flour uncooked split peas ground up in the blender—what an aromatic flour that makes! You can also use any kind of dried beans, lentils, or barley.

You can grind coffee in the blender—though not all blenders are well suited to the task. Buy whole coffee beans and grind each day's supply as you need it. And you can make it as fine as you like, depending on the kind of coffee maker you use. (Actually, the finer the grind, the fuller the flavor.)

When you make bran or corn muffins, mix the wet ingredients for the batter in the blender. Pour this into the flour mixture and mix quickly by hand. There's less chance of overmixing the batter this way.

You can also use the blender to mix pancake batter—everything goes in for about 15 seconds.

Overcooked steak or a leftover piece of roast are the fixings for a first-rate pâté. Cut the meat into small chunks and feed the pieces into the blender with some Worcestershire sauce, a little mayonnaise, any spices you like, a bit of salt and pepper. Cover little bread squares or crackers with this to serve as canapés with drinks, or as appetizers, or with soup. Or use as a sandwich spread.

Put leftover cooked fish into the blender and make it into a pâté, just as you would meat or chicken. Add mayonnaise or other moisteners, herbs, and other flavors. This is especially good for a celery or egg stuffing, or for a canapé spread.

When making a white sauce, pour all the ingredients, including the butter, into the blender and set it going. When it's thoroughly mixed, pour into a wet rinsed-out pan and heat, stirring with a whisk, until it's thickened. You won't have to worry about lumps and it's easier than melting the butter, adding flour, mixing, adding warmed liquid, etc. Try it.

Make your own bread crumbs by breaking up slices of stale bread, including the crusts, and dropping the pieces into the blender with salt, pepper, powdered garlic, and dry cheese or any herbs you have on hand. (Cut the cheese into small pieces first.) In this way you get more variety than with store-bought bread crumbs—and for less cost.

Aerate fruit drinks in the blender. Orange juice made from frozen concentrate is twice as tasty if you blender it before serving. You can fizz up tomato juice in the same way.

Vegetables, fruits, meats, or chicken can be puréed in the blender, then frozen in small quantities (in ice cube trays, for instance) to be used as baby food.

Many a blender will clean itself. After you've used it, put in some water and a tiny bit of soap or detergent and turn it on. Run until the blades are clean. Rinse well.

If the blade attachment of your blender can be removed, always wash it in hot water immediately after you use the blender and let the blades drain right side up. Don't let the blades stand when they're dirty or they're likely to clog and gum up, making cleaning difficult.

If the blades do become stiff, put the attachment in a container and cover it with cooking oil. You can do this every few months, letting the blade attachment stand overnight. Then drain, wash and rinse. This will allow the blade mechanism to turn freely and with less resistance when the blender is on.

Don't put egg whites in the blender if you want to beat them to stiffness; a blender can't whip much air into the foods it grinds.

Turn the blender off before you insert a scraper or spoon to dislodge food from the sides of the jar and remove the instrument before you turn the blender on again.

BLUEBERRIES: see BERRIES

BONES
Put beef bones, cut into small pieces (the butcher will do this for you) in a shallow pan in a 400° oven and roast them until dark

brown. Stir occasionally. Use these bones in your stock pot; they give splendid flavor and color.

Never throw away the carcass of any roast bird. Simmer the bones for a couple of hours in seasoned water (with a few vegetables and onions thrown in). You'll have a wonderful stock. Do the same with steak bones, ham bones, or the bone from a leg of lamb.

BOTTLES: see JARS AND BOTTLES

BOUILLABAISSE
The secret of a great bouillabaisse is the variety of fish in it—a minimum of 6 kinds, bouillabaisse afficionados say.

Because bouillabaisse contains olive oil, you have to cook it at a rapid boil for the first 10 minutes or so. This breaks up the oil droplets so that they form the necessary emulsion with the other ingredients. (You must add any tender-fleshed fish—and all shellfish—later.)

BOUILLON
See also *Consommé.*

To make any kind of bouillon, whether canned or homemade, fat-free, refrigerate it well and when thoroughly chilled, pour through a fine handkerchief draped over a strainer.

To clarify a quart of bouillon, beat 2 teaspoons of water with an egg white and the shell of an egg broken into small pieces. Stir this into the bouillon and boil it for a minute or two, then strain through a fine handkerchief draped over a large strainer.

Keep a can of clear beef or chicken bouillon in your refrigerator so that it's chilled and ready when you need stock. Clear it of fat as described above.

Don't use more than 2 bouillon cubes in any dish—too many give a strong, unpalatable flavor.

Use bouillon (canned or homemade) instead of water to add to gravies, meats or vegetables, and to cook rice.

BOUQUET GARNI: see HERBS AND SPICES

BOWLS

Substitute a large round plastic bowl for the usual heavy mixing bowl when you're beating cake batters, etc. It's much easier to lift for pouring and washing (and it's not as hard on the wrists, the housewife's favorite site for bursitis).

BRAISING

When braising meats, use a heavy pot which is just large enough to hold the food to be cooked. Never put in more liquid than will come halfway up the food. Too big a pot (and consequently too much liquid) will boil or poach the food, giving it an entirely different taste.

BRANDY

See also *Flambée Dishes.*

Use brandy in cooking in most of the ways you use wine—it is, after all, distilled from wine. You need less, since the flavor is more highly concentrated. Its alcoholic content is also greater than wine, so be sure to cook off the alcohol, slowly, if using brandy in a gravy. This isn't necessary, of course, in a dessert sauce.

Try rubbing a chicken well with some good brandy before you roast it. You can then season it further, if you like.

BRASS: see COPPER

BRAZIL NUTS: see NUTS

BREAD

See also *Blender, Bread Crumbs, Corn Bread, Flour, Rolls, Yeast and Yeast Dough.*

A 1-pound loaf of bread makes about 15 medium-thick slices.

The sides of a loaf will brown almost as well as the top if baked in an anodized (dull-finish) aluminum, dark metal or glass pan. If you have a new bread pan which is shiny, use it first for cooking other than bread baking, or put it in a 350° oven and bake it empty until it has lost its sheen.

Use solid shortening rather than oil to grease bread pans, and grease them generously, then flour. You'll find bread very easy to remove from the pan when baked.

When baking bread in an aluminum foil pan you barely need to grease it, but before you use it for bread baking, take a very thin nail and punch many holes around the sides (from the inside out) so that the sides of the bread will brown better.

A 2-pound coffee can makes a great pan for baking a 2-pound loaf of bread. Remove both ends, grease the inside well and flour; then stand it upright on a cake pan or cookie sheet. Press the dough down in the can and cover it with a towel. Let it rise until the dough reaches the top or even a little above it. Put the cookie sheet with the can upright on it in the oven and bake as you would any other bread. When you've removed the bread from the oven take a sharp knife and slice off one (or both) of the protruding ends of the bread; then shake the can gently to dislodge the loaf—you'll have a nice cylinder of bread.

Here's an unusual bread for you: When the dough is ready for the final rising, press in only half the amount of dough, and then spoon a thin layer of cooked, seasoned ground meat on top of this. Put the remainder of the dough on top of the meat layer, press down gently, and let the whole thing rise. Then bake as usual. What a wonderful bread!

Italian-style breadsticks can be made from any bread dough. After the dough has risen, pull off pieces about the size of walnuts and roll them into pencil-thin ropes. Put them on lightly greased cookie sheets, pressing the ends down firmly. Brush with milk or beaten egg yolk and sprinkle with caraway, poppy, or sesame seeds (and salt if you like). Bake in a hot oven till crisp.

Kneading

An enamel tabletop is a good surface to knead bread on. If you don't have one, get a large enamel tray. (These are also marvelous for rolling pastry, as they tend to stay cool.)

Heavy doughs, such as pumpernickel, whole wheat or rye, are often hard to handle when you begin to knead them. First oil your hands a little and kneading will be much easier.

Here's how to knead bread (or any yeast) dough: form the dough into a fairly flat ball and place on a lightly floured surface. Put the heel of your hand down into the center of the ball and push hard against the dough, away from you. Turn the dough ball slightly and repeat. Continue in this way, occasionally turning over the whole mound of dough.

Air bubbles in dough can be broken if you throw the dough hard against the kneading surface several times.

If dough becomes sticky at any point, sprinkle flour lightly over it or rub flour into your hands while kneading.

You can often mix and knead bread dough in the same bowl. Use one of those huge 17- or 18-inch stainless steel bowls for mixing and kneading. This has another advantage: You can move the bowl to a higher or lower surface, thus varying the height at which you work to ease the strain on your back and shoulder muscles.

Bread dough contains enough flour when it becomes elastic and firm upon kneading, and does not stick to your hands or to the kneading surface.

If the dough begins to stick to the surface, you may need to sprinkle a little flour over the board occasionally. If any dough sticks to the board, scrape it up with a metal spatula and push it back into the ball.

The harder you work (knead) bread dough, the better it will be. It's probably impossible to be too rough with it. The dough is thoroughly kneaded when it's dry and satiny—after about 10 minutes of kneading, or 200 "kneads."

Bread dough has been kneaded enough if the dough springs back quickly after you dent it with your finger. Another test: cut the dough apart with a knife and check whether there are any large bubbles. If the dough is fine-grained, you've kneaded it enough.

35

If you have to keep dough in the refrigerator for a few days, remove and knead it slightly every day, to release the carbon dioxide accumulated from the yeast. Then brush it lightly with oil and replace in the refrigerator.

You can freeze yeast dough, but it's better to make the bread or rolls and freeze after baking. Frozen dough has a long way to go before reaching the proper temperature for rising.

Rising

Set yeast dough to rise in a warm place, about 80° to 85°. (Don't set it on a hot radiator top—this is usually too hot and the temperature will kill the yeast.) If you have no warm place to set your bowl of dough, either put the covered bowl in a larger bowl of warm water or put it on a rack in an unheated oven, set a large pan of boiling water on the oven floor, and close the door. You may need to replace the hot water once or twice.

You'll have no trouble getting bread dough to rise easily if you put it in a warm oven. For either a gas or electric oven, bring the temperature to warm (but not so warm that you can't rest your hand comfortably on the baking rack). Turn off the heat and put in the bowl of dough to rise. Check after 30 minutes—you may need to warm the oven slightly again. (Remove the bowl before rewarming the oven.)

If you use plastic wrap to cover a bowl or pan of bread dough while it's rising, oil the underside of the plastic first, otherwise the dough will stick to it. If you've forgotten to do this and the dough does stick, dip the blade of a table knife in oil and use this for removing the dough from the plastic.

You'll get a lighter loaf of bread if you knead the dough again a short time after the dough has completed its first rising. Allow the dough to rise once more before you put it in the pan for the second and final rising before baking.

If you're making a single loaf of bread, you need not grease a separate bowl for the dough to rise in. Instead, oil the baking pan and let the dough do its first rising in this. When it has risen, take it out of the pan, knead it a little, sprinkle the oiled pan with a little flour, and replace the dough for the second and final rising. When it's risen and ready to bake, put the pan in the pre-heated oven. (Actually, you can do this if you're baking 2 loaves. Divide the original dough into halves after you've kneaded it and let each half rise in its own baking pan, as above.)

When making bread in a cold kitchen, warm all the ingredients, including the flour and the mixing bowl in a low oven before mixing. Your dough will rise higher.

If your bread tastes "yeasty," the dough has probably fer-mented too long. Don't let it rise as long the next time.

To test when bread dough has risen enough, press two fingers lightly into the dough about ½ inch deep. If the depression remains, the dough is ready. (By this time, it has probably doubled in bulk.)

Don't add any more flour to the dough after it has risen—it will give your bread dark streaks.

Once you've put your bread dough in the pan just before baking, don't let it rise too much. If you do it will fall in the oven and the dough won't be able to support itself because of the excess carbon dioxide inside. A loaf should rise to about double its volume, no more.

When you make slashes across the top of the dough for French or Italian bread, be sure the cuts are shallow—use a very sharp knife or a razor blade. Cuts that are too deep allow some of the gases to escape before they've had a chance to hold the dough high during baking.

Dough

See also *Flour, Yeast.*

If the prospect of wrestling with a big lump of dough discour-ages you from bread making, you might try this. Most bread recipes are for 2 loaves, but you can halve the recipe and make a single loaf. Not only is it much easier to work with a small ball of dough, but also the smaller the volume of dough, the faster it rises. The entire bread-making session will take less time. And for many people, a single loaf of bread is enough.

Yeast dough, especially heavy bread dough (dark pumper-nickel or 100 percent whole wheat), will rise more quickly if you double the amount of yeast. This won't change the taste of the bread, although it may be slightly coarser.

Too much salt in bread dough will slow the rising action of the yeast.

When making rye bread, remember that too much rye flour will keep the dough from rising properly. Use rye flour in the proportion of no more than (and often somewhat less than) 1 to 2 of white flour.

Add a little sugar to bread dough if you want it to rise more quickly. (Sugar also gives bread a soft brown outer crust.)

For half the amount of white flour in your bread dough, substitute barley or dried beans or lentils, or any dry cereal such as oats or Wheatena that has been finely ground in the blender. Mix well in the blender with the white flour. Your bread will be very tasty indeed.

Add a teaspoon of garlic powder to your flour when making bread. You'll have a lightly garlic-flavored bread that is delicious, especially warmed or toasted.

If you want to add more gluten to your bread flour but still don't want the dough to be coarse, substitute ½ cup or so of sifted whole wheat flour for the same amount of white flour. If you have siftings left over in the sieve (and this depends on the size of the openings in the sieve), use these siftings—called bran siftings—in other breads or add to your bread crumb supply.

Sugarless varieties of crisp dry cereal add a fine touch to bread dough. Substitute ½ cup or so, just as it comes from the package, for ½ cup of flour.

Some bread bakers feel that the chlorine in our water supply systems inhibits the growth of yeasts. This may be true, but there's no need to buy spring water for making bread. Chlorine is volatile, so it will disappear if you boil the water for a few minutes, especially in the small quantities used for bread dough. (Be sure to cool the water to body temperature before you add yeast, however, or you'll kill the yeast.)

If you want to make a crusty bread with a wheaty flavor, use water as your liquid. If you like a soft crust with a creamy white crumb, use whole or skimmed milk.

Bread made with milk has a softer, more tender crust than bread made with water. This is one reason that bakers often prefer to use milk if the dough is intended for rolls.

Don't imagine that you have to limit yourself to water or milk for the liquid when making bread. Although most recipes call for one of these liquids, you can substitute others. A rich strong broth is marvelous in a bread dough, so if you have some soup around, strain it and use a cup or so—whatever volume of liquid the recipe calls for—in your bread. Or don't even strain it; put it in the blender and use the purée. You'll need a little less flour if you do this.

You can also use vegetable juices of any kind (including the water you cook vegetables in) when making bread. And if the bread is a sweet one, use fruit juice.

Yeast breads are moister when made with potato water (water in which you have boiled potatoes) than when made with other liquids. The potato water makes the bread last longer and gives it a slightly greater volume, but a coarser texture.

Bread dough has absorbed enough flour to make it ready for kneading when it forms a shaggy mass in the bowl and pulls away from the sides. Add more flour during the kneading process until the dough just ceases to be sticky.

A batter bread is one that requires no kneading The unbaked dough has a higher proportion of liquid to flour, but you pour it into the baking pan much as you would a cake batter. The baked loaf is more moist than a kneaded bread and also somewhat coarser.

When making a fruit bread with baking powder dough, let the mixed dough stand in the baking pan for 20 minutes before you put it in the oven. This seems to mellow and ripen the bread, giving it a richer flavor.

You'll get a nice moist loaf of bread if you add a ½ cup of well-cooked, blendered rice to your bread.

A little mashed potato added to bread dough will give the bread a most attractive flavor.

Use little or no shortening when you make the dough if you want a bread that's dry and crispy like some Italian or French breads. Remember, this type of bread dries out much faster than regular bread.

Baking

If you want to serve freshly baked bread or rolls at your dinner party but don't have time to make them on the day of your dinner, make them days ahead and *partially* bake them. Then wrap them individually in aluminum foil or waxed paper and freeze. Thaw them on the morning of the day of your dinner. Just before they are to be served, put them in the oven and finish baking. They'll taste exactly as though you'd started from scratch the same day.

If you have to make bread on a day when you know you're going to be rushed, measure out all the ingredients the night before, refrigerating those which need it. Then in the morning you can just go to it. This is a great time saver.

For a soft glaze on top of a loaf of bread, brush the surface with an egg white lightly beaten with 1 tablespoon of water before putting the loaf in the oven.

If you want to have an interesting speckled crust on the top of bread or rolls—the kind of crust on Dutch bread—brush the surface with beaten egg white at 20-minute intervals or so during the final rising.

For professional-looking crusts for breads or rolls, brush the tops with milk and dust with flour before baking.

For a shiny crust (such as on a rye bread), brush the top of the loaf with a mixture of 1 egg beaten with 1 tablespoon of milk before putting the bread in the oven.

For a crisp crust, brush the top of the loaf with cold water just before putting it in the oven.

To get a very crunchy crust on breads and rolls, baste them with ice water after they've been baking for 10 minutes. You can also put a pan of water in the oven with the baking bread or bake the bread longer at a slightly lower temperature. It's the humidity that gives the "crunch."

If you like a soft crust on a bread, brush the top lightly with melted shortening or oil several times while the bread is baking or once when it's out of the oven but still warm.

When baking bread in glass loaf pans, the oven should be 25° cooler than when baking in metal pans.

Some breads rise higher and are lighter in texture if you place them in an unlighted oven, then light the flame and bake. You can't always predict which flour combinations will react this way, so experiment with your recipes.

If you want to bake a round loaf of bread, bake it in a casserole dish, 1½- to 2-quart size.

To prevent the crust of a bread from cracking, make shallow, diagonal slashes across the top of the unbaked loaf just before you set it in the oven to bake.

Bread containing whole eggs tends to brown quickly. If you see this happening, cover it lightly with aluminum foil halfway through the baking period.

If the bread you're baking seems to be developing a hard crust too soon, cover the entire bread with a large heat-proof bowl or a pot, and continue baking. Remove the covering about 10 minutes before the bread has finished baking.

If bread seems to be browning too fast, cover it loosely with aluminum foil during the last 20 minutes of baking.

Bread is fully baked if it gives off a hollow sound when you remove it from the pan and tap the loaf on the bottom and side. If it doesn't sound hollow, bake another 5 minutes and test again. (You don't have to put it back in the pan for this second baking—stand it on a wire cake cooler in the oven. This is also a nice device for baking a loaf with browner sides and bottom.)

After baking a bread always remove promptly from its pan and let cool on a rack. Cooling in the pan will make the sides and bottom soggy.

If your bread doesn't seem completely baked when you remove it from the pan, let the bread continue baking, out of the pan, on the oven rack.

Bread baked in a heavy metal pan will not readily brown on the sides and bottom.

No two ovens bake alike. Every bread baker has to adapt the bread recipe, temperature, and baking time to the oven. Don't be afraid to make changes and substitutions if your bread doesn't turn out the way you want it the first time. Just keep track of which substitutions help to produce the desired results.

Storing, Cutting, and Reheating

Never wrap a newly baked loaf of bread until it's thoroughly cooled; otherwise it will sweat and become soggy.

Bread will keep well at room temperature for 3 days if wrapped tightly in plastic wrap.

Bread made without oil or fat (like French and Italian bread) is delicious but it gets crusty and dry after a few hours. It will keep much better if you wrap it carefully in aluminum foil and freeze it. When wanted, put the foil-wrapped bread in a 350° oven for 10 minutes (more, if the bread is frozen). When you open it, you'll find it almost as good as fresh-baked.

To keep bread for any length of time, wrap it as airtight as possible to prevent drying and put it in your freezer. You can do this with sliced or unsliced bread.

Unsliced bread is very easy to slice when frozen. Not only that, frozen bread can be cut into much thinner slices than fresh bread.

However, remember that whole wheat and other dark breads are almost impossible to slice when they're thoroughly frozen. Slice the breads before you freeze them. And if you slip small pieces of waxed paper between the slices, they will be easier to separate.

Frozen bread slices will thaw at room temperature in 15 minutes, or you can put them into the toaster while still frozen.

Put a whole frozen bread, unthawed, into a 400° oven for 15 to 20 minutes. You'll find the bread will taste freshly baked and will remain soft for about a day.

Warm or freshly baked bread is difficult to slice without mangling it unless you have an *exceedingly* sharp knife, or an electric knife or heat the blade of the knife first.

Nut bread is hard to cut when fresh—it crumbles easily. Cool for several hours or overnight before slicing, or put it in the freezer for an hour and you will have no trouble with crumbling.

To reheat bread in the oven, sprinkle it lightly with water and put it in a brown paper bag in a low (300°) oven. Check after 15 minutes. This will restore the fresh flavor without overcooking the crust.

If you want to put slices of bread under the broiler (for cinnamon toast, or bread with any covering) first cut off the crusts—they burn.

Save all bread trimmings and crusts you have left over from making sandwiches or anything else. Put them in a plastic bag and freeze. When you've accumulated enough, use for making bread crumbs, bread pudding, stuffings, or mix them with ground meat in a meat loaf.

To avoid unpleasant cooking odors, put several slices of stale bread in the water when cooking strong-flavored vegetables such as broccoli, cabbage and Brussels sprouts. Skim off with a strainer after cooking.

Odds and Ends

To butter very thin slices of bread (when making hors d'oeuvres, for instance), start with an unsliced loaf. Slice off the end of the loaf (you can use it for croutons) and spread softened butter on the cut end of the loaf. Slice as thin as you wish, butter the next cut end, and repeat to the end of the loaf.

If you have a few slices of bread that you won't be eating, set them in a very low oven (200° F or less) until they're crisp and tanned. This is Melba toast, and it will keep for weeks.

Dice bread crusts and sauté them in oil or butter with any spices or flavorings you like. They make wonderful croutons for soup or salad. And if you don't want to make croutons immediately, freeze the diced crusts until you're ready.

The sandwich syndrome makes us think bread has to be cut into slices. If it's Italian or French bread, tear it into chunks to eat. You get more of the substance, taste, and aroma this way. And if you've just baked a bread, cut it into large cubes instead of slices to get the really homemade flavor.

BREAD CRUMBS

See, also *Blender, Breading*.

1 pound of bread will yield about 9 cups of soft crumbs.

1 slice of fresh bread broken into soft crumbs will yield about ⅔ cup, lightly packed.

1 slice of toast or dried bread will yield ⅓ cup of fine crumbs.

2 ounces of dried bread, crushed, will yield about ¾ cup of fairly fine crumbs.

To make fresh (soft) bread crumbs, cut off the crusts of day-old white bread and crumble the bread gently. Then rub through a very coarse strainer. (Keep the crusts for future use: see under *Bread*.)

To make fine crumbs from dried bread, use either stale bread or white bread toasted lightly and allowed to dry at room temperature or in a very low oven until all moisture is gone. Cover the bread with a dishtowel and either roll hard with a rolling pin or hit lightly with a hammer. You can also break up the pieces and put in a blender. If after pulverizing, you suspect they're not completely dry, spread them shallowly on a cookie sheet in a 250° oven for about 10 minutes. Store in well-sealed jars. They'll keep their flavor for several months, especially if refrigerated.

3 slices of fresh white bread, finely chopped or crumbled, will give you 1¾ cups of soft crumbs; 3 slices of well-dried white bread will give you ½ cup of dry crumbs.

If you have extra slices of bread, dry them, grate them, and add to your bread crumb supply.

To make bread crumbs, dry out slices of bread by putting them into a wire lettuce basket or a string shopping bag, and hang in your kitchen until the slices become crisp. Exposing them on all sides this way will give you uniform drying.

You can also dry slices of bread in a very low oven until they're thoroughly crisp.

If you don't have a blender, put thoroughly dried slices of bread in a clear plastic bag, press the air out, and close the open end. Crush with a rolling pin until the crumbs are very fine.

You can grate bread crumbs as you need them by storing a well-wrapped roll or two in the freezer. Grate the frozen roll over the surface of the dish you want the bread crumbs on, much as you would grate a piece of cheese.

If you're out of bread crumbs and don't even have any stale bread around, use dry cereals. Any of them can be tossed into the blender, and spiced and flavored in any way you like. If you don't have a blender, cover them with a dish towel and run a rolling pin over them.

For buttered crumbs, toss soft bread crumbs in melted butter (about 1 tablespoon of butter to 1 cup of soft crumbs). You can also add 2 tablespoons of melted butter to 1 cup of dry crumbs—these are very good, but different from soft buttered crumbs.

Add dried herbs, seasonings or grated cheese to home-made bread crumbs and you'll always have seasoned crumbs ready to use—at a tiny fraction of what you'd pay if you bought them.

Try putting prepared bread stuffing in your blender and using it for breading chops.

If you're running low on flour, substitute very fine bread crumbs, plain or toasted, for all or part of the flour in cookies—they'll taste a little like macaroons. Add ½ teaspoon almond extract, and they *will* taste like macaroons.

Very fine bread crumbs used in place of flour are particularly good in a hearty cake like applesauce or nut cake.

Fine dry bread crumbs make a good thickener for creamed sauces in casseroles or *à la king* dishes. Use them wherever you like a toasted flavor in a sauce.

BREAD DOUGH: see BREAD, FLOUR, YEAST AND YEAST DOUGH

BREADING

Corn flakes ground into fine crumbs give a nice crunchy coating for chicken or fish.

You can make a breading (of crumbs, flour, etc.) adhere very nicely to fish fillets, chops, or chicken pieces if you first cover the pieces of food with a mixture of 2 parts skimmed milk powder and 1 part water. Let the pieces stand in this coating for 5 minutes, then shake well before dipping them in the breading. Fry or sauté.

A bread crumb crust will adhere better to chicken, fish, chops, etc., if you put the breaded food in the refrigerator for an hour or so before frying or sautéing.

BROCCOLI

1 bunch of broccoli (about 1½ pounds) will serve 4 people generously.

When you buy broccoli, look for bunches which are a rich, dark green, with tightly closed green buds. Over-aged broccoli is lighter in color, the buds are yellowish and open and may even show small yellow flowers. This is tougher, stronger in taste and has much less flavor than proper young broccoli.

If you divide broccoli into 3-inch-long flowerets, it will cook more quickly and consequently stay greener. Cook the stalks too, but first peel off the thick skin.

If broccoli stalks are *very* thick, either split them lengthwise up to the buds or cut them into cubes and cook them with the buds.

A couple of slices of stale bread in the cooking water will minimize the cooking odor of broccoli. Skim the bread from the surface with a small strainer or slotted spoon after the broccoli is cooked.

If you're going to use broccoli in a mixed dish, parboil it first for 5 minutes in salted boiling water. Beware of overcooking—it should be slightly crisp.

If broccoli loses its bright green color, it's overcooked.

If you want to cook and serve broccoli whole, try cooking it covered, standing up, like asparagus. The water should come just up to the buds—the steam will cook them. Lift the cover now and then to keep the buds green. They taste best when slightly crackly, so don't worry about their being undercooked; 10 to 12 minutes is usually all it takes.

BROILING
See also *Beef, Chicken, Fish.*

Broiling is a cinch as long as you don't place the food too close to the heat source, and as long as you baste frequently. The basting liquid should be largely fat or oil.

Warm the basting oil or marinade because a cold liquid added to broiling meats will slow the browning.

Rub surfaces of a broiler—pan or grill—with vegetable oil before you place the meat or chicken on it. This will prevent sticking and also make cleaning easier, especially for barbecue grills; rub them well with vegetable oil before you use them.

A good way to broil, with little mess, is to line a cake or pie tin with aluminum foil, then stretch another piece of foil straight across the top, tucking the edges firmly around the rim. With a skewer, make small holes in the stretched piece and broil on this surface. You can discard all the foil afterward.

If the meat you're broiling is fatty, drain off the fat occasionally to prevent its catching fire. If the fat *does* catch fire, clap a large pot lid down over it. This almost always cuts off the oxygen supply and smothers the fire. If this doesn't work, throw a handful of baking soda on the flames.

If you put a few slices of bread in the broiling pan under the rack, they'll soak up the dripping fat and lessen both smoke and fire hazard.

When you broil meat, turn it only once. Cook the second side a slightly shorter time than the first.

If you're broiling meat which is more than 1 inch thick, don't turn the heat too high or the outside will burn before the inside is cooked.

You should baste most broiling meats from time to time during cooking.

When you broil steaks and chops, make slashes about 1 inch apart on the fat surrounding the meat—this will keep the edges from curling.

You can tell that broiled red meat has reached the medium-rare stage when tiny drops of pink juice show on the surface of the side being cooked. If you press it with two fingers it should feel neither soft (too rare) nor firm (well done). Get used to detecting the doneness of broiling meat by pressure.

Serve food at once, as soon as it leaves the broiler. There's absolutely no way it can be kept both crisp and hot. Have your diners in their places before you remove the food from the broiler.

As soon as you've removed meat from the broiler, sprinkle the pan with salt or detergent, then cover with wet paper towels. You'll find it much easier to clean later.

For rotisserie broiling, use only tender cuts of meat, or meat which has been tenderized in a marinade. Center the meat on the spit to insure proper balance. If you're broiling poultry, tie the bird compactly so the wings or legs don't trail.

When you're basting with a sauce during rotisserie broiling, do this only during the last half hour of broiling—otherwise you'll overbrown the outside of the meat.

If you're charcoal-broiling meat whose fat drips down on the coals, flick drops of water on the little bursts of fat fire which don't go out at once. Professional charcoal-broilers keep a pan of water beside them for this purpose while they cook.

BROTH: see SOUPS AND STOCKS

BROWNING
See also *Sautéing*.

Brown all meats in a heavy low-sided pan and use a high flame so that the steam formed will dissipate before it has a chance to steam the meat.

Add about ½ teaspoon of sugar to the fat in which you brown meat, and the meat will become a beautiful mahogany color.

BROWN SUGAR: see SUGAR

BRUSSELS SPROUTS
Fresh Brussels sprouts are tight, firm and green. If the leaves are loose, pale or yellowed, they're not fresh.

1 quart of sprouts will serve 5 or 6 people.

Wash Brussels sprouts under cold running water, and drain them. Pull off the loose leaves. Cut a little cross at the bottom of each stem end.

Before you cook Brussels sprouts in any manner, blanch them: drop them into rapidly boiling salted water, bring it quickly to a boil again, then drain and spread them out on a towel to cool. From here on, follow your recipe or cook as you like—but don't overcook. People who say they don't like Brussels sprouts usually have had them overcooked. After blanching, Brussels sprouts should rarely be cooked more than 7 to 10 minutes. They should be served slightly crisp.

Put a couple of slices of stale bread in the cooking water to minimize the odor of the cooking sprouts. Remove the bread with a small strainer or slotted spoon.

Nutmeg and grated cheese are marvelous additions to Brussels sprouts dishes.

BUNS
To reheat breakfast buns (especially cinnamon buns, which are usually quick to harden), put a pan of hot water in the oven while they heat. This will soften them up.

49

BURNED POTS

Sprinkle powdered cleanser or baking soda liberally over the burned portion of the pot, then add only enough water to moisten the powder or soda well. Cover the pot with plastic wrap so that the moisture won't evaporate and let stand several hours or overnight. You can sometimes lift the burned portion out of the pot with only a little scraping. If the pot is very badly burned it may need two such treatments.

BURNS

Both well-seasoned cooks and novices have gotten superficial burns from spattering grease or from hot utensils. Immediate rinsing with ice cold water for 5 to 10 minutes or application of cold compresses will help lessen pain and prevent blistering. More serious burns should be seen by a physician.

BUTTER

See also *Margarine.*

There are 2 cups of butter in 1 pound.

¼ pound of butter (1 stick) equals ½ cup, or 8 tablespoons.

⅔ stick of butter equals ⅓ cup.

It's a good idea to keep a can of butter on your pantry shelf for emergency use. Canned butter is absolutely delicious—you can buy it at gourmet food shops.

One reason for buying sweet butter rather than salt butter is that salt can disguise off-flavors. Salt butter can be a little rancid without its being detected. This is not so with sweet (unsalted) butter. For this reason, sweet butter is often stored more carefully, and is apt to be fresher. (You can freeze it to keep it fresh.)

To make your own butter, pour pure, heavy, untreated (not ultrapasteurized) cream in the blender and whip until butter forms. This takes a very short time. You may need to turn the blender off and push the cream down against the blades once or twice. Then scrape the butter onto a piece of kitchen muslin, fine cheesecloth, or large white handkerchief, and squeeze to drain out the moisture. If you don't want sweet butter, add a little salt. Pat into a bowl and chill.

To cut serving slices from a standard stick of cold butter, put clear pastic wrap or the butter wrapper itself around the knife blade and you'll make nice clean cuts without sticking. You can also heat the knife blade for a clean cut.

To soften ice-cold or frozen butter quickly, grate it with a coarse grater or against the underside of a strainer with large holes and leave it at room temperature for a few minutes. It'll be just right for creaming with sugar to make a cake batter, for example.

To make browned butter, be especially careful to heat the butter very slowly so that it browns evenly. To make butter quite brown, lift the pan from the heat every now and then, swirl it, and sniff it to be sure it isn't beginning to burn. Take care not to overdo it—if it burns, it's useless.

When melting butter over direct heat, it won't be as likely to burn if you add a little cooking oil. Be sure to keep the heat low.

To get packed butter or shortening out of a measuring cup, hold the lower part of the cup in a pan of hot water for only an instant.

When you use butter for sauces, use sweet butter if you can: it has a finer flavor than salt butter.

For clarified butter (pure butterfat with none of the milk solids in it), use the following method, which is quicker and less messy than most: Put the butter in a small pan, then set the pan in a larger one containing hot water, and heat until the butter melts completely. Let the pan of butter cool to room temperature, and then refrigerate it. The pure butterfat will solidify and you can lift it off. (Don't throw away the white residue; it's full of protein and flavor. Keep refrigerated and add it to cooked vegetables or use in delicate butter sauces.)

Another way to clarify butter: heat it very gently only until it melts. Set it to one side of the stove, keeping it warm, until the clear liquid portion rises to the top. Skim this off carefully for use in delicate butter sauces.

Clarified butter can be heated to a higher temperature than regular butter without burning because the milk solids have been removed.

When sautéing in butter, the time to add the food is when you've brought the butter to a foam and the foam has begun to subside.

To make whipped butter at less than half the store cost, let a stick (½ cup) of butter come to room temperature, then whip it to lightness with an electric beater. If you wish, slowly add 8 tablespoons of cooking oil, 1 at a time, beating well after each addition. After everything is well whipped, remove the mixture from the bowl with a rubber spatula and store in a container in the refrigerator. The volume of butter will have doubled. And it will stay spreadable even when cold.

If you use whipped butter in baking (uneconomical, but sometimes there is no choice), weigh it, don't go by volume.

Try making up herbed and other flavored butters, then store them in small glasses in the coldest part of the refrigerator (you can also freeze them). They're useful to have on hand when you want a good sauce for a hot vegetable without having to go to a lot of trouble.

BUTTERMILK: see MILK

BUTTERSCOTCH BITS
A 6-ounce package of butterscotch bits equals 1 cup.

CABBAGE

1 pound of cabbage will yield 5 firmly packed cups of shredded cabbage. This will cook down to a little over 3 cups drained, unless you overcook it—then it will be less.

When you choose winter cabbage, look for a tight, firm head. The exception is young spring cabbage, which is softer.

It's likely that a cabbage is coarse and has a strong flavor if the stems of the outer leaves have begun to detach themselves from the main stem.

To serve in some kinds of salad, you may want to blanch the cabbage by quickly parboiling; then rinse in cold water, drain, and refrigerate it before cutting.

For a very crunchy salad, soak the cabbage (cut in half) in salted ice water for an hour or so. Chilling also makes it easier to slice in thin strips.

Shred cabbage very fine to use in salad. Let it stand in ice water to crisp, then wrap in a dishtowel and refrigerate until ready to use.

Don't shred cabbage too fine if you're going to cook it.

If you want cabbage to be less gassy, parboil it for 5 minutes, rinse in cold water, then cook it again in fresh water to the consistency you like.

For most dishes, you should cook cabbage uncovered for no more than 6 to 8 minutes (depending on how thin you've cut it). It should be slightly crackly to the teeth.

Put a couple of slices of stale bread in the cooking water to minimize the odor of cooking cabbage.

Try steaming cabbage instead of boiling it. Steam shredded cabbage for about 10 minutes, or cabbage cut in large chunks for a little longer.

Red cabbage will keep its color while cooking if you add 1 tablespoon of either vinegar or lemon juice or ¼ cup of wine to each 2 cups of cooking water.

If you want whole cabbage leaves for stuffing, here's how to remove them: bring water to a boil in a deep pan; stick a fork into the base of the cabbage and submerge the head in the boiling water for 1 minute; remove, drain and carefully pull off the leaves which have softened. Return the rest of the head to the boiling water and repeat the process until you've removed all the leaves you need.

Another easy way to separate cabbage leaves to prepare stuffed cabbage or cabbage rolls is to wash, dry, core, and freeze the head of cabbage. Defrost it, and the leaves will separate easily.

Here's how to stuff cabbage leaves: place the stuffing in the center of each leaf, then either fold the leaf over on all sides to form an envelope, or roll the leaf up, tucking in the open sides if you wish. Cut long green scallions lengthwise into strings and use these to tie the cabbage rolls or envelopes. Cook as your recipe directs.

CAKE

See also *Baking Powder, Baking Soda, Blender, Cupcakes, Fats and Oils, Flour, Fruitcake, Icing, Sugar.*

Before you bake a cake, assemble all your ingredients, bowls and utensils. Grease and flour the cake pans and light the oven. Then get to work, with everything proceeding in one continuous motion.

You can bake a 1- or 2-egg cake calling for 2 cups of flour or less in an 8-inch square cake pan, or in two 8-inch round ones. For every ½ cup of additional ingredients (flour, nuts, fruit, etc.), use a pan size that is 1 inch larger either in length or width, or use an additional smaller pan.

Grease the bottom and sides of a cake pan with shortening before you line the bottom with waxed paper. Then grease the surface of the paper, pour in the batter, and bake. With this method you can cool the cake in the pan and when you remove the cake, the waxed paper will stick to the pan rather than to the cake.

Use solid vegetable shortening when you grease a cake pan. Oil tends to burn, especially on any surface which the batter doesn't cover.

To keep your hand clean when you grease cake pans, slip it into a small plastic bag, dig out a bit of shortening, and grease the surface. You can replace the bag in the can to use the next time.

After you grease a cake pan, put a little flour in it and bang the pan around briskly until the sides and bottom are lightly coated. Empty any excess flour into the sink, then pour in the batter. The cake will rise more evenly at the sides and it will also be easier to remove from the pan.

Don't grease the pans you bake sponge and angel food cakes in.

You won't have to grease your fruitcake tin if you line the inside with brown paper. After the cake is baked, leave it in the pan on a cake rack to cool. Then remove the cake—the paper will pull off easily.

You can bake cakes in cans from coffee or other foods. If you use a can, don't fill it any higher than you would any other pan, or the cake won't bake through. (After the cake has cooled, you can return it to the can for storing.)

Never try to fill a high narrow pan with cake batter designed for a low flat one. The batter will seldom bake through.

You can also use a jello mold to bake a cake if you grease and flour it thoroughly before pouring in the batter. (If the mold has an attractive design on the bottom it will be transferred to the top of the cake. Instead of icing the cake—which would destroy the design—try sprinkling the mold well with brown sugar (as you would for an upside-down cake) before you pour in the batter.

Before you make an upside-down cake, line the pan with aluminum foil. Cool the cake for 10 minutes after baking, cover the top with a serving plate, invert, and peel off the foil carefully. The top of the cake will look unruffled and professionally baked.

When you bake chocolate cake or chocolate cupcakes, dust the greased pans with sifted cocoa. It adds to the looks as well as the flavor.

Cakes containing molasses will be less likely to stick to the baking pan if you line the pan with waxed paper before pouring in the batter.

When you're using honey or molasses in a cake recipe, measure the oil or other shortening in the measuring cup first. Use the same cup for the honey or molasses, which will then pour out easily without sticking to the inside of the cup.

A square layer cake is nice for a change. Instead of pouring batter into traditional round pans, pour it into the 8-inch square ones that many cooks use for noodle or potato puddings. Or use a couple of loaf pans, taking care not to fill them higher than you would a cake pan. This will give you an oblong layer cake.

If you're going to sprinkle chopped nuts in a buttered pan before you pour in the batter or dough, butter the pan well, sprinkle the nuts over the bottom, and chill before pouring in the batter or dough. The nuts will adhere to the pan surface better.

Mixing

Unless a recipe calls for all-purpose flour, don't substitute it for cake flour. It's made from harder wheat and you'll get a heavier-textured cake.

If you add cocoa to a cake recipe which doesn't call for cocoa, decrease the amount of flour by 2 tablespoons for each ¼ cup of cocoa.

If you substitute oil for solid shortening in a cake batter, use about ⅓ less than the amount of solid shortening suggested.

Use fine granulated sugar for cakes. (Put granulated sugar in the blender for a little while.)

For maximum lightness in a cake, especially sponge cake, have the ingredients at room temperature, or even warmer. Warm the bowl in which you do the mixing.

Add all spices and flavorings, liquid or powdered, to the shortening when you begin to mix a cake batter. The flavors will be distributed more evenly throughout the batter.

You can make a pretty fair cake flour by substituting cornstarch and all-purpose flour. To get 1 cup of "cake flour," add 3 table-spoons of cornstarch to about ⅞ cup of all-purpose flour, then sift. This isn't perfect, but it can sometimes get you out of a hole.

For most cake batters, use 1½ teaspoons of baking powder for every cup of flour.

You can almost always substitute 2 egg yolks for 1 whole egg in a cake recipe.

When a recipe calls for egg yolks and egg whites to be beaten separately, always beat the whites first (it usually doesn't matter if they stand for a short time). Then you won't have to wash the beater before beating the yolks. If you beat the yolks first, you *do* have to wash the beater, because the minute any trace of egg yolk touches the white, you'll never be able to whip the whites to frothiness.

It's much easier to cream butter and sugar together if you sprinkle a few drops of water over the mixture.

If butter is very cold (or even frozen) and you've forgotten to soften it to use in a cake batter, grate it with a coarse grater or against the underside of a strainer that has large holes and leave at room temperature for a few minutes. You'll find butter just right for creaming with sugar.

Another method if you have to cream sugar and butter together when the butter is cold, is to put the mixing bowl over fairly hot water and beat until the butter softens. Then set the bowl in a larger bowl of cold water and continue to beat with the sugar until the mixture becomes fluffy and a pale lemon color.

If you need eggs at room temperature and have forgotten to remove them from the refrigerator, put them in warm water for 10 minutes.

When you add eggs to cake batter, separate the yolks from the whites and mix the yolks in first. After the batter has been mixed and all the other ingredients included, beat the whites until fairly stiff and fold them in last. You'll get a lighter, softer cake.

Most cakes calling for vanilla extract will taste better if you double the amount of extract. These days vanilla extracts seem rather weak.

In most cake recipes, you can substitute buttermilk for regular milk and your cake will be much lighter. Add ¼ teaspoon of baking soda to the dry ingredients for each ½ cup of buttermilk you use.

Sponge cakes, which tend to be somewhat bland, will have a very pleasant flavor if you add 1 teaspoon of anise to the batter.

If you're mixing batter by hand, use a wire whisk and you'll avoid lumps.

You can keep nuts and raisins from sinking in a cake if you heat them first, roll them in flour, then add to cake batter at the end of mixing.

A quick way to mix cake and cookie batter and still get a light texture is to have a quart-sized screw-top jar handy for mixing all the dry ingredients. Shake everything up well and pour into the mixing bowl. Then use the blender to mix all the wet ingredients—milk, eggs, shortening, extracts, etc. After everything is thoroughly mixed, pour the contents into the bowl of dry ingredients and mix. In no time you've got your batter ready, and you'll be surprised at how fine the texture will be. (Keep the screw-top jar on the shelf with your other cake ingredients—there's no need to wash it each time you use it.)

You can prepare the dry and wet ingredients of a cake batter separately, ahead of time, well before you put them together to make your cake. Mix the dry ingredients in a screw-top jar and set aside until needed. The wet ingredients (milk, eggs, shortening, extracts, etc.) can be mixed in a screw-top jar and refrigerated for as long as 4 days before you use them.

If you have to make a cake on a day when you know you're going to be rushed, measure out all the ingredients the night before, refrigerating the wet ingredients. Then in the morning you can just go to it. This is a great time saver.

Always insert the beaters in an electric cake mixer before you plug it in.

After you've finished beating a cake batter with an electric mixer, hold the beaters less than an inch above the batter and set the mixer at the lowest speed. Most of the batter clinging to the blades will spin off, and with little spatter.

Don't overbeat sponge cake batter or it will lose its lightness. Mix thoroughly, but stop as soon as all the flour has been incorporated into the batter.

Beat a couple of tablespoons of creamy peanut butter into the batter of a white or golden cake, then bake as usual.

The best fruitcake batters are very stiff. The right amount of liquid to use when you're making a fruitcake is only enough to allow you to mix the dough, with its burden of fruit, in the mixing bowl.

An angel food cake will be lighter and finer if you use superfine sugar. Or put the sugar in a blender for a few seconds at moderate speed.

Baking

Bake your cake as soon as possible after the batter is mixed or it will become heavy and coarse-textured.

After you've poured batter into a cake pan, tap the bottom lightly to release any large air bubbles.

After you've poured angel food batter into its pan, cut through it several times with a knife or spatula to prevent large air holes forming.

Put your angel food cake in a cold oven—*then* turn on the heat. Try this method. It works!

Cake pans shouldn't touch one another in the oven—or the oven walls.

Most cakes should be baked in the center of the oven, but angel and sponge cakes should be baked on the lowest rack.

Bake a loaf cake at 350° for 45 to 60 minutes.

Cake layers should be baked at 375° for 25 to 30 minutes.

Some types of cake seem to "hump" during baking. Most of these will remain level if you cover the pan with aluminum foil during the first part of the baking period. Then remove the foil for the last 10 to 15 minutes so that the top of the cake will brown.

Too much flour, or too hot an oven, will sometimes cause a cake to "hump" in the middle.

If the surface of your cake cracks, the chances are that your oven is too hot.

If a cake is higher on one side than on the other, either your stove needs leveling or the heat in your oven is unevenly distributed. Call a professional stove man to give your oven a complete examination.

Chocolate cakes burn rather easily, so watch them carefully while they're baking. You may have to turn the pan slightly every 15 minutes, or lower the flame after the first 15 minutes.

To test for doneness, insert a thin skewer or toothpick into the center of the cake. If it comes out clean and dry, the cake is done.

If your cake is too dry you may have used too much flour in proportion to fat, not enough liquid or baked it at too high a heat.

If a cake is too coarse in texture, you probably undermixed it or used too little baking powder.

If the surface of your cake seems to be browning too quickly, cover it lightly with aluminum foil for the last 5 minutes of baking.

If you have trouble with cheesecake cracking while baking, it may be because your oven was too hot. Another way to avoid this problem is to bang the pan gently several times on a level surface—after you've poured the cheese filling into the shell—to force out possible air bubbles.

A cheesecake should always cool to lukewarm in the oven with the door open. Then it should be refrigerated.

Very few cakes won't benefit by turning the cake pan halfway around toward the end of baking. This allows all sides of the cake to get the same amount of heat.

Most cakes should be cooled first in their pans. But a freshly baked cake removed from its pan won't stick to the cooling rack if you oil your palms with cooking oil and rub the surface of the rack.

Cooling

Let your cake remain in the pan for at least 15 minutes after you take it out of the oven.

A cake will be less likely to stick to the pan if you put it on a wet towel to cool as soon as you take it out of the oven.

If you bake cakes on baking paper (white unglazed paper sold in kitchen-supply stores) you can remove the paper easily if you set the cake, paper side down, on a well-soaked towel until you see the edges of the paper begin to curl. Lift the cake and peel off the paper.

To cool an angel cake, turn the pan upside down as soon as you remove it from the oven. Slip the tube opening onto a bottle to hold the pan up while it's cooling.

Never try to remove an angel cake from the pan until it has thoroughly cooled. Then, to loosen it, slide a straight knife or spatula firmly against the sides of the pan, moving it up and down in very short strokes.

In general, the way to remove a cake from its pan is to run a blunt knife blade around the sides of the pan, pushing against the pan rather than the cake. Shake the pan lightly up and down several times, giving it a sharp tap or two on the bottom if necessary, then invert the cake quickly onto a wire cake cooler.

After you remove a cake from the pan, let it finish cooling on a wire cake cooler or a dishtowel folded several times so that the air can circulate under it.

Never invert a cake onto a plate until it is thoroughly cooled, otherwise it's likely to stick to the plate.

Serving and Storing

A freshly baked cake can be brought hot and steaming from the oven and cut at once into individual portions and served as a pudding dessert. Pour any hot sweet sauce over it. This is a good tip to remember for a cake that didn't quite make it, but is still edible.

Before you remove a cake from the pan to the serving plate, sprinkle the plate with a little granulated sugar. This will keep the cake from sticking to the plate.

When you cut a cake with a knife, the pressure often causes the cake to mat. This won't happen if you get yourself a cake cutter, a metal gadget with a handle and a series of long tines. It's particularly handy for cutting angel food cake.

Or wash a serrated or straight knife blade in very hot water, dry it quickly, then slice.

A cake will stay fresh for several days, especially if it's been cut, if you put half an apple with it and keep it covered.

Don't ice cake or coffee cake before you wrap and freeze it. Make the icing and freeze it in a separate container. Ice the cake after both the icing and the cake are defrosted. A coffee cake that's been frozen can be heated first, before icing. It will look and taste freshly baked.

If your freezer is a very cold one, remove an ice-cream cake to the refrigerator about ½ hour before you serve it, to make cutting and eating easier.

You can freeze an iced layer cake or a portion of one if you wrap it carefully.

If you freeze and then thaw an angel cake it will slice neatly, without crumbling.

If you're going to cut just a couple of servings from a cake and store the rest for a while, cut the cake in half and take the portions from the middle. Then press the 2 halves together: the cake will stay moist and soft.

Don't throw out stale cake—you can make a fine dessert with it. Soak pieces of the cake in rum, then mix this into a thick vanilla pudding and chill well. Cover with whipped cream or decorate with split almonds, or serve with fruit syrup. This becomes a dish for entertaining.

Crumble dry, leftover cake, add some sherry to the crumbs, and use this as a topping for dessert soufflés and cream desserts.

CAKE FLOUR: see FLOUR

CANAPÉS: see HORS D'OEUVRES, SANDWICHES

CANDLES

Candles will burn more slowly and last longer if you put them in the freezer the day before they're needed. There's one caution, however. Very thick candles may crack when frozen. Put them in the refrigerator instead.

CANS AND CANNED FOODS
See *Muffins*

See *Bread* for how to use a 2-pound coffee can to bake bread.

See *Cake* for how to use any size can to bake cakes.

Look at the weights on can labels and compare brands, weights and prices before you buy. "Drained weight" and "net weight" don't mean the same thing. In any canned product that comes packed in water or syrup, what you're interested in is the drained weight—the weight of the solids, not the liquids.

Always wash the tops of cans with soap and water before you open them. Many stores spray their shelves with insecticides.

Shake most cans vigorously before you open them, and you'll find that the contents are more likely to empty out cleanly.

Generally, canned goods stay wholesome for about a year, so it's a good idea to write on the cans the date you bought them.

Store canned foods in a cool, dry place. Cans rust in high humidity. Too much warmth may cause the contents to deteriorate as the weeks pass. (Too cold isn't good either—if the contents of a can freeze, throw the can out.)

In an emergency, you can often use a clean can in place of a small pot on the stove or in the oven to heat food.

Use cans for storing foods in the refrigerator or the freezer. Cover with aluminum foil and use stick-on labels to mark each can before storing. A word of caution: Don't save any cans for storing whose opened metal edges are jagged. Save only those cans that have perfectly smooth openings.

One reason cans are good for storage is that you can strain hot liquids or fats directly into them without fear of cracking or breakage. And when you freeze foods in cans, you can stand the cans directly in a pan of hot water to defrost the contents.

Use the 4- or 6-ounce cans that mushrooms or tomato paste come in for freezing small amounts of rich stock to use in gravy or sauce, or for adding to soups. There's no need to thaw a large container of stock when you need only a little.

Small-sized cans are also excellent for freezing egg whites, lemon juice, or individual portions of baby food that you've prepared.

For freezing individual servings for a meal, 8-ounce and 10-ounce cans are perfect. When the time comes for thawing and heating, put the can in a low oven or in a pan of water on the stove over low heat. You can sometimes stand a can directly on a very low burner. This usually works best for frozen liquids or foods that contain a good portion of liquid.

When you're heating an opened can of food in a pot of water, the can is likely to bounce around a bit unless you place something between the bottom of the pot and the bottom of the can. A good object to use is a flat key, the type that opens a sardine can.

The opened ends of clean cans make nice cookie cutters.

CANTALOUPE: see MELONS

CAPERS
Try to buy small capers—they're more subtly flavored and more tender than larger ones.

Capers come packed in salt or vinegar. In either case, soak them well in cold water before using.

CAPON: see CHICKEN

CARAMEL
You can make caramel (burnt sugar) for coloring stock, soup or gravy by mixing 1 tablespoon of sugar with 1 tablespoon of water and heating this mixture until the water evaporates and the sugar begins to brown. Don't let it brown too much. Double or triple these amounts, depending on your needs.

To caramelize a metal mold, put ½ cup of granulated sugar with 2 tablespoons of water in the mold and boil over medium heat, swirling the mixture in the mold frequently until the sugar turns light brown. Hold the mold in a pan of cold water for a couple of seconds to cool it slightly, then raise it, turning and tilting in all directions so that the bottom and sides are lightly covered with the caramel.

CARAWAY: see HERBS AND SPICES

CAROB: see COCOA

CARROTS

1 pound of carrots will serve 3 or 4 people.

1 pound of carrots will yield 3½ to 4 cups, sliced or diced.

1 pound of cooked carrots, drained and mashed, makes 1⅓ cups; 1 pound of raw carrots, grated, makes about 3 cups.

For serving as a vegetable, buy young slender carrots. They're sweeter. Older ones which are thicker, tougher and sometimes deeper in color are best for soups and stews.

If you can buy carrots with their leafy tops on, do so. They're more likely to be fresher than those wrapped in plastic bags. Remove the greens before storing.

Use a potato peeler to cut carrots into fine thin shavings to serve with greens in a tossed salad.

If you want to make carrot curls, slice the carrots lengthwise into several thin strips to within ½ inch of the small end. Soak them in ice water until they curl. Drain and store in the refrigerator until it's time to serve.

If the carrots you're cooking do happen to be old tough ones, cut them in quarters lengthwise and cut out the long woody middle section. Use only the outer part for cooking. (Add a little sugar or honey to the cooking water.)

If you scrub carrots and boil them whole, then rinse them in cold water, you can easily rub off the skins. It's not necessary to peel them first. If the carrots are young, leave the skins on—the whole carrot is more tasty.

Cooked mashed carrots can be used interchangeably with pumpkin in a recipe calling for mashed pumpkin.

Small cooked carrots—or larger ones cut into 2- to 3-inch lengths and whittled a little to round the edges—make a lovely garnish. Butter them lightly and dust them with very finely chopped parsley

CARVING
See also *Turkey*.

Carving knives should be very sharp (see *Knives*).

If you know how to carve well, you can get more servings out of a piece of meat or fowl.

It's easiest to carve on a board. Things slip on a platter.

With 2 knives you can be a good carver. Use a long thin flexible knife with a rounded end (called a *tranche-lard* in French) for slicing, and a shorter, firmer one with a pointed end for cutting off legs and wings and separating chops.

When you carve, use a 2-tined fork to hold the meat, and whenever possible cut away from you.

CASSEROLES
You can bake many casseroles ahead of time, minus the last 20 minutes of cooking, then refrigerate. Forty minutes before it's time to serve the casserole, put the oven on low (so that glass or ceramic dishes won't crack) and bake, gradually bringing the oven up to cooking temperature. If you're still worried about a dish cracking, put it in the oven on a wooden board, such as a cheese-cutting board.

Baked clay (ceramic) or glass casseroles should never be placed over a direct flame. Use an asbestos pad or a "flame tamer." If you intend to freeze a casserole, line the dish with aluminum foil, then fill, cook and freeze. After the casserole is frozen remove it from the dish, foil and all, and store in the freezer, well wrapped. This frees the dish for other uses.

Never soak any clay casserole dish which is partially or wholly unglazed (rough, porous)—unglazed clay absorbs water, and the dish may become useless.

CAULIFLOWER
An average cauliflower (about 1½ pounds), served as a vegetable, will feed 3 to 4 people.

When you buy cauliflower, pick one whose curd (flower head) is white or near white and hard. Avoid any with a yellowed surface or a covering of small gray specks—this means it isn't as fresh as you'd like it to be. The innermost green leaves surrounding the head should cling to it and be bright green.

Don't cook cauliflower in an aluminum pot; it will darken the vegetable.

Cauliflower will stay nice and white if you add a little sugar, lemon peel or vinegar to the cooking water.

Cauliflower will stay white and taste sweeter if cooked in half milk and half water without a cover. Or cook it in milk alone. (Use the milk for a sauce or as the base for a cream soup.)

Some cauliflower come with lots of bright green leaves that make good eating. Blanch them lightly and serve with butter, or stuff them just as you would cabbage leaves.

Don't discard cauliflower stalks when you cook the head (or curd). Trim off the dry, fibrous parts, blanch, and cut up to serve cold in salads. Or cook them, cut into strips or slices, and serve with a white or hollandaise sauce.

If you're going to cook cauliflower whole, trim it at the stem end and make a crosscut here with a sharp knife to facilitate the cooking of this harder portion.

Parboil a whole cauliflower for 8 minutes in boiling salted water, then drain and cool quickly in a pot of cold water. For further cooking, simmer it in fresh water or steam. If you're going to bake or use in another fashion, do the 8-minute parboiling first.

Cauliflower will cook more evenly if you divide the head into small flowerets. Peel the stalk to expose its center, then slice. If the leaves are firm and young, cut these up and cook them with the rest.

Cauliflower should be barely tender when you're ready to serve it. Don't overcook!

CAVIAR

There are several kinds of black caviar (eggs from sturgeon or similar fish), three of which are best known in this country.

They're graded in order of the size of the grain, Beluga being the most highly prized; Ocietrova is next and Sevruga third. They're all expensive and delicious. The best way to serve black caviar is the simplest: open the container and surround it with cracked ice; set it beside toast fingers or small butter sandwiches, and separate dishes of minced onions, minced hard-cooked egg white and sieved hard-cooked egg yolk. And you know what goes best with this? Champagne.

Red caviar (salmon eggs) is the least expensive kind of caviar. Don't knock it. It can be served in the same way and with the same delight as black caviar.

When you use caviar in a mixed dish, as for canapés, add it just before serving, otherwise the oil will smear or discolor the other ingredients.

CELERY

1 large stalk of Pascal, or green celery, diced, will give you about ¾ cup.

Pascal celery contains more vitamin A than white celery.

You can stuff celery with practically any sandwich spread or cracker dip.

The quickest and most thorough way to rid a celery stalk of strings is to scrape it from top to bottom with a short-bladed knife.

You can make celery crisp for the table by standing it up to its leaves in a pitcher of cold salted water in the refrigerator. Add some lemon juice to keep it white.

To make celery curls, cut cleaned celery into 4-inch pieces. Then cut each piece into narrow strips down to about an inch from the end. Soak these in ice water for half an hour or so, and they'll curl.

When you cook celery, use a small amount of water and a low flame. Boiling too fast makes celery tough.

Save your celery leaves. Use them in soups and stews. If they're fresh and green, cut them into your tossed salads.

Dry celery leaves, then rub them through a sieve. Save this

powder to use as a flavoring in soups, stews and salad dressings.

Make your own celery salt at a fraction of what you'd pay for it at the store. Dry celery leaves thoroughly, crush them to a powder or rub them through a sieve, and mix with salt.

Maybe you've never heard of celery fritters, but try them. Cut up those tough outside stalks of celery which you might not otherwise use, and make fritters—using any fritter recipe—to accompany meats and chicken. They're really good.

CEREALS

To prevent cereals, such as rice, flour, oats and grits, from becoming infested with fly-eggs and other insects, pour them from the boxes or bags they are packaged in and store in large tightly closed jars. Or place each package in a large plastic bag and twist the top closed with a rubber band.

When you cook cereal, add it slowly to rapidly boiling water so that the boiling won't be disturbed. This will prevent gumminess. Be sure you use a large enough pot to allow for rising at the sides without overflowing.

You can use many dry cereals as crumbs if you put them through a blender. They're excellent in meat loaf, hamburger and as a substitute for bread crumbs. They're good added to bread dough, too. You can also make crumbs by rolling crisp cereals in a dishtowel with a rolling pin.

To crisp cereal, pour into a cake pan and heat in a moderate oven.

Leftover cooked cereal can be chilled, cut in slices, and sautéed like scrapple. Dip the slices in beaten egg and crumbs first. This can be a very healthful starch substitute at a meal. (And it really tastes good.)

CHARD: see SWISS CHARD

CHEESE
See also *Soufflés.*

If you're learning about cheese, don't be put off by the way some kinds look. Many cheeses taste their best when they look their worst. Experiment with different types, one at a time.

Cheese which you intend to serve at the table should always be at room temperature. Remove it from the refrigerator 1 hour or more ahead of time.

Cheddar Cheese

4 ounces of grated Cheddar cheese will give you about 1 cup.

Cottage Cheese

There are 2 cups of cottage cheese in 1 pound.

Cottage cheese is a soft uncured cheese made from skimmed milk, but most has some cream and a little rennet added. It's sometimes called pot cheese.

Creamed cottage cheese contains at least 4 percent butterfat, and usually has some salt added to it.

Although cottage cheese breaks down when it's been frozen and thawed, it can be used in cooking. After thawing, it's easy to whip until creamy.

Farmer cheese is pressed cottage cheese which has been made with some whole milk, thus it has a somewhat higher fat content than cottage cheese.

Store containers of cottage cheese upside down in the refrigerator so the cottage cheese will stay moist.

Pot cheese is a nonfat, no-salt cottage cheese that has had much of the moisture pressed out.

Cream Cheese

There are 4 ounces of cream cheese in ½ cup.

To use cream cheese as a spread, let it come to room temperature and mix it with a very small amount of any of the following: milk or buttermilk, sweet or sour cream, yogurt, onion juice, Worcestershire sauce, mayonnaise, soft butter, clam or vegetable juices, herbs, spices.

Serving

Cream cheese and cottage cheese are wonderful spreads for hot waffles, or pancakes. You can sprinkle brown sugar over the cheeses, or use them with fruits or syrups.

To serve Roquefort cheese in cubes or squares, use a fork when you cut it. The cheese will retain its natural crumbly texture.

Use a potato peeler to cut cheese into strips for garnishing.

Storing

After you cut a piece of cheese, butter the edge of the remainder which is to be stored and it will be less likely to dry out and lose its proper consistency.

The best wrapper for storing cheese in the refrigerator is aluminum foil. It keeps the odor in and prevents drying.

If mold forms on the surfaces of hard cheeses such as Parmesan, Swiss, Cheddar, Romano, just cut or scrape it off. The cheese is still good.

Many cheeses—particularly Swiss, all the French, Italian and Greek natural cheeses, and Cheddar—can be frozen and will keep well.

You can freeze an unopened package of cream cheese. When thawed, it's not quite as smooth-looking as before, but it's perfectly good and tasty for all cream cheese uses.

Most firm cheeses will keep easily for 2 months in the refrigerator if bought fresh and kept unopened in the original wrapping.

The best way to store an opened piece of cheese in the refrigerator is to use a jar—one with an opening large enough to accommodate the width of the piece of cheese. Set the cheese, standing up, on the inside of the jar lid, then invert the jar and screw it onto the lid. Store in the refrigerator, lid end down. You have an airtight and odortight covering. And you can see what's in the jar.

Grating

1 pound of firm cheese equals 4 cups grated; 2 ounces will give ½ cup.

¼ pound of Cheddar cheese, grated, will yield about 1½ cups, loosely packed.

1 pound of American cheese will give about 5 cups of grated cheese.

Any firm cheese can be hardened (by exposure to air) and grated.

The two most common cheeses for grating are Parmesan (mildly flavored) and Romano (sharp). Also try grating Swiss, Gruyère and Cheddar for use on casseroles and vegetables.

If you use a large amount of grated cheese in your cooking, buy grating cheese in blocks and grate it yourself. You'll save half the cost and have double the flavor.

To dry cheese for grating, wrap it tightly in folded paper toweling and when the towel has absorbed a lot of oil, remove it and rewrap the cheese in fresh paper toweling. Repeat this until the cheese is dry enough to suit you. (Keep the cheese at room temperature during this procedure.) This is a good device for removing oil—hence calories—from cheese for eating, too.

Before you grate cheese, brush a little oil on the grater with a pastry brush. You'll find the cheese will wash off the grater easily.

It's easier to use a blender than a grater to grate very dry cheese and get fine-grained grated cheese. Cut the cheese into small cubes (so they won't get caught in the knife blades).

If you're going to mix grated cheese into a hot dish, toss it in just before serving, otherwise it will become stringy.

Stand a wide-mouthed funnel in a tall glass or jar and grate the cheese into it. This will prevent the cheese from flying out every which way as you grate.

If you don't have a grater, you can scrape Romano or Parmesan or any other hard cheese with a 4-tined fork.

If you need to grate or shred a very soft cheese, try putting it in the freezer for about 30 minutes first.

If you freeze Roquefort, blue, or Gorgonzola cheese, it will grate very nicely into a salad dressing or into any dish calling for finely crumbled cheese.

Any dried-up cheese (Swiss, American, Cheddar, etc.) can be grated and used over vegetables, soups, etc.

Another use for dried-up cheese is to cut it into small chunks and put the pieces in the blender with some slices of raw onion and add some sour cream or yogurt. This makes a marvelous canapé or sandwich spread.

Cooking

Italian Fontina cheese melts more smoothly and is less stringy than mozzarella.

For a cheese sauce that won't curdle, first make the sauce without the cheese. When the sauce is cooked and nearly as thick as you want it, fold in the freshly grated cheese. Don't boil the cheese sauce after this step.

When cheese is added to a soup, the grated cheese you buy tends to make it cloudy. If you want a crust of cheese to float on top of a soup, grate it fresh. Use Swiss, Parmesan, Romano, Cheddar or Gruyère.

Cheese will melt smoothly in a milk sauce if you add the cheese to the cold milk and then heat it slowly while stirring.

Don't cook any cheese at a high temperature; it becomes tough and stringy. A double boiler is the safest pot to use if you're making a cheese sauce.

Put a slice of Swiss or Gruyère cheese over a cooked vegetable and heat it in the oven until the cheese melts, or put it under the broiler until the cheese browns lightly.

CHEESECAKE: see CAKE

CHERRIES

A pound of fresh stemmed cherries will give you about 3 cups; pitted, about 2½ cups.

A paper clip makes a great cherry pitter. Open it out into a hook and use it to pierce the cherry and push the hook under the pit. Just give the clip a twist and with the other hand pinch just behind the pit. It comes right out. And it's fast.

CHESTNUTS: see NUTS

CHICKEN

See also *Birds, Frying, Garlic, Leftovers, Sautéing, Stuffing.*

When you buy a whole chicken, count on ½ pound per person.

2 pounds of unboned chicken breasts will give you about 1½ pounds of meat after boning.

Try to buy fresh-killed chickens rather than frozen or cold-storage ones. They really have much more flavor. Cold-storage chickens are sometimes chemically treated to slow down decomposition. You can be sure a bird is fresh-killed if it hasn't been eviscerated before you buy it. If you live in a city, fresh-killed chickens can be bought at kosher meat markets. Some small regular butcher shops also carry them—but not supermarkets, unfortunately.

To insure tenderness in a chicken (for frying or broiling) buy one which weighs 3 pounds or less, unless you intend to stew or roast it.

In a young and tender chicken the skin under the legs and wings will break easily, and the breastbone will be flexible.

A medium-aged chicken (3 to 4½ pounds) still has a somewhat flexible breastbone, and skin which is also a little delicate (it should break without too much pull). Some of these can be fried, but most are best for roasting.

An old chicken (a fowl) costs less per pound than a young chicken for frying or broiling, has a rigid breastbone, is well over 4 pounds, and is lumpily fat around the tail. Get a chicken like this for stewing and soup making.

A capon is a gelded rooster. Although it has large deposits of fat all over its body, these contribute to its flavor. A capon averages more meat per pound and is also tenderer and juicier than any other fowl. Capons weigh from 6 to 8 pounds.

Preparing

You can marinate an older chicken so that it's as tender as a young one. Use a warmed mixture of oil, wine, and herbs. Pour this over the bird and let stand for about 4 hours at room temperature, turning now and then. You can also marinate it in the refrigerator for a day. You'll be surprised at how tender the chicken will be.

A rather tough chicken can also be tenderized if you marinate it overnight in the refrigerator in nothing more than seasoned white wine or dry vermouth.

An old bird can also be made tender by long gentle simmering. Stew a cut-up bird in about 3 cups of water with any vegetables and flavorings you like. Cover and simmer—never boil—for a couple of hours. The chicken will end up very tender indeed.

It's much easier to bone chicken breasts if you freeze them slightly.

Chicken halves will broil evenly if you split the meat partway at the leg joint where the thighbone and backbone meet.

Rub the entire surface of a chicken with a little salad dressing (this can contain a little mayonnaise if you like) before you put the bird in the oven. It's not only tasty, but it also keeps the chicken moist.

If you like Southern-style fried chicken, don't dry the chicken pieces after you've washed them. Roll them in a mixture of 1 cup seasoned flour and 1 teaspoon of baking powder. Fry in 1 inch of hot fat.

You can make a flour coating for chicken crispier and lighter if you mix a little cornstarch well into the flavored flour (about 2 teaspoons of cornstarch to ½ cup of flour).

To get a crisp, dry coating on chicken, sauté the pieces (turning them once) only enough to cook slightly. Put them in the oven to finish cooking and browning.

You can get a nice cracker crumb coating on fried chicken by dipping the pieces in evaporated milk before rolling them in the cracker crumbs. Let stand about 10 minutes before frying or sautéing.

Store uncooked chicken in the refrigerator covered with a damp dishtowel. Air should reach the bird or an unpleasant odor develops. Don't store a chicken for more than 2 days before you cook it.

Sometimes you may need to scald a chicken a little to remove some of its feathers. Add a teaspoon of baking soda to the scalding water and the feathers will come out easily. You can use tweezers or a strawberry huller to pluck out the pinfeathers.

It's not very hard to eviscerate a chicken yourself. Make a slit at the tail, large enough for your hand to reach into comfortably.

Pull out the organs gently but firmly, starting at the top, exerting pressure with your fingertips only where the tissues are attached to the inner wall of the body. Take care not to press hard in the liver region by the gall sac—any part of the bird on which the dark yellow fluid in the gall sac falls is useless and has to be discarded. Rinse the cavity well after you've removed the innards.

Here's how to cut a whole chicken into parts: bend the wings and legs so you can tell where they join the body, and with a sharp knife cut through the skin here. Locate the joints and then sever the wings and legs from the body. If you want to detach each thigh from its drumstick, move the thigh and drumstick against one another until you've located the joint. Cut through the skin and meat and move the thigh again, until you see the joint. Cut through it. On either side of the breast, below the ribs, cut through the skin and soft bones to the back. Bend the lower portion of the back up, snap it and cut free from the upper part. Cut each side of the breast free from the back by inserting your knife through the opening which is just below the joint from which you detached the wing. Cut downward through the points where the ribs are attached to the breastbone.

To truss a chicken, twist a pipe cleaner around the legs, or tie them together with white thread or dental floss. Spread the wings outward, then bend the second joint out and fold it under from the back—the wings will stay in place, close to the body. A large bird which requires longer roasting should have the wings tied close to the breast to keep the breast juicy. Use white string or dental floss. Also tie the ends of the drumsticks together.

If you can, season all poultry the day before you cook it. The dish will be much more flavorful. Be sure you remove the bird from the refrigerator at least an hour before cooking.

Don't add salt to a roasting or braising chicken until shortly before serving. Salt coaxes the juices out of meats or fowl, and unless you're making soup or stock, you want these juices to stay inside the chicken.

One of the best herbs to use with chicken is tarragon. Soak a teaspoon of dried tarragon in ½ cup of dry white wine for ½ hour, pour the mixture over the chicken, then cook it any way you have in mind.

Dry vermouth, a very full-flavored wine, is great for cooking chicken—you need very little other seasoning. Vermouths contain many roots and herbs and are more full-bodied than other dry white wines. (You also need less than if you were using other types of wine.)

Try rubbing a chicken with some good brandy before you roast it. You can season it in other ways at the same time.

If you want a crisp brown crust on roasted or broiled chicken, rub mayonnaise all over the skin before cooking.

There are many ways to prepare a chicken for roasting. One is to make a thick flour and water paste and to cover the bird with it before you put it in the oven. It will dry and harden and keep the bird juicier. (Take the coating off about 20 minutes before the bird is done so that it can finish browning.)

When you're making chicken croquettes or patties, they'll be easier to handle if you dust your hands well with flour. Also, form the croquettes well ahead of time, then chill them thoroughly. They'll keep their shape better.

Cooking

A 4- to 5-pound chicken should be roasted at 350° for 1½ to 2 hours.

A large chicken may be roasted breast-side down for the first 40 minutes. This will keep the breast from drying out. Then turn the bird breast-side up to complete the roasting.

Broilers have very little fat on them. Oil or butter a broiler well before cooking. Baste often and keep your eye on it.

When you broil chicken, don't place it too close to the flame, or the outside will char before the meat has had a chance to cook inside.

To test a roast chicken for doneness, stick a skewer into the thickest part of the leg—if the juice which runs out is clear (not pink), it's done. You'll also note that the meat has shrunk back somewhat from the ends of the drumsticks.

You don't need a special mallet to flatten chicken slices, such as boned chicken breast, for sautéing. Put the pieces of chicken between sheets of waxed paper and hammer with the underside of a small heavy frying pan.

When you sauté chicken, heat the fat only moderately hot. Chicken sautéed in fat that is too hot gets an unpleasant flavor. Cook it skin-side down at the start so that the skin won't shrivel before it has cooked and browned.

Dark meat takes a little longer to cook than light. When you sauté chicken, cook the thighs and drumsticks about 4 minutes longer than other parts of the bird.

To test sautéed chicken for doneness, prick it with a sharp-tined fork: if the juice which rises is clear and untinged with pink, it's cooked enough.

There's a combination of frying and sautéing which cooks chicken pieces deliciously. Here are the steps to give you tender juicy chicken: put about 1 inch of fat in a heavy frying pan and heat it—but not to smoking—then add the chicken pieces. Cover the pan. During the cooking, turn the chicken only once. Keep the lid on until close to the end of cooking. Drain the chicken pieces well or pat them dry with paper towels.

When you bread or flour chicken pieces before frying, refrigerate them for 1 hour or more and you'll find that the covering will adhere better during cooking.

When you fry chicken pieces in deep fat, watch for them to rise to the surface. This indicates that they're done. You'll see that they're a nice golden brown.

If you're cooking chicken for chicken salad, let it stand in its broth for an hour before you cut it. It will not only have more flavor, but also a velvety texture.

Canned chicken is very soft. Don't expect to use a whole canned chicken in any intricate dish and have it hold its shape.

If you want to render chicken fat, melt the pieces of fat, stirring over a very low flame until you feel you've liquefied all the fat you can. Strain and cool.

See *Soups*, for what to do with a chicken carcass. Never throw it away until you've cooked everything out of it.

Chicken bones and skin, unlike meat bones, should be browned in a pan on top of the stove instead of in the oven before going into soup or stock. Poultry bones dry out and scorch in the oven.

Save chicken skin if you remove it before you cook chicken. Add to bones or meat waiting for the stock pot, freeze for future use, or use it later to make the greatest chicken broth ever by simmering in lightly salted water for an hour—it has lots of flavor. (You can remove the fat from the broth after it has been refrigerated.)

If you can get chicken feet (a kosher butcher may have them, and will charge very little) they make excellent stock, broth or consommé. Have the nails chopped off, scrub the feet and cook until they fall apart, then strain and refrigerate. Skim when cooled.

You can cook chicken feet, necks and backs (all very inexpensive) with a few cups of water in a pressure cooker for a little over 1 hour, until the bones are the consistency of soft chalk, at which point they are a very nutritious meal for a dog.

To sauté coated chicken pieces quickly and still get a crusty skin, cover the pan during the first half of the cooking. If you like a tender skin, cover the pan during the last half of the cooking.

The dark meat of a chicken has more flavor than the white. If you're adding pieces of chicken to a soup, it will have a richer taste if you include a lot of the dark meat (drumsticks and backs).

Chicken gizzards are the toughest part of a chicken. By cutting them in pieces and simmering until tender in a little liquid or stock, you can shorten the cooking time if you are using them in a stuffing or for a fricassee.

CHICKEN LIVERS
See also *Liver*.

Collect and freeze all chicken livers which come with the chickens you buy. After a while you'll have enough for a main dish.

Before you use chicken livers, examine each one to make sure no part of the skin of the gall sac adheres to it. This skin is yellowish in color and will ruin the dish if any part remains.

When you cook chicken livers, brown them first quickly at high heat, then cook gently at low heat, also for a short time. Handled this way, they won't lose any of the blood and juices which keep them tender.

If you want to use the blood from chicken liver in a sauce or gravy, add ¼ teaspoon of lemon juice so that it won't curdle.

CHILI SAUCE
See *Ketchup*.

Once you've opened a bottle of chili sauce, refrigerate it. Otherwise both the flavor and the color will deteriorate.

CHINESE FOODS
Visit a Chinese or Oriental food shop for some new food ideas. You'll find many kinds of noodles including shrimp noodles; bean curd (to serve in soup or salad); fresh bean sprouts and bamboo shoots for mixed vegetable dishes and salads; fresh or dried ginger root for seasoning stews, chicken and fish; fresh baby pea pods (snow peas) for stews, soups and salads, and as a vegetable in itself; many kinds of dried beans; Japanese and Chinese mushrooms, both dried and canned (and wonderfully chewy); plus many kinds of canned, dried and fresh fish and meats.

CHIVES: see HERBS AND SPICES

CHOCOLATE
4 ounces of chocolate, grated, will give you ¾ cup.

2 ounces of chocolate, melted, will give you ¼ cup.

Use a potato or vegetable parer to make chocolate curls for decorating cakes and pies. You can use bars of sweet, semi-sweet or bitter chocolate. The chocolate should be at room temperature or even very slightly warmer. You can adjust the thickness and length of the curls by the pressure of your strokes.

Once you've melted chocolate to use in cooking, keep the pan of chocolate over warm water until you're ready to use it.

When you melt chocolate to add to cake batter, add a little flour to the residue in the pan after you've poured the chocolate from it; mix thoroughly, then add it to the batter. This will remove almost all the chocolate from the pan.

For a quick icing, put a piece of sweet or semi-sweet chocolate on top of a hot cupcake as soon as you've taken it from the oven. Cover with a little aluminum foil; then, when the chocolate has melted, spread with a knife.

CHOCOLATE CHIPS
A 6-ounce package of chocolate chips will give you 1 cup.

CHOPPING BLOCK
Get yourself a wooden chopping block; it's very handy in the kitchen. They come in all sizes. You'll use it for everything from rolling dough to cutting vegetables to carving meats.

Scrub your chopping block after each use, then wipe it dry. Don't let water remain on it for very long. Once every 6 months cover it with vegetable oil and let it stand overnight, then wipe off the oil. It will last indefinitely.

CHOU PASTE
See also *Cream Puffs*.

Chou paste is the dough from which cream puffs, éclairs and other types of filled puff shells are made.

You have to beat cream puff dough (chou paste) very, very thoroughly if you want the puffs to be really light and glossy.

Bake chou paste in a hot, preheated oven so that it puffs at once, the puffs increasing 4- or 5-fold. Watch them—if they begin to brown too quickly, reduce the heat after 10 minutes or so. But don't take them from the oven until they're dry and light when you hold them in your hand; if they're still moist inside they'll collapse when cool.

A properly baked puff is puffed high, medium tan in color, and gives off a light papery sound when you flick it with your fingernail. (This is something like the sound a properly baked meringue gives.)

You may find that very large puffs have moist centers when the outside has baked thoroughly. So that the puff doesn't collapse upon cooling, slice off the top and remove all the moist dough with your fingers. Then return the puff to the hot turned-off oven for 10 minutes, leaving the door ajar.

If a puff seems done but shows beads of moisture, it's probably underbaked. Return it to the hot oven, turn off the heat and leave it in for about 5 minutes with the door ajar.

You can freeze puff shells. When you remove them from the freezer, put them in a preheated 425° oven for about 4 minutes, and they'll be dry and crisp again.

Cool puff shells thoroughly before you fill them or they'll get soggy.

CHOWDER: see SOUPS AND STOCKS

CINNAMON: see HERBS AND SPICES

CLAM CHOWDER

There are three things a clam chowder—any kind of clam chowder—must have: clams, onions and salt pork. Not bacon, salt pork.

If you're using unshucked clams for a chowder, scrub them well with a brush under cold running water and drop them, a few at a time, into ¼ potful of boiling water. Remove them with a slotted spoon or a small strainer as soon as they open (a couple of minutes at most), take the clams from the shells and set them aside. When you're all through let the broth in the pot settle and pour it off carefully (there'll be sand at the bottom). Use this broth in your chowder, adding the clams whole—if they're small—or minced, just before serving, so they won't toughen. If you're using very large chowder clams, cut away the tough muscle portions and just use the soft belly.

If you add a can of whole or minced clams to your chowder just before serving, it will give a richer flavor and very tender clams.

CLAMS
See *Shellfish.*

Different types of clams come from different waters. These are the chief types from Eastern waters: the hard-shelled chowder clams, cherrystones and littlenecks are all the same clam (Quohog or Quahog) at different stages of development, the littlenecks being the youngest and tenderest. There are also soft-shelled clams (Ipswich) with long gray necks, often called steamers. And there are razor clams (a great delicacy) from the same waters.

Clams from certain waters, or at particular times of the year, may contain a lot of sand. They'll usually discharge their sand if you cover them with a mixture of 1 gallon of water to ⅓ cup of salt and let them stand completely undisturbed for about an hour.

The traditional method of de-sanding clams is to sprinkle them liberally with cornmeal, then cover with fresh water and let stand about 3 hours.

A clam is alive—and therefore fresh—if its shell is tightly closed. Never use an opened clam which won't close on handling or one which floats when placed in water.

If you want to store fresh unopened clams in the refrigerator, put them on the lowest shelf, covered with a wet dishtowel. They can stay there as long as 2 weeks, if necessary, but examine them daily and discard any which have opened and won't close. Naturally, the sooner you use them, the meatier they'll be and the better they'll taste.

Opening hard-shelled clams at home is tricky if you've never done it before, but here's a way that works: scrub the clams thoroughly with a brush under cold water, then let them stand quietly out of water for 5 or more minutes until they're slightly relaxed. (When a clam is handled roughly it "clams up" and holds its two shells so tightly closed that it's hard to wedge a knife blade between them.) With a little practice you'll be able to tell that the clams are relaxed by the width of the crack between the shells. Pick up the clam lightly and place it in your left hand in the crotch between your thumb and index finger, crack side facing out. Take a short strong knife and place it quickly to the center of the crack (the side of the knife, not the point) and push in *quickly*, using your right-hand index finger to give force to the thrust. Run the blade forcefully down and then along the entire crack, cutting the muscle at the back which holds the shells together. If you're too slow with the thrust, the clam will tighten again and you'll have to set it aside to relax once more. This sounds involved, but it isn't, and with a little practice you'll be an expert clam opener in a short time.

Here's another way—the lazy man's way—to open clams, and for serving on the half-shell it takes an expert to tell the difference. After you scrub the clams, drop them, about 3 at a time, in boiling water for about 15 seconds. Remove them quickly with a slotted spoon or small strainer and open with a knife, as described above. Dropping them in boiling water for a few seconds relaxes the muscles just enough for you to slip the knife blade in easily, but not enough to cook them even slightly. But beware of leaving them in the water any longer, or they'll be poached.

To store clams on the half-shell, open them, taking care to retain as much of the liquid as you can, then place them in a flat pan or dish and cover with clear plastic wrap to keep them from drying. Refrigerate, but serve them the same day they're opened.

Heat toughens clams quickly, so avoid overcooking. They're done in 3 minutes or less.

CLARIFYING

You can clarify hot fat, consommé, broths, etc., very easily by letting them drip through a paper coffee filter that has been fitted into a funnel with a narrow neck.

CLEANING TIPS

Keep a small soaped sponge near the stove to wipe up grease spatters and avoid bigger cleanups later.

A toothbrush is ideal for cleaning a strainer, scrubbing a grater, cleaning the blades of a blender, and a dozen other kitchen uses. Keep one near the sink.

Keep some coarse sand handy. It's marvelous for scouring the insides of bottles you can't otherwise get at. Fill the bottle about a quarter full of sand, add a little soapy water, screw the cap on, and shake like crazy. Pour the contents into a strainer, then rinse the bottle and the sand well. Let the sand dry and store it again for future use.

Or you can tie tiny pebbles or coarse sand very loosely in a small piece of nylon stocking knotted at both ends and use to clean a bottle or jar. Shake well with soapy water and you'll see the inside of the bottle get clean as a whistle. Pull out the knotted stocking, rinse under running water, and hang it up to dry.

If you want to keep your drinking glasses absolutely free of marks, dry them with a dish towel in each hand so that your fingers never touch the glass.

Those flat, green sheets of hard sponge that are meant for cleaning cars without scratching the finish are good for scrubbing enameled pots and nonstick-coated pans. They're like nonscratching scouring pads. Cut the big sheet into handy-sized pieces—6 inches by 3 inches, for example.

Don't throw away those plastic mesh bags that onions and potatoes often come in. Use them to put soap ends in. Cut the bag to size, knot the ends, and you've got something with which to wash dishes and scrub things. (These mesh bags are also handy for drying vegetable pieces and mushrooms in.)

Put soap ends in a quart container half full of water and keep adding bits of soap as they're left over. In time you'll get a thick, soapy fluid that is great for certain cleaning chores. For example, you can use it for cleaning a jar or bottle you can't get your hand into. Fill a jar or bottle with the fluid and let stand overnight, then pour the soap back into the storage container and rinse the jar or bottle with hot water. It almost always comes out sparkling clean.

When you have to clean a doughy or floury counter top, or any surface made messy by food preparation, dust it first with salt. The flour or food remnants will never stick to the cloth or sponge when rinsed out.

Perform potentially messy food chores in or over the sink: measuring flour, pouring soups and sauces from pots into other containers, flipping eggs or omelets. If you should have an accident, think of the cleanup work you'll be spared.

To freshen smelly household sponges, soak them for several hours in a solution of 2 tablespoons of baking soda to 1 pint of water.

To make your kitchen smell nice (or to cover up an unpleasant odor), put a teaspoon of whole cloves and a slice of orange rind in a cup of water, bring to a boil, then simmer for 10 minutes.

COCOA

See also *Chocolate*.

There's 1 ounce of cocoa in ¼ cup; 1 pound of cocoa equals 4 cups.

Cocoa is chocolate with most of the fat (cocoa butter) removed.

To substitute cocoa for chocolate in a recipe, use ¼ cup of cocoa plus 1 teaspoon of butter or oil for each ounce (square) of unsweetened chocolate.

If you add cocoa to a cake recipe which doesn't call for it, decrease the amount of flour by 2 tablespoons for each ¼ cup of cocoa you add.

When you make hot cocoa, simmer the cocoa powder in water alone for about 5 minutes before you add milk and sugar. This breaks down the starch and you'll have a more velvety cup of hot chocolate.

If you don't want skin to form on top of a cup of hot cocoa, beat it until it's frothy as soon as you make it.

Add a tablespoon or two of strong coffee to your hot cocoa. Good!

Some people can't eat chocolate or cocoa. They can try a substitute, however. Use carob powder in place of cocoa in any recipe for cakes, cookies, or brownies. Carob powder is available in many supermarkets. Use the same amount of carob powder as you would cocoa, but cut down a little on the sugar called for in the recipe because carob powder contains some natural sugar.

COCONUT

When you're picking out a coconut, look for a heavy one that sounds full of liquid when you shake it.

Once a coconut is opened it won't keep for much more than a week in the refrigerator, but you can freeze the pieces. They'll be less likely to dry out if you submerge them in coconut milk and store in containers.

To remove the coconut meat from its hard shell, cover the pieces with boiling water and simmer for 8 to 10 minutes.

If you want freshly grated coconut, cut the coconut meat into small pieces and drop them in the blender. This is easier than—and every bit as good as—grating the pieces by hand.

Don't throw away shredded coconut if it begins to dry out. Toast it by spreading it on a cookie sheet, and heat in a moderate oven. Shake the pan occasionally so the coconut browns evenly. Use as a dessert topping on cookies or sprinkled over a cake icing.

COFFEE

1 pound of coffee, brewed, will give 40 to 50 cups.

If you have to buy coffee for long storage, buy whole coffee beans. They oxidize less rapidly than ground coffee. (See *Blender*.)

Unopened cans of coffee will retain their flavor longer in the freezer.

For drip, percolator, or vacuum-type coffee makers, use 1 heaping tablespoon of ground coffee for each ¾ cup of cold water.

Even though many fancy coffee makers are on the market, you might discover that boiled coffee can give you a first-rate cup of java. Use the finest grind. You'll not only get a delicious cup of full-flavored coffee, but you'll also find it economical—no need to use a full coffee measure per cup of water. A little more than half a coffee measure (the equivalent of 1 rounded tablespoon) is enough for 1 cup of rich boiled coffee.

And here's how to make boiled coffee without any fancy paraphernalia: Put ground coffee and cold water into a pot, allowing a few inches at the top so the contents won't boil over. Bring to a rolling boil and remove the pot at once from the heat. Allow it to quiet, then return it to the heat once more. As soon as the coffee starts the second boil, remove the pot from the heat and let stand for about 1 minute. Then pour into cups. There's no need for a strainer because after the second boil the grounds always sink to the bottom.

Coffee that has overboiled and become bitter (though this shouldn't happen) can be made palatable if you add ¼ cup of club soda to each 1½ measuring cups of hot coffee. Stir well.

It may surprise you to learn that regular instant coffee (not decaffeinated) contains quite a bit less caffeine than the equivalent amount of regular brewed coffee.

Mix regular coffee with an equal amount of decaffeinated coffee and you can halve the amount of caffeine you take in—and still get the taste of coffee.

The nearest thing, in taste, to brewed coffee is freeze-dried coffee. In freeze-drying, the coffee bean isn't heated as long as regular instant coffee. (But freeze-dried coffee is usually more expensive than regular instant coffee.)

If you're going to serve coffee in demitasse cups, you can use regular coffee if you make it half again as strong as you usually do.

Make frozen cubes of very strong coffee; put a couple in a cup and pour boiling water over them. You have instant real coffee.

1 pound of medium-ground coffee will give you 4½ cups.

The flavor of ground coffee will keep better if you store the opened container in the refrigerator covered tightly—when it's exposed to air its volatile oils evaporate and it always loses some flavor. (If you don't use it up quickly, keep it in the freezer.)

There's no unanimity about how coffee should be made. Most experts agree it's best when you make it in a nonmetal container, with the coffee grounds not in contact too long with the water. They favor the drip method, using an enamel or glass pot.

If you make drip coffee, stir the coffee in the pot before you pour it, otherwise the best part remains at the bottom of the pot.

You can make instant coffee very palatable if you add the coffee to a pan of boiling water and let it come to the boil again. Then pour.

If you're pouring hot coffee into a glass containing ice cubes, stand a long-handled metal spoon in the glass first, then pour. Otherwise the glass is quite likely to crack.

Pour freshly made or leftover coffee into an ice cube tray and freeze. Keep the frozen coffee cubes in a plastic bag in the freezer and use these for icing iced coffee—you won't dilute the coffee.

You'll get the freshest and best-tasting coffee by buying whole beans and grinding them in your blender before brewing. No preground coffee can equal this.

COLD FOODS
Generally, dishes to be served cold need more seasoning than those you're going to serve hot, since warmth naturally releases the bouquet in foods, herbs and spices.

If you want foods for picnics or school lunches to stay cold longer, put the opened insulated carrier you intend to use in the freezer and let stand overnight. Then in the morning pack the cold food in it quickly and close. (This is also true for thermos bottles.)

COLE SLAW
Try preparing cabbage for cole slaw by putting it through the coarse or medium blade of the meat grinder. This will save you a lot of time, and the cabbage won't crush.

COLLARDS
You can use collard greens for rolling and stuffing just as you do cabbage. And you don't have to blanch the collard greens first as you do with cabbage: Just wash, fill, and roll. They'll soften properly during the cooking.

CONSOMMÉ
See also *Aspics and Gelatin Dishes, Bouillon.*

Consommé is clear broth which contains gelatin so that it jells when cold.

Chicken feet or a veal knuckle cut in two by your butcher are the best things to use if you want a consommé which jells naturally.

To jell a clear broth which has had no bones cooked in it, use 1 tablespoon of unflavored gelatin for each 2½ cups of liquid. (You might like a little more or a little less liquid—the thickness one wants in a consommé is a matter of taste.)

COOKIE SHEETS

When you buy cookie sheets, try to get stainless steel instead of aluminum. Aluminum sheets eventually warp and buckle as the years pass, and give an uneven surface.

It isn't necessary to grease cookie sheets if the cookie dough has a lot of shortening in it (as most cookie doughs do).

If you must, grease cookie sheets with a solid vegetable shortening or sweet butter (butter adds more flavor to the cookies). Don't use a liquid fat for greasing; the area between the cookies will burn during baking, and it will be almost impossible to clean.

If you flour a cookie sheet after you've greased it, cookies made from thin batters will be less likely to thin out and spread during baking. A greased, floured sheet is also best for any dough which contains chocolate bits—if the chocolate comes in direct contact with a cookie sheet it's likely to stick and burn.

Don't knock yourself out to scour cookie sheets. They do a better job of baking cookies when they're not shining and gleaming. As long as they're clean, you can forget the baked-on stains.

COOKIES

See also *Cookie Sheets, Cupcakes, Fats and Oils, Nuts.*

You can often make cookies using a recipe for cake dough: Eliminate practically all of the liquid from the cake recipe and use only half as much baking powder as the recipe calls for. Substitute some all-purpose flour for cake flour.

If you use cooking oil instead of solid shortening in cookie dough, the cookies will be more tender. Conversely, a solid shortening makes cookies crunchy.

Put ¼ cup or so of almonds, pecans, or walnuts in the blender, grind them quickly to a rather coarse powder, and add to the cookie batter. Use a little less flour than the recipe calls for. Whoever eats these cookies is in for a delight.

Whole bran and wheat germ are nutritious and economical substitutes for nuts in cookies.

If refrigerator cookie dough seems a little too soft to form into cylinders, don't be tempted to add more flour to stiffen it. Instead, stick the bowl of dough in the freezer for about an hour. You'll find the dough easier to handle.

To form refrigerator cookie dough into cylinders, push the dough into long, narrow cans that have had both ends removed. Store these in the freezer (for future use) or the refrigerator. Use cans from concentrated frozen juices or the elongated cans asparagus, etc. comes in. Save one end of the can. When you're ready to slice the dough into cookies, push in at one end of the can with the can end. Slice off the dough at the other end as thin or as thick as you like. Use a cheese cutter or a buttered knife for this.

Almost any cookie dough makes a dandy pie pastry, especially for open-faced tarts, etc. Knead the dough a little, roll it out, and fit it into a pie pan just as you would pastry dough.

The opened ends of clean cans make neat cookie cutters.

Here's a suggestion for cutting out cookies: Roll the chilled cookie dough between 2 sheets of waxed paper and slip this into the freezer for 15 minutes. Remove, pull off the top sheet, and cut out the cookies.

To flatten thick drop cookies before baking, slip a piece of nylon stocking over the bottom of a glass. Dampen the stocking and use to tamp down the cookies to the thickness you want.

Cookie batter thins and spreads out on hot cookie sheets, so either cool the cookie sheets before you use them again or have an extra one that can cool while the other is in the oven.

If you let brownies cool completely in the pan before cutting them, you'll be able to cut the squares neatly without tearing.

Cookies made with oil will keep for at least 2 weeks in a cookie jar. But butter cookies, unless you freeze them, will develop an off-flavor after a week.

Cookies that have become hard can be softened if you store them for a day or so in a closed container with half an apple.

You can also soften cookies that have become too crisp or dry by storing them overnight in an airtight jar with a slice of fresh bread.

If you make cookies with honey instead of sugar, you'll find them at their best about 2 weeks after you bake them. They ripen. Store the cookies, separated by squares of waxed paper, in closed jars in a cool place.

A quick way to put a nice topping on cookies without making an icing is to cover the cookies with jelly or preserves before you bake them. The cookies, when cool, will have a tasty glaze on them.

Whip an egg white lightly, then brush it over the cookies and dust with granulated sugar before baking. This gives a shiny sweet crust to the cookies.

The flour used in most cookie doughs is all-purpose flour rather than cake flour. Cake flour is usually too tender for cookie dough.

If you're out of flour you can often substitute fairly fine plain or toasted bread crumbs. The cookies will taste a little like macaroons. Add ½ teaspoon of almond extract and they *will* taste like macaroons.

Cookie dough takes about half as much baking powder as cake dough.

Before you mix brown sugar with butter or margarine for cookie dough, run it in the blender for a little while. This breaks up lumps and makes it easier to cream into the shortening.

You can substitute many kinds of dry cereal for nuts in cookies.

Oatmeal cookies will taste better if you toast the oatmeal first. Sprinkle it over a pan and put it in a low oven for about 10 minutes.

If you roll cookie dough between sheets of waxed paper you can avoid adding more flour to the dough; also, it won't stick to the rolling pin. This is easier if the dough is chilled lightly first—all cookie doughs are handled more easily if they're chilled.

Rolled cookie dough—like pie pastry—shouldn't be handled too much, nor should it contain too much flour, or it will toughen.

When you use your hands to shape cookies—especially if the dough contains a lot of shortening—wet your hands with cold water from time to time and the dough won't stick to your palms.

Dip your cookie cutter in either powdered sugar or warm water, and the dough won't stick to it.

When you flatten balls of cookie dough before putting them in the oven, you'll often get better results if, instead of using the traditional flat side of a knife dipped in water, you wet your fingers and use them to flatten the dough. The dough won't stick to your fingers, whereas it sometimes does to the knife.

Use a wet knife to cut refrigerator cookie dough into slices, and they'll cut cleanly, without ragged edges.

Baking

Not all ovens maintain a constant temperature throughout prolonged baking—many ovens get hotter as time goes on. This matters more with cookies than with other kinds of baking. If you're baking several batches of cookies, check the temperature from batch to batch. You may need to set the regulator back, or else bake the later batches a shorter time than you did the earlier ones.

If you bake cookies on baking paper you can easily remove the paper afterward by setting the cookies, paper-side down, on a well-soaked towel until the edges of the paper curl upward. Lift, and peel off the paper.

If you find that your cookies are too crisp, you may have used too much sugar or too little fat in the dough. Also try storing them in an airtight place.

If your cookies come out too soft, you may have used too much liquid for the amount of flour.

Never put cookies in a container for storing until they've thoroughly cooled.

Soft cookies, such as ginger cookies, should be separated from one another in the cookie jar by squares of waxed paper, otherwise they're likely to stick together.

Many cookies stored in airtight containers will remain soft. Some, like ginger cookies, become downright limp—many people like them this way. And some become sticky, especially those containing a lot of egg white.

COOKING FOR ONE

If you live alone and don't enjoy having to create daily menus for yourself, a freezer can be your best friend. Cook for four, or any number in a particular recipe. After cooking, save one serving for immediate eating and freeze the other servings, wrapped individually (see *Cans and Canned Foods* for how to make this easy). You'll not only eat well, but also spare yourself from cooking three other separate meals.

If you don't drink much milk, but use only a little in your coffee, you can still buy it by the quart and not worry about its going sour. Pour the quart of milk into 3 or 4 small bottles or jars with good screw tops. Allow a couple of inches of room for expansion on freezing. Set them in the freezer. (Milk defrosts at room temperature in a few hours, and perhaps a day in the refrigerator. If you want to hasten thawing, stand the bottle or jar of milk in a pan of cold water and shake the bottle or jar now and then. Once thawing starts, you can add a tiny bit of warm water to the pan. Let it stand and again give the bottle or jar an occasional shake. The milk will thaw in less than an hour.)

Buy a pound of good steak—the very best quality, if you like—and divide it into thirds. Eat a portion the day you buy it—or the day after—and wrap and freeze the rest. (Unless you weigh over 150 pounds or are engaged in strenuous physical work, this amount of meat is all most people need at a meal. Eat plenty of vegetables with it.) Out of that pound of steak you've got three meals for a moderate cost.

COPPER

If you're out of copper polish, dissolve a scant tablespoon of salt in ⅓ cup of vinegar, dip a soft cloth into the mixture, and rub the copper surface. Rinse well and dry. This really does the job.

Or you can do a great job on copper by rubbing it with a piece of well-salted lemon rind. This works on brass, too.

If you haven't any copper cleaner, you can clean copper-bottomed pots and other kitchen utensils with toothpaste and a damp cloth.

CORKS

An easy way to get a cork out of a wine bottle is to dip a cloth in near-boiling water and quickly wrap it around the neck of the bottle near the cork. Then insert the corkscrew. The hot cloth will make the glass expand just a little.

CORN

A 1-pound can of whole kernel corn, drained—or a 1-pound can of creamed corn—will give you about 2 cups.

5 to 6 ears of fresh corn will give you about 3 cups of kernels when cut from the cobs.

To remove the silk from an ear of corn, wipe downward toward the stem end with a clean damp cloth, or use a stiff vegetable brush.

Refrigerate corn as soon as possible after it has been picked. Corn begins to lose sweetness immediately, at room temperature.

Never buy corn that's been husked—it has little flavor.

Here are a couple of ways to tell whether corn is fresh: the butt end (where the corn attaches to the stalk) should be white and moist. If it's dry or brownish, the corn has probably been around for a while. Also, look at the "flags"—the small, fine, narrow leaves that stand out near the top of the ear. These will shrivel and become brittle if the corn isn't fresh.

Examine the teeth on an ear of corn before you buy it by tearing back the green husk a little. If the teeth are a very dark yellow, the corn is past its prime and will be starchy rather than sweet. If the teeth are very small and nearly white, the corn is probably too young to have developed much sugar yet.

Some corn contains cutworms. You can tell whether an ear is affected by lifting the corn up by its silk. If the silk remains attached when you raise it, it is unlikely that there are cutworms inside.

If you can't use corn the day you pick or buy it, stand it—with the husks still on—in a little water in the refrigerator, stemside down. It will keep well for a day or two.

Cooking

Don't add salt to the water in which you cook corn—it toughens it.

Put the tenderer green husks from inside the corn into the cooking water. This adds beautifully to the flavor.

There are several good ways of boiling corn. But remember, corn is an exception to the fact that most vegetables become softer with continued cooking. Like eggs, ears of corn toughen with overcooking. Test an ear from the pot occasionally. Corn of different kinds and from different areas varies in tenderness. In general, corn should be just tender enough to eat.

To boil corn, shuck and put it in a large pot. Cover with boiling water, put a lid on the pot and light the flame under it. As soon as the water returns to a boil remove the pot from the heat, still covered, and let it stand about 8 minutes. Test, drain and serve. (Cooked this way, the corn can stand in the hot water for as long as 20 minutes and still have good flavor.)

Here's another way to cook corn which uses very little water. Take the tender inner husks, wet them, and line the sides and bottom of a heavy pot. Put the shucked corn on this and cover with more husks. Cover the pot tightly and set over a low to medium flame. When the lid of the pot feels hot to the touch, turn the flame as low as possible and cook for about 12 minutes longer.

If you have to cook corn a little ahead of time, bring the water to a boil, add the corn, cover, and turn off the heat. Let it stand until you're ready to serve. It will rarely need more cooking.

Try roasting corn in your oven. Pull out the silk but leave the husks on. Roast at 325° for about 50 minutes. Remove the husks (wear rubber household gloves—they're hot!) and serve. This method gives a much better flavor than boiling.

An old-fashioned method of cooking corn on the cob is to cook it in half milk and half water. It helps to keep the corn tender.

CORN BREAD

Try mixing ⅓ cup of crumbled crisp-cooked bacon into a corn bread batter before you pour it in the baking pan.

Corn bread won't stick to the baking pan if you grease the pan and then sprinkle it well with fine cornmeal.

Don't bake corn bread in a pan that is too thin or the outside will be overdone before the inside has baked.

CORNMEAL

Stone- or water-ground cornmeal is made from the whole corn (including skin and germ) and is more nutritious than the dry granular "new process" kind. But stone-ground doesn't keep as long, so buy it in small quantities.

Cornmeal gives a tougher, coarser covering than crumb or flour coatings for fried, baked or broiled foods. This is fine for some things—a cornmeal coating has a distinctive flavor—but for a thin light crust you might want to use fine bread crumbs or flour or cracker meal.

Cornmeal won't form lumps if mixed well with a little cold water before you add it to any hot or boiling liquid.

CORNSTARCH

See also *Thickeners.*

Cornstarch gives a clear quality to a soup or sauce, while flour makes it opaque. One tablespoon of cornstarch equals 2 tablespoons of flour for thickening power.

CORN SYRUP: see SYRUPS

COTTAGE CHEESE: see CHEESE

COVERS

If you need a cover for a pie plate or a low baking dish and your pot covers don't fit, try inverting a pot or frying pan over the top.

If you need a cover which makes a very tight seal over a pot, cover it with a sheet of waxed paper, then put a pot cover over this. You'll find that the heat and moisture will stay in very well.

Always lift the lid of a cooking pot away from you to avoid steam burns.

CRAB

¾ pound of cooked crabmeat equals 1½ cups.

The cooked meat of 6 hard-shell crabs equals about 1 cup.

It's the meat of the blue crab which is generally sold in fish markets, cooked and packed in containers. It comes in lump or flake forms. Lump is usually preferred for crabmeat cocktails, and is more expensive. But before you buy a container of it, have your fish man empty the can in front of you; sometimes the top layer may be lumpy but the portion underneath may not. It's better to discover this at the market than in your kitchen.

Blue crabs are also sold as hard-shell crabs or, in the spring or early summer, soft-shell crabs, after they've shed their hard shells but before the new ones have grown.

Alaskan king crab, available both frozen and canned, is really more like lobster in taste and texture (though not as tender) than like ordinary blue crab. Blue crab is much sweeter and tenderer, and much the better of the two.

If you buy whole crabs, they'll usually be cleaned for you at the fish market. But if you must clean them yourself, here's how to do it for both hard-shell and soft-shell: wash them free of sand under cold water, and with a small knife, remove the spongy substance under the side joints and the pouch between the eyes (or remove the entire head from just below the pouch). All the rest is edible.

Whether you buy canned or fresh crabmeat, always finger through it carefully to remove the bits of shell which seem always to be there, especially in the fresh-packed variety.

Soak any kind of canned crabmeat for a short time in icy water to remove the tinny taste which it sometimes has. Crabmeat rinsed this way is more like fresh crabmeat in taste.

If you buy live soft-shell crabs, to get a particularly succulent flavor, submerge them in seasoned milk or eggnog 2 or 3 hours before killing and cooking.

Crabmeat, like all seafood, is very delicate. Never overcook it.

CRACKERS

Crackers of all kinds, plain or sweet, salted or seasoned in other ways, can be ground in a blender or placed in a plastic bag and rolled with a rolling pin to give you crumbs to use in meat loaf, meatballs, chicken croquettes, fish patties, and for a variety of toppings for baked vegetables, meat pies or puddings.

The meal of slightly sweetened crackers often gives a good taste to a ground meat dish.

When crackers get limp, crisp them in a preheated 300° F oven for about 5 minutes.

CRANBERRIES: see BERRIES

CREAM

See also *Sour Cream.*

If you're not completely certain about the freshness of cream, beat in a pinch of baking soda. The cream won't curdle, even when you add it to hot coffee.

Whipped cream will be fluffier and less likely to liquefy later if you use confectioners' instead of granulated sugar when you sweeten it.

Whipped cream will retain its lightness, height and texture for a day or more (refrigerated) if you add 1 teaspoon of corn syrup to each ½ pint of cream before whipping. This will add almost no perceptible sweetness to the taste.

For maximum frothiness in whipping, use day-old rather than fresh cream.

If you see signs of the cream becoming buttery during whipping, add 2 tablespoons of cold milk and whip again, carefully.

Cream whips best if you don't whip too much at a time. A good rule of thumb is to see that the height of the cream to be whipped doesn't completely cover the blades.

Cream doubles in volume when it's whipped.

If you use an electric beater for whipping cream, circulate it around the bowl by hand so that you can reach all parts of the bowl. Use a rubber spatula to bring the edges of the cream into the center.

Cream for whipping should be heavy cream. If you can, avoid containers labeled ultrapasteurized or whipping cream. They contain additives such as algin and monoglycerides—substances no one needs in pure heavy cream.

Most of the "whipped cream" that comes squishing out of a nozzle is part air, part added chemicals, and—I suppose—part cream. Avoid it like the plague.

Keep heavy cream refrigerated until the very last minute before you whip it. The colder the cream, the easier it is to whip and the less likely it is to turn to butter during energetic whipping.

Whipped cream is easier and faster to make if *everything*—the cream, bowl, and beaters—has been chilled. This is especially true in a warm kitchen, where the cream is likely to turn to butter before it's thickened. You can also set the whipping bowl in a bowl of ice cubes as you whip.

The best way to eliminate spatter when whipping cream is to start out slowly. If you're whipping by hand, save the frenzy for later when the cream begins to thicken. If you're using an electric mixer, don't turn it up to whipping speed until the cream starts to thicken. Once thickening begins, there's very little spatter. This method may take a little longer, but you don't have to wash your walls afterward.

You can avoid spatter by whipping cream in a high narrow bowl instead of a low wide one. Circulate the beater as you whip.

You can also cut down on spatter when you're whipping cream, if you cut a piece of waxed paper or plastic wrap large

102

enough to cover the bowl, make 2 holes in it for the stems of the beaters, push the stems up through the holes from below, attach them to the beater, then whip the cream under this covering.

If you want to whip a small amount of cream, put the cream in a cup and use only 1 blade of the electric beater.

If you plan to fold whipped cream into other ingredients, remember that it will hold its stiffness only if the other ingredients are very cold.

When you use cream in any dish cooked on top of the stove, avoid boiling or it will curdle. Always cook dishes containing cream over a low flame, and stir constantly.

Try undiluted evaporated milk (or even evaporated skimmed milk) as a substitute for light cream. These can be used very successfully in sauces, with a great saving of calories.

Instead of serving plain cream with coffee, pass around a bowl of unsweetened whipped cream, as they do in Vienna. A generous teaspoon on each cup of coffee looks and tastes wonderful.

Serve a dollop of slightly salted whipped cream on tomato soup or any creamed soup. You can dust paprika, curry powder or finely minced chives over it.

You can freeze leftover whipped cream by spooning dabs of it on waxed paper and putting these in the freezer. When they're frozen, put them in a plastic bag and keep in the freezer to use for dessert toppings. They take from 10 to 15 minutes to thaw.

If you plan to serve whipped cream over a sweet dessert, don't add sugar to the cream when you whip it. It's often not necessary, and the contrast can be delightful.

Never pour whipped cream on a hot dessert before you serve it; the cream will liquefy. Instead, serve it at the table.

Here are a couple of uses for whipped cream that may not have come your way. Mix a little into the juices of stewed or sautéed mushrooms, fold in the mushrooms, and serve. Also, whip and lightly salt some heavy cream and beat into hot mashed potatoes.

You can freeze heavy, medium, or light sweet cream, but you can't freeze sour cream. It becomes liquid and will not thicken.

(You can, of course, still use sour cream that has been frozen in cooking.)

Use sour cream (plus ¼ teaspoon of baking soda) to replace the water or milk in bread dough. It will give you a very tender loaf.

CREAM CHEESE: see CHEESE

CREAM OR CUSTARD DESSERTS

Don't keep cream pies or any cream- or custard-filled desserts at room temperature for long. Bacteria love them as much as you do, and grow quickly. Refrigerate right away and keep cold until serving time. Their refrigerator life is at most 3 days.

CREAM PUFFS

See also *Chou Paste*.

Don't fill cream puffs until shortly before you serve them, otherwise they're likely to become soggy. You can make the filling early and refrigerate it. Fill the puffs 1 hour or so before the meal at which they'll be served.

To fill a cream puff or an éclair, cut a very small hole in the side or end and press the filling in, using a pastry bag. A shortcut is to slice off the top, fill the puff with a spoon, then replace the top and ice or sugar it—but this isn't quite as professional.

CRÊPES

See also *Fillings*.

Never overbeat crêpe batter—this toughens the crêpes. Whip only until the batter is smooth, the same consistency as light cream.

To test for proper consistency, 1½ tablespoons of crêpe batter, immediately tilted around in the prepared hot pan, should give you a 5-inch crêpe.

If you let crêpe batter stand in the refrigerator for 1 hour or more after mixing, your crêpes will turn out smoother and more velvety.

If you're making crêpes for dessert, use 3 parts milk and 1 part water for the liquid, and they'll be lighter. You'll get a heavier crêpe (for filling or an entrée) if you use only milk or light cream for the liquid.

A crêpe should be made in a heavy-bottomed pan the same size as the crêpes you want to make.

Butter a crêpe pan with a pastry brush.

The trick in making a successful crêpe is to see that the bottom of the hot buttered pan is coated quickly with the batter before it begins to set. Lift the pan from the flame in order to tilt it all around quickly. You'll need very little batter for a single crêpe—only enough for one thin coating.

To turn crêpes (or omelets) easily without using a spatula (resign yourself to sacrificing a few crêpes and give yourself 20 minutes for practice), prepare a small cast-iron omelet pan or a crêpe pan (as recommended under *Omelets*), make up your batter, and cook one side as any crêpe recipe directs. Then hold the pan over the kitchen sink and flip the crêpe up with a turning-over motion of your wrist. The secret is to flip it high—don't hold back. It will turn over in the air and you should have the pan ready underneath to catch it. Discard anything that falls in the sink. A few tries will have you catching the crêpe upside down beautifully. Pretty soon you won't have to move from the stove to do it. (The knack stays with you.)

You can make crêpes many hours in advance, fill, and reheat them. You can even freeze them unfilled, of course. Separate them between squares of waxed paper, then wrap the whole very well.

Try using crêpes in place of store-bought lasagne noodles the next time you serve lasagne.

Crêpes, which you can freeze (stored between layers of waxed paper), sometimes crack in the freezer when they're laid flat. Try rolling them instead. Arrange the crêpes in layers of 3 or 4 with waxed paper between each crêpe, roll, and snap a rubber band around each roll. Store in the freezer. Crêpes thaw nicely at room temperature without breaking.

CROQUETTES

A croquette mixture should consist of about 2 cups of finely diced solids to 1 cup of thick cream sauce, formed into cakes, balls or cones, coated and deep-fat fried. The softer the mixture, the more delicate the croquette.

Make your croquette mixture well ahead of time so you can chill it thoroughly. Croquettes are much easier to handle when they're cold. They also hold together better while being cooked.

Dust your hands with flour when you form croquettes and they won't stick to your hands.

If your croquettes are very creamy, dip them twice in beaten egg and crumbs, allowing them to dry after each dipping. This will seal the soft insides. Don't forget to chill them well after this.

You can mash canned or baked beans, season them and make them into delicious croquettes. (Dip them in egg and crumbs, then deep-fat fry.)

You can roll croquettes, particularly fish croquettes, in potato chip crumbs. Run over a bag of potato chips with a rolling pin until the crumbs are as fine as you want them.

CROUTONS

Make your own croutons—the ones you buy are always a disappointment. Butter both sides of 2 or 3 slices of bread, season if you want, then cut them into small cubes. Scatter the cubes on a cookie sheet and heat them in a 375° oven for about 15 minutes, or until they're lightly browned.

If you're adding croutons to a salad, do it just before serving, after the salad is tossed and the dressing has been added, otherwise they'll be soggy.

CRUMBS AND CRUMB CRUSTS

See also *Pies.*

15 graham crackers pounded to fine crumbs will give you 1 cup. For coarse crumbs, 12 graham crackers should do it.

22 soda crackers pounded to fine crumbs will give you 1 cup.

Cracker crumbs are quick and easy to make, and much less

expensive than those you buy. Just throw some crumbled crackers into the blender and grind to whatever fineness you like. If you're going to use the crumbs as a coating for fried or sautéed foods, toss in some caraway seeds, or sesame seeds, or paprika, or herbs of any kind.

Food to be floured or coated with crumbs for frying or sautéing should be allowed to stand at least 30 minutes after being dredged. The coating will adhere better during the cooking.

Hard, dry cookie crumbs are delicious when mixed into a regular dough. They give the cookies a crunchy texture, rather like ground nuts.

If a recipe calls for graham cracker crumbs, it's usually advisable to crumble the crackers with your hands (or with a hammer over waxed paper) instead of in the blender. When the crumbs are too fine, they tend to "mat" and become limp when mixed with moist ingredients.

Sometimes a graham cracker crust pie can be cloyingly sweet, especially if the filling is rich. When you make your crumbs, substitute ⅓ cup of soda cracker or saltine crumbs for the same amount of graham cracker crumbs. If you use saltines, omit the salt called for in the recipe.

An easy way to lay a crumb crust evenly along the bottom and sides of a pie plate is to press the crumbs down with another pie plate a size smaller.

CUCUMBERS
When picking out cucumbers, choose the smaller, thinner, greener ones. Large thick cukes, and those showing much yellow on the surface, tend to be pulpy and tough inside and full of large seeds.

Many cucumbers these days are sold with a paraffin coating to slow their deterioration. The only way to remove this is to peel them. Try to buy them unwaxed—ask for pickling cucumbers.

You can give a professional look to cucumber slices if you take a sharp-tined fork and score the cucumber from top to bottom (pressing in at the top and drawing the fork down toward the bottom of the cucumber, making sharp lines). Do this all the way around the cucumber, then slice it crosswise.

To make peeled diced cucumbers very crisp for salad, sprinkle them with salt and refrigerate in a bowl for a couple of hours. Drain them (they will have released quite a bit of water) and dry with paper towels or a dishtowel. Then refrigerate again until you're ready to combine them with the salad.

Here's how to prepare cucumbers for cooking so they won't be mushy: peel, slice down the middle and remove the seeds. Then salt them well and let stand for an hour or more, to draw out excessive water. Wipe off the salt and dry with a dishtowel. Now they're ready to cook.

Try cooking cucumbers as you would eggplant. You can stuff and bake them, boil them and serve with a sauce or cream and then broil them.

Did you know that a long thin slice of peeled cucumber added to a highball glass masks the alcohol taste of a mixed drink? This is especially true if the drink contains gin or rum. Add a few slices to a punch bowl, for those who don't like the taste of alcohol.

CUPCAKES
See also *Cake, Icing.*

If you bake cupcakes or muffins in muffin papers, be sure you peel the paper off while the cake is still hot. Otherwise you can have a terrible time getting it off.

To make cupcakes all the same size, use an ice-cream scoop or a quarter measuring cup to ladle out the batter. For large-sized cupcakes, use a half measuring cup.

Fill cupcake tins about ¾ full.

To make cupcakes into cookies, cut the cupcakes crosswise with a sharp knife after they're thoroughly cooled. Cover the slices with icing.

Moist, crumbly cupcakes are often hard to remove from their tins. Set the cupcake pan in the freezer for a couple of hours and the cupcakes will ease out nicely with the help of a knife.

CURRY: see HERBS AND SPICES

CUSTARD
See also *Pies.*

The term *boiled custard* is a misnomer. A custard shouldn't really boil. If it does, it's likely to scorch. Keep at a simmer.

To make a custard with eggs rather than cornstarch or flour, the ratio should be 1 egg or egg yolk to every ½ cup of liquid. With this rule, you can make varying amounts and sorts of pie fillings, custard desserts, and vegetable quiche-type dishes. Add solids as you wish.

If you've made a custard that won't thicken properly—never mind the reason—must you pour it down the drain? Not on your life. Pour the custard into a bowl and put it in the freezer. Take it out after an hour or so and beat it. Return to the freezer. After a couple of hours, remove from the freezer and beat it again. What have you got? You've got a pretty decent ice cream, that's what.

You can also use an undercooked custard or a custard that won't thicken properly to pour over a pudding or ice cream.

To see if a baked custard is done, insert a knife blade near the edge of the custard (not in the middle). If the knife comes out clean, the custard is done. The middle part of a baked custard firms during cooling. Remove a baked custard from the oven as soon as it passes the knife blade test. If a baked custard "weeps" or is runny, you've probably baked it too long.

When you serve baked caramel custards, you can make sure the caramel is liquefied and flows nicely over the unmolded custards if you make the custards a day ahead and let them chill in the refrigerator until the time of serving.

If you scorch the milk you're heating for a custard, discard it. It won't taste good. You can avoid this by heating it in a double boiler.

If you plan to unmold a baked custard, beat the eggs only lightly before you add them to the liquid. This will keep the custard firm when it is baked. (Too much beating produces a light, porous custard.)

For a rich brown custard crust, beat the eggs until they're frothy before you add them to the milk.

Custard made of egg yolks, sugar and milk will be less likely to curdle if you beat 1 teaspoon of cornstarch or flour into the cold milk for every 4 egg yolks you use.

Never cook custard over high heat or it will curdle. Stir it continually while cooking—either in a double boiler over boiling water or with an asbestos mat or flame tamer under the pot.

If your custard begins to curdle during boiling due to excessive heat, pour it at once into a cold bowl, and beat it hard with a whisk.

Boiled custard is done when you've cooked it just until the bubbles disappear. It is at this moment that it leaves a light coating when you let it run off the back of a metal spoon.

As soon as a boiled custard is done, you want to prevent its continuing to cook. Take the pan from the heat at once and set it in a larger pan of cold water.

When cooking a baked custard for a pie, you can prevent the pastry from getting soggy after you've slipped the custard onto the crust if you heat the milk to its boiling point before slowly combining it with the beaten eggs when making the custard. This will give the custard a slightly crisp undercrust.

For baked custards, put the custard cups in hot, but not boiling, water when you put them in the oven. If you use boiling water the custards will be porous on the bottom and sides.

Refrigerate custards and custard-filled desserts at once, and keep cold until serving. (They should not be refrigerated for longer than 3 days.)

CUTTING BOARD
Brush cooking oil over the surface and sides of a new wooden cutting board and let it stand for about a week. If dry spots appear on the board (this means the oil has seeped into the wood), put more oil on it. Wipe the board with paper towels and it's

ready for use. Repeat this every 6 months or so and the board will not warp or split. (Never let a cutting board soak in water.)

If possible, position your cutting board so it overhangs a table or counter top slightly. This arrangement comes in handy when sweeping peelings and other odds and ends straight into the garbage. (And the food itself, which you've cut on the board, can be swept into a dish or pot.)

DANDELION GREENS

The only dandelion greens to use in salad or as a cooked green are very young tender ones—the kind that are available in early spring. Too many of the greens you see in markets are well beyond this stage, and are bitter and tough.

DATES

8 ounces of pitted dates will give 1½ cups chopped.

Put dates (and other sticky fruits) in the freezer for 1 or 2 hours and you'll be able to cut and chop them much more easily. Also, dip your knife or scissors in hot water now and then while you're cutting.

If you're using chopped dates in a cake, toss them in flour before you add them to the cake batter so that they don't sink to the bottom during baking.

DEFROSTING: see FREEZER AND FREEZING

DESSERTS

See also *Cake, Custard, Ladyfingers, Pies.*

The fillings of many pie recipes can be baked as is without a crust. Many of these baked fillings can be cut into wedges and served; others can be treated as hot puddings to be served with a spoon, and topped with anything you like.

For an unusual dessert, freeze washed and drained berries in a flat serving dish, then at serving time remove from the freezer and pour cream over them. The cream will freeze slightly to the berries. The combination is wonderful.

If you've made a fancy gelatin or similar kind of dessert that you'd like to arrange on a serving plate in advance, unmold the dessert hours earlier and invert a large bowl over it. Keep it chilled and safe in the refrigerator.

DILL: see HERBS AND SPICES

DISH TOWELS

To quickly cool any cooked foods (boiled potatoes, asparagus, broccoli for salad, etc.), spread them out on a dish towel.

Small terry cloth hand towels are less expensive than terry cloth dish towels, although they're about the same size. In fact, the hand towels are usually more attractive. So the next time you need terry cloth dish towels, try the linen department instead of kitchenware. And look for white sales.

If you have a few badly stained cotton or linen dish towels that have had their day, don't use them as rags—yet. Save these old dish towels to wipe off chicken and meats before cooking them. Toweling is much better than paper towels for this chore. Dish towels are also great for cooling freshly baked cookies on, or for the quick drying of mushrooms.

If you have an old, worn linen table cloth, consider cutting and hemming usable parts of it for dish towels. Real linen dish towels cost a bundle these days, and in any case it takes months of use before new linen dish towels become soft and absorbent. You can use parts of soft cotton tablecloths, too. Age lends cotton a wonderful absorbency.

DISHWASHING

Because sponges crumble, a good way to handle them for dishwashing is to enclose 1 or 2 in an 8-inch piece of nylon stocking, tying a knot at each end. You can also enclose a small piece of soap with them.

Use scissors to cut a square of steel wool into halves, or even quarters, when you need it for dishwashing. You can extend the life (and minimize the cost) of a box of pads.

Here's a good quick way to wash dishes (especially if you have only a small space to work in) and one that also uses less water:

lather a sponge or dishcloth copiously and then scrub rinsed glasses, silverware and dishes without running water, setting each to one side as soon as it's been soaped. Then rinse under hot running water, and set them to drain. This is *quick*.

You should wash the following items immediately after using them: knives, all kitchen things made of wood or with wooden handles, electric beater and blender blades, strainers, wire whisks.

As soon as you've removed meat from a broiling pan or roaster, sprinkle the pan with salt or a detergent, then cover with wet paper towels. You'll find it much easier to clean later.

Dishes or utensils which have held eggs are easier to wash if you rinse them first with cold water to prevent the eggs from coagulating and sticking to the dishes.

Before you wash heavy pots and large platters, put a folded Turkish towel or a rubber liner across the top of one side of your sink. Rest the pot or platter on this when you wash it.

DOUGH: see BREAD, CHOU PASTE, PASTRY DOUGH

DOUGHNUTS

The more egg yolk you use in doughnut batter, the less fat the doughnuts will absorb in cooking.

Doughnut dough should be as soft as possible; use as little flour as you can get by with and still be able to handle it.

Let doughnuts stand for about 15 minutes before frying after you've formed them. They'll absorb less fat.

If you add 1 tablespoon of vinegar to the fat before you heat it for frying doughnuts, you can eliminate most of the odor of hot fat which spreads so easily through the house.

Doughnuts will also absorb less fat if you heat the cooking fat to 370°–375°.

When you fry doughnuts, turn them frequently in the hot fat and they'll be less likely to crack.

If you want doughnuts to have a soft crust and less fat on the outside, lift them straight from the frying fat and dip them in boiling water. Then set them to dry.

Sugar doughnuts by shaking them one at a time in a paper or plastic bag with a little confectioners' sugar.

For quick doughnuts, cut circles out of the centers of refrigerator biscuits and then drop the biscuits into hot fat, as you would regular doughnuts.

To make firm doughnuts, refrigerate the dough for 8 to 12 hours before you form and fry the doughnuts. Put only a few doughnuts at a time into the hot fat to prevent the temperature of the fat from suddenly cooling. Fat that's too cool results in greasy doughnuts.

Add a good-sized piece of stick cinnamon or 5 or 6 whole cloves to the cooking fat to give your doughnuts an interesting flavor. Of course you can always add a little ground cinnamon, cloves, mace, or nutmeg to the dough when you're mixing it.

If you've made more doughnuts than you can use right away, freeze the leftovers. Be sure to wrap them airtight. And don't ice them first. Thaw, then crisp them lightly in the oven before icing them.

DRIED FRUITS
Shake raisins and other dried fruits with flour before you add them to dough or puddings so that they won't sink to the bottom during baking.

Dried fruits sold in bulk usually need to be soaked in cool water at least an hour, or until they're plump, before you cook them. Take care not to overcook.

When you buy candied fruits to use in fruit cakes, try to get them at a store which carries them in bulk, like a fine candy store or food specialty shop. The ones you buy in glass or plastic jars often have a terrible chemical taste, possibly because of the preservatives added. They can ruin a fruit cake.

DUCK
See also *Stuffing*.

For trussing, see *Birds*.

1 duck will serve 2 people.

When you buy a fresh duck, look for a young one—the only kind worth roasting. It should have a soft flexible beak.

All ducks have excess fat in their body cavities. Remove it before cooking.

A roast duck doesn't have to be greasy. Prick with a sharp-tined fork around the wings and legs, particularly close to where they're attached to the body. A great deal of fat will run off during roasting.

There are at least two good ways to braise a duck. One is to cook it on top of the stove for a short time at high heat, turning often. This pulls out a lot of the fat, which should be poured out of the pan. Then lower the heat and continue braising as your recipe directs. The second way to braise is to prick the duck as for roasting, then sear it in a hot preheated oven for about 20 minutes. (This also releases the fat, which should be discarded.) Then put the pot on top of the stove and braise as directed.

DUMPLINGS

You won't have any trouble getting dumplings to drop from a spoon into boiling liquid if you keep dipping the spoon in the boiling pot.

Drop soft dough dumplings from a spoon onto chicken or meat which is simmering in a broth, not into the broth itself. Dumplings are delicate and need support while they cook.

Simmer dumplings for 10 minutes without a cover, then 10 minutes longer with the cover on. (Don't lift the cover during this period.)

When you drop dumplings into a pot of liquid, don't crowd them. Put in only enough to cover the surface without causing others to submerge.

ÉCLAIRS: see CHOU PASTE, CREAM PUFFS

EGGPLANT

A 1-pound raw eggplant, diced, will make about 2 cups; and 1¾ cups cooked.

Avoid eggplants that are wrinkled or dull-looking. They're likely to be limp and pulpy inside. Be sure the skin is tight and shiny.

Try to use eggplant within a couple of days after you buy it. If refrigerated for more than 3 or 4 days, eggplant loses flavor.

When you buy eggplant, get the heavier, not necessarily larger, ones—they're meatier. Actually, you should pick ones which are on the small side because they're generally sweeter.

You can use a potato peeler to pare an eggplant. (If you're slicing it, it's sometimes easier to slice first, then peel the slices.)

Drop eggplant into salted water as you peel it, and it won't discolor. (When you drain, press it well with absorbent toweling.)

It is not necessary to peel eggplant. You can often bake and eat it, skin and all. It tastes much better and is very nutritious.

Because some eggplants, especially older ones, have a slightly bitter flavor, many cooks slice them thickly, sprinkle the slices with salt, then let them stand under a weight for 1 hour or so. This pulls out excess water. Wipe them dry, and use less salt when you cook them. (To weight them down, spread them flat, covered by a tray, with some bottles of water on the tray.) It's not always necessary to salt and weight down eggplant slices, especially if the eggplant is young. Often you can just slice and cook as directed.

Sliced eggplant absorbs fat easily. You can counteract this blotter effect if you dip the slices in batter (or in egg and then in seasoned flour or crumbs) and cook in *very* hot, but not smoking, fat or oil.

EGGS

See also *Custard, Egg Whites, Egg Yolks, Meringues, Omelets, Sauces, Thickeners.*

There's no difference nutritionally between white and brown eggs, nor between fertilized or unfertilized eggs.

To qualify as jumbo, a dozen eggs must weigh at least 30 ounces; extra-large eggs must weigh at least 27 ounces per dozen; large eggs must weigh at least 24 ounces per dozen; medium eggs must weigh at least 21 ounces per dozen.

2 medium eggs, unbeaten, give about ¼ cup.

The contents of a large egg weigh about 1½ ounces, of which the white weighs 1 ounce (2 tablespoons) and the yolk ½ ounce (1 tablespoon).

Generally, when you buy medium eggs you get more for your money. Only rarely will you have to add an extra egg to a recipe to make up for size. Many recipes are constructed with medium eggs in mind.

When you buy eggs look for the date on the egg carton and choose the ones dated closest to the day you buy them. The date may be stamped on the carton (the fairest dating method, as far as the consumer is concerned) or it may be coded by number ("63" means 63 days from January 1, i.e. March 4). Unfortunately, few consumers know about this code, but you can figure it out.

Don't wash eggs before you store them. The dull natural coating (the "bloom") helps protect their freshness.

Here's a fair rule of thumb for telling old eggs from fresh ones: The shells of old eggs tend to become shiny and smooth; fresh eggs have a rough, chalky appearance.

The older an egg, the larger is the air space within the shell. If an egg rattles when it's shaken, it's not fresh.

If you're not sure how fresh an egg is, put it in cold water. A completely fresh egg will lie flat on the bottom. A moderately fresh egg may have one end slightly raised. You know what it means if it floats.

Eggs which are too fresh won't whip to as much frothiness as eggs several days old.

If you spill a raw egg where it's difficult to pick up, cover it with salt and let it set; then pick it up with damp paper towels.

When you break open an egg, the yolk is less likely to break if you hit it obliquely rather than straight across.

Break an egg by cracking it on the side of the bowl or some other blunt (rather than sharp) edge—you're less likely to break the yolk in the process. After you've emptied the shells, run your finger around the inside of each half to detach all the egg white.

If you open a fresh egg into a dish you'll see an upstanding yolk surrounded by a thickened white portion with a more watery white around the outsides. An egg with a flat yolk and a wholly watery white isn't fresh.

When your recipe calls for several eggs, break each one into a saucer separately before you add it to the rest. One bad egg can ruin everything if you break it into the main bowl.

If eggs are at room temperature before you fry or boil them, the whites will be less likely to be tough. So remove them from the refrigerator a couple of hours before using.

If you need eggs at room temperature and have forgotten to remove them from the refrigerator, put them in a pot of fairly warm water and let stand for 10 minutes.

If you want eggs for thickening, beat them only slightly. If you want them to make a mixture light, beat them to frothiness.

Avoid beating eggs directly into any hot mixture—they'll curdle. Either cool the mixture first or add small amounts of the hot mixture to the eggs, beating well between additions. After the eggs are fairly well liquefied by the mixture, combine the two and beat again.

Salt toughens eggs. Add it to egg dishes only after they're cooked.

Cook all egg dishes at low or moderate heat, otherwise they'll toughen.

When you serve egg dishes use stainless steel flatware instead of silver. The sulfur in egg yolks discolors silver.

You can often substitute 2 egg yolks for a whole egg in a cake recipe. Add a little extra milk.

To make egg threads (as for Chinese dishes or soups) beat an egg well, then pour it into a wide hot oiled pan. Let it spread over the surface in a very thin layer. Cook until firm, turn out on a board and shred.

Some recipes call for beaten eggs and others call for unbeaten eggs. The addition of beaten eggs produces lightness in a batter; and unbeaten eggs make the ingredients adhere to one another (as in meat loaf).

If you've overfried an egg and no one will eat it, just mince it up, add a little mayonnaise, and you've got egg salad for a sandwich.

An egg glaze (for painting the surface of unbaked bread, pie, or any pastry before baking) is made by beating 1 egg with 1 teaspoon of water. This gives a shiny, brittle crust.

Butter or any kind of fat should be heated to the bubbling point before you add the eggs.

Separating

Chill eggs before you separate the yolks from the whites. Yolk membranes are firmer in chilled eggs and are not as likely to break.

If you have trouble separating eggs, you might try breaking them, one at a time, into a narrow-necked funnel. The yolk will remain above and the white will slip through.

When separating the yolk from the white, there's no better method than to make a bowl of one hand and pour the raw egg gently into it. The yolk will stay in your hand and the white will drip through your fingers. It doesn't take long to master this simple technique. And you don't have to worry about breaking the yolk, as occasionally happens when you shift the egg from one half shell to the other. Those shell edges are sharp.

When a recipe calls for egg yolks and egg whites to be beaten separately, always beat the whites first (it usually doesn't matter if the whipped whites stand for a short time). Then you won't have to wash the beater before you tackle the yolks. If you beat the yolks first, you *do* have to wash the beater because the moment any trace of the yolk touches the white, you'll never be able to whip the white to frothiness.

If you've separated an egg and see a bit of yolk in the white, remove the bit of yolk by touching it lightly with a moistened cloth.

Boiling

Remove eggs from the refrigerator at least ½ hour before boiling, since very cold eggs may crack when you put them in boiling water.

If you puncture the rounded end of a cold egg with a pin, it will be less likely to crack when you put it in boiling water.

If an egg cracks while boiling, immediately pour a large quantity of salt on the crack, lowering the flame first. This will often serve to seal the egg and stop a lot of the white from escaping.

When you boil a cracked egg, add some lemon juice or vinegar to the water—this often prevents much of the egg from oozing out. (If you have an egg which may have been cracked for some time, especially if you bought it that way—throw it out. It could contain harmful bacteria.)

When it's important to boil an egg for a certain number of minutes, place the egg, at room temperature, in water which has reached the boiling point. Reduce the heat to a simmer and start counting the time.

It's important to know that eggs begin to cook while the water is heating, so if you time eggs from the point at which the water reaches a boil, the smaller the amount of water you use, the more accurate your timing will be. Use only enough water to just cover the eggs.

To soft-boil eggs, lower them carefully into boiling water, reduce the heat to a gentle simmer and cook for 3 to 4 minutes.

Cook medium-boiled eggs the same way as you would soft-boiled eggs, but for 6 minutes.

When you're making soft- or medium-soft-boiled eggs, remember that large or jumbo ones should be boiled 1 minute longer than small or medium ones.

Coddled eggs are eggs which are soft-boiled until the whites are firm and the yolk liquid, about 5 minutes in boiling water at once lowered to a simmer.

It's hard to tell a hard-cooked egg from a raw one on the refrigerator shelf. If you think the problem will come up, add ½ teaspoon of turmeric or some beet juice to the water in which you cook the eggs.

Another way to distinguish between a hard-boiled egg with its shell on and an uncooked one: spin it on its end—an uncooked egg won't spin.

To hard-boil eggs, lower them carefully into boiling water, reduce the heat at once to create a gentle simmer, and cook the eggs for 10 minutes. Plunge the eggs into cold running water and they will be easier to peel.

Plunging hard-boiled eggs in cold running water while they are still hot will also prevent a greenish ring from forming around the yolk.

To ease the shelling of hard-boiled eggs, put a tablespoon of vinegar in the water in which you boil them. After they're cooked, crack them gently all over and they'll practically leap intact out of their shells. (Even cold hard-boiled eggs are easy to peel if boiled in water with vinegar.)

It's hard to peel a hard-boiled egg neatly when the egg is under 3 days old, especially when the hard-boiled egg is cold. When you're boiling eggs for this purpose (as for Easter eggs) use slightly older eggs.

You can hard-boil eggs so that the whites are firm and the yolks thoroughly cooked but still creamy. Place the eggs in a pot, cover with cool water and bring the water to a boil. Cover the pot at once with a tight-fitting lid, turn off the flame and let stand for 25 minutes. Eggs cooked in this way are very good for stuffing or slicing.

You can slice hard-boiled eggs so that the yolks won't crumble if you keep dipping the knife or egg slicer in cold water.

When you're making stuffed eggs, slice off a tiny piece from the rounded bottom of each hard-boiled half so that when you stuff and arrange them in the dish they'll stand without any trouble.

Cold hard-boiled eggs are easier to slice without crumbling than hot eggs. If you need sliced eggs for sandwiches, or for a garnish, etc., hard-boil, peel, and refrigerate them for a few hours before slicing.

If it's important to you that the yolks of hard-boiled eggs be exactly centered (in making stuffed eggs, for example), stir the water from time to time while the eggs are cooking.

A pastry blender is a quick and efficient tool to use for mincing hard-boiled eggs for egg salad, etc.

Another way to prepare eggs for mincing is poaching instead of hard-boiling them. You won't have to bother with peeling the eggs and it's quicker. If you poach the eggs in broth, they'll have more flavor.

For very good stuffed eggs, mash the hard-cooked egg yolk with a little anchovy paste. Set a small sprig of parsley in the center of each stuffed egg.

Frying

If you like fried eggs with the whites coagulated but the yolks still liquid, use a cover while frying, lifting it often to see that you don't overcook. Or, when the yolk has almost reached the consistency you like, turn the egg over in the pan with a spatula (flipping might break the yolk) and slide it at once onto your plate.

Fried eggs continue to cook after they've been removed from the pan, so fry them just short of the point you like before sliding them off onto a plate.

Poaching

For poaching, the fresher eggs are, the better. The whites of fresh eggs coagulate quickly to surround the yolks with a protective coating which helps keep the yolk membrane from breaking.

When you use an egg poacher, be sure you butter the rings well before you open the eggs into them.

129

Here's how to poach an egg when you have no poacher: bring water with a little white vinegar or lemon juice added (to keep the whites from spreading) to a rolling boil, then lower the flame until the water begins to simmer. Make a whirlpool with a spoon and open the egg into the center of the whirlpool. Move the spoon gently and swiftly around the edge of the pan, keeping the whirlpool going in one direction. Poach for 3 to 3½ minutes. Remove the egg with a perforated spoon.

You can poach eggs in many liquids other than water, such as tomato juice, soup or stock, beer, wine, milk. You can also serve the poached eggs with a sauce made from some of the thickened liquid. Use a butter and flour or cornstarch thickening. Have the thickened butter ready while you're poaching the eggs.

If you've poached eggs and can't serve them right away, slip them into cool water and reheat in hot salted water (but don't let them cook) when you're ready to serve.

Scrambling

For velvety, creamy scrambled eggs, cook them very slowly, starting with a cool buttered pan. Add 1 tablespoon of cream or evaporated milk at the very end. Stir in, and serve.

Scrambled eggs are always at their most tender if you cook them over hot water in the buttered top of a double boiler. This assures a constant low temperature.

If you're making scrambled eggs in a pan over direct low heat, remove the pan from the heat while the eggs are still slightly underdone. Scrambled eggs continue to cook in the hot pan even when you remove them from the fire.

If you cover scrambled eggs in the top of a double boiler and let them stand over warm water (no flame) they'll stay moist and creamy—for a reasonable time—until you want them.

A tablespoon of sherry does wonders for scrambled eggs and omelets. Beat it into the eggs before you cook them.

Shirring

Shirred eggs are broken whole into buttered ramekins or other oven dishes and either baked or broiled. They're usually covered with cream or melted butter while cooking.

Shirred eggs are easier to control when broiled. Baking tends to toughen them.

If you do bake shirred eggs, set the ramekins in a pan of warm water so that the outside of the eggs won't overcook before the inner portion is ready.

EGG WHITES
See also *Meringues.*

There are about 8 medium egg whites to a cup (less if the eggs are large).

1 egg white equals about 2 tablespoons.

Egg whites will beat up more quickly if you add a pinch of salt to them.

If you lift the beater up and down occasionally while mixing egg whites, you'll get more frothiness. This method incorporates more air into the mixture during the beating process.

Egg whites can be frozen. Drop them in a glass or plastic container, allowing a little room for expansion as they freeze. Cover and label the number of egg whites the jar contains. They'll defrost at room temperature in about an hour and can be used in the same ways as fresh egg whites.

Freeze egg whites in ice cube trays if the trays have individual plastic cups that hold one ice cube each. Pour one egg white into each cup, slide the tray carefully into a plastic bag, and set it in the freezer.

You can't whip egg whites to stiffness if they contain any egg yolk. Should even the tiniest bit fall in, the best way to get it out is to take a large piece of eggshell and gently and carefully scoop up the bit of yolk. It should enter the inside of the shell readily, if you're careful.

Egg whites at room temperature will whip to greater frothiness than cold ones.

Add ⅛ teaspoon of baking soda to egg whites if you want them particularly high and frothy.

Stiffly beaten egg whites won't "leak" if you add ¼ teaspoon of cream of tartar or ½ teaspoon of white vinegar to every 4 whites before you whip them.

Don't beat egg whites in an aluminum bowl or they will acquire a grayish color.

Don't try to whip egg whites to stiffness in a blender. It won't work. The blades can't pull in enough air to lighten them.

To whip 1 egg white, put it in a cup and use only 1 beater of your electric mixer.

Stiffly beaten egg whites will have more body if you whip in a little sugar toward the *very end* of beating. Never add sugar to egg whites until you've beaten the whites to where they stand up in peaks. Then add the sugar a little at a time, whipping as you go. If you add sugar too soon, or too much at any one time, you'll get a thin marshmallowy sauce which won't thicken.

When you use an egg white to clarify broth or consommé, take care not to overbeat it. Egg white should be beaten only until it begins to froth, before adding to the broth or consommé.

If you have any egg whites left over from a recipe which called for egg yolks, use them in fruit whips, white cakes, cake icings, baked meringues, angel food cakes, meringue toppings for puddings and pies, soufflés, or hard-boiled and finely chopped, then minced with parsley for a garnish.

Here are some uses for leftover egg whites, besides the traditional fruit whips, angel food cakes, meringues, etc.:

Chicken or Fish

Cover cooked chicken or fish with a well-beaten meringue into which you've whipped a couple of teaspoons of sour cream and any herbs you like. Then dust lightly with grated cheese and paprika, and pop into the oven or under the broiler until lightly browned.

Cookies

Substitute 2 egg whites for 1 whole egg in a cookie recipe. You'll get different, but good cookies. Or whip an egg white lightly, then brush it over the cookies and dust with sugar before baking. This gives a shiny sweet crust to the cookies.

Macaroons

These are variants of baked meringues, with ground nuts and a little flour and flavorings added.

Marshmallow Sauce

This is often what you end up with when you bollix up a meringue by adding the sugar too soon. But it's great over puddings, cake, or ice cream. Spice up the sauce with cinnamon, nutmeg, or vanilla.

Mayonnaise

You can make a pretty fair mayonnaise by substituting a couple of egg whites for egg yolks.

EGG YOLKS

See also *Custard*.

The color of an egg yolk depends on what the hen was fed. It has nothing to do with the nutritional value or age of the egg.

To make egg threads to blend into a soup, Chinese style, heat a little butter in a pan. When the butter begins to bubble, pour in 1 or more egg yolks that have been beaten with a little cold water. Immediately tilt the pan so the yolk mixture coats it entirely—the thinner the better. As soon as the sheet of yolk is lightly cooked (no longer runny), turn it out on a cutting board. Cut into very thin strips with a sharp knife. Add to a clear soup—any soup, actually—before serving. If you like, when you first beat up the yolks, throw in some finely cut chives, fresh dill, or parsley. Egg threads can turn a good soup into a memorable one.

You can substitute 2 egg yolks for 1 whole egg in a cake recipe. Add a little extra milk or other liquid.

Here are some uses for egg yolks if you have them left over from recipes calling for whites alone. Use them in Béchamel sauce, Mornay sauce and custards, or add them to puddings such as cornstarch pudding (without boiling), cake frostings, mayonnaise and salad dressings, and sponge cakes. Hard-boil them and push them through a strainer for a garnish; use them in place of whole eggs in cakes (add a little more milk for moisture); as sauce thickeners; or beat them and add in a thin stream to boiling soup.

133

When you blend egg yolks into a hot mixture, add small amounts of the hot mixture to the eggs first, beating well each time. When the egg yolk mixture is fairly liquid, you can add this to the hot one, stirring constantly; but don't ever let the mixture come to a boil, or it will curdle.

If you want to hard-boil whole egg yolks separately from whites, bring water to a boil, then turn off the flame and drop the yolk in carefully. This will keep the membrane from breaking. Heat the water again slowly and simmer for 8 minutes. Any white which clings to the yolk can be removed easily.

If you're going to store 1 or more egg yolks in the refrigerator for a few hours before using them, rinse the storage cup or jar before you slide the yolks in. A dry container is more likely to cause the yolk membrane to break.

You can store broken egg yolks in the refrigerator for use in cooking or salad dressings. Add ½ teaspoon of cold water for each yolk, beat them well and store covered. Use them within 1 week.

You can also store unbroken egg yolks intact, without the membranes breaking, if you pour ½ cup of cool water into a jar and dissolve ⅛ teaspoon of salt in it. Slip in the whole yolk. The salted water should entirely cover the yolk. Drain carefully before using. Refrigerated, it will stay fresh for 1 week.

If you want to freeze egg yolks, mix them with a little sugar or salt to prevent coagulation, then cover and freeze. Or mix ½ teaspoon of honey well into every 6 yolks before freezing and they'll thaw smoothly without forming a "skin" or becoming gluey. Use these in any recipes calling for egg yolks.

Any mixture containing egg yolks will curdle when boiled. If a sauce contains egg yolks, use a low flame or cook it in the top of a double boiler. Stir constantly.

ELECTRIC MIXER

Use your electric mixer to mash boiled potatoes (using a fairly deep bowl to avoid spatter). You can also use it for mashing other soft vegetables such as cooked carrots or turnips.

Use an electric mixer to remove the strings from cooked mashed pumpkin—the strings will adhere to the beaters.

You can avoid spatter when you're whipping egg whites, cream or batters if you cover the mixer with a dishtowel, or cover the bowl with a piece of waxed paper and make 2 openings for the beater stems to fit through. Stick the stems through the holes, attach the beaters, and beat as briskly as you want with no spatter.

ELECTRIC PERCOLATOR
Your percolator will have a sweet clean interior if you fill it occasionally with hot soapy water and 2 tablespoons of baking soda, then perk it for 10 minutes. Drain, refill it with hot water and perk 5 minutes more. Rinse.

ENAMELWARE: see POTS AND PANS

ENERGY SAVERS
When you're cooking something in the top of a double boiler, boil a few eggs in the bottom part for free. You can always use hard-boiled eggs for salads, sandwiches, etc.

After you've finished using the oven, don't waste the accumulated heat. Slip a pan of diced or sliced vegetable bits into the oven to dry as the oven cools. This is a good thing to do with a leftover half onion or a couple of aging carrots. You'll have dehydrated vegetables for stews and soups that will cost you next to nothing. Be sure the oven isn't too hot, even though you've turned off the heat, otherwise the veggies may brown or char when what you want them to do is dry.

When you use the oven for any purpose—baking or roasting—sneak a cake or some cookies in. You can bake them for nearly free. While they're in the oven, adjust the temperature to suit them—the food you're roasting won't mind.

A stew or soup will generally continue to simmer on top of the stove for 10 minutes after you've turned off the heat, so you can lessen the amount of heat you use by this length of time. This adds up!

135

If you have a self-cleaning oven (which holds heat longer than a regular oven because of extra insulation), you can turn the heat off at least 10 minutes before the final cooking time, and the food will continue to cook.

Defrost frozen foods before cooking and you'll shorten cooking time and energy used.

A good general rule for most top-of-stove cooking is to keep the heat as low as possible and still maintain the cooking. This saves money and energy, and lessens the likelihood of scorching.

ENGLISH MUFFINS

If you're going to freeze English muffins, first tear or slice them in halves, then put the halves into a plastic bag. The frozen halves can go directly into the toaster.

The frozen halves of English muffins won't stick to each other if you stack them all with their cut surfaces *up*, one on top of another.

EVAPORATED MILK: see MILK

FATS AND OILS

It may be economical to buy cooking oil in a 48-ounce bottle, but a bottle that size is unwieldy. So for daily use, pour some of the oil into 1-pint or even ½-pint narrow-necked bottles (use a funnel). Keep the large bottle on your storage shelf for refilling the smaller bottle as needed.

Strain, cool, and refrigerate any fat or oil that you've used for frying or sautéing. Store it in a covered jar in the refrigerator or freezer. It's not only economical but it's also already flavored and you may need to add very little seasoning to what you're cooking when you use it.

You can substitute vegetable oil for solid shortening in much baking and general cooking. If you're making this substitution in a cake, cookie, or pancake batter, use 1 or 2 tablespoons less oil than the amount of solid shortening called for.

The temperature of hot fat has reached 365° F if a 1-inch cube of bread dropped into the hot fat browns in 1 minute.

Never pour water or other liquids or wet foods into hot fat. The fat will rise and overflow and may very well catch fire. Furthermore, you might get burned. Also, never cover a pot in which you're deep-fat frying. The steam won't be able to escape and the result can be the same as adding liquid to hot fat: dangerous spattering.

You can make walnut-flavored oil rather inexpensively (real walnut oil costs a fortune). Toast ⅓ cup of walnut pieces in the oven or in an unoiled skillet until they're a little dark. Stir now and then—be careful not to let the nuts burn. Grind them in the blender with ½ cup of cooking oil and let them stand in a jar for a day or two. Strain the oil through several thicknesses of cheesecloth or through a white handkerchief. Use the oil in salad dressings or for sautéing. It's delicately flavored and delicious. Refrigerate it, and be sure to shake it well before use.

You can clarify hot fat by straining it through a coffee filter placed in a narrow-necked funnel.

To clarify fat, drop a few slices of raw potato in it, bring to a boil, then strain through several thicknesses of cheesecloth or through a white handkerchief draped over a sieve.

Sometimes you will want to clarify fat further to rid it of very fine particles. In such cases, first let the strained fat cool to room temperature, then add one or two cups of hot water and heat the mixture just until it boils. Cool, refrigerate, and then remove the clear fat from the top.

Since vegetable fats and oils don't absorb fish odor, you can often reuse them after you've strained them.

The best way to remove fat from hot liquids is to pour the liquid into a jar or narrow bowl and let cool; then refrigerate until the fat has hardened and you can remove it with a knife or spoon.

Store cooking fat in the freezer and it won't get rancid before you've used it all.

Don't pour fats down the kitchen drain—that's asking for trouble. If the fat is one which will congeal when cold, pour it into a can and stand it in the refrigerator or freezer until it hardens. Cover and discard with your garbage. If it's a liquid fat, either flush it down the toilet or pour it into a disposable screw-top jar and discard that with your garbage.

FIGS
Fresh figs don't keep well. Plan to eat them immediately after you buy them.

FILLINGS
If you have a runny filling for a crêpe, dumpling or any filled dough preparation, freeze the filling until it's partially congealed, and you'll find that it will hold together until the dough is sealed and in the cooking pot.

FIRE

If grease catches fire, clamp a large pot lid down over it at once to cut off the oxygen supply; or pour baking soda on the flames, and they'll disappear.

Keep a small spray fire extinguisher within easy reach in your kitchen. Read the directions for use every now and then so that you won't have to stop to read them if you need it quickly.

FISH

See also *Bouillabaisse, Fish Stock, Frying, Leftovers, Mousse, Sauces and Gravies, Sautéing, Shellfish, Sole, Soups, Tuna.*

When you buy a fish you can tell it's fresh if the eyes are bright and bulging, the body is stiff—not limp—and the flesh is firm: it should spring back when you press with your finger. The scales shouldn't come off easily when you rub them with your hand.

When you buy salt cod, be sure the pieces are white and thick. Don't buy thin yellowed pieces—they'll be tough and stringy.

Make sure the fish you buy hasn't been previously frozen. Many frozen fish, fresh-looking in the showcase, are poorly flavored. Buy fish in season, when you can get them freshly caught.

When you buy fish, allow ½ pound per person.

Have your fish man leave on the top and bottom fins. These are attached to the bones, and make removing them easier after you've cooked the fish. Many cookbooks will direct you otherwise, but try this first.

Freeze fish bones, especially the carcasses of large fish, and use them later when you're making fish stock or seafood chowder.

Even if you buy fish fillets, search carefully with your fingers for small bones before cooking.

Examine a fish for scales before you cook it. Using a serrated grapefruit knife, hold the fish by the tail on a flat surface and scale it upward, toward the head.

You can eliminate fishy odor from some fish (trout and mackerel, for example) if you skin them before cooking. Your fish man

141

will usually do this for you if you ask, but if you have to do it yourself, cut the skin all the way around, behind the head. Then grasp the skin with a dry cloth or rub salt on your fingers (to get a good grip) and pull straight back.

Fish, such as salt cod, dried herring and finnan haddie, all need soaking for 3 to 6 hours to de-salt (the amount of time depends on the fish; some cod needs overnight soaking); change the water a couple of times. Then they're ready for cooking. Don't use salt in the dish.

Don't soak or cook salt cod in metal bowls or pots. The metal often discolors the fish.

Fish deteriorate rapidly, so plan to cook them the day they're bought or caught. If you must store them overnight in the refrigerator, wrap very well so their odor won't spread to other foods.

Very little fish odor will cling to your hands if you dip your hands in cold water before you handle the fish.

Leftover cooked fish (salmon, halibut, etc.) can be frozen. When it's thawed it flakes as beautifully for a salad as freshly cooked fish.

Cover frozen fish with milk and defrost in the refrigerator. Drain and pat dry before cooking. The flesh will be firmer and have a pleasant taste.

Also, when you thaw frozen fish, don't thaw it completely before you cook it. The juices that are still partly frozen inside the fish will remain there when the outside is cooked, and the whole piece of fish will be moister.

If you let frozen fish thaw slowly in the refrigerator, there'll be less leakage than if you thaw it at room temperature.

If you must thaw frozen fish quickly, let it stand under cold—never warm—running water.

Use frozen fish immediately after you've thawed it.

Lemon is the master of fish. Sprinkle fish with lemon (or lime) juice and let it stand in the refrigerator for ½ hour.

Remove fish from the refrigerator ½ hour before you cook it.

For a variation on a butter sauce or a white sauce to be served with fish, use white wine instead of milk and add a teaspoon or more of prepared mustard.

A large number of fish and shellfish recipes are inter-changeable. If a recipe calls for shrimp or lobster, you can often substitute fish fillets. The cooking time may need to be modified, but the method and the sauces won't. The final dish is just as delicious.

You can make a chowder from canned tuna. Cook and dice some potatoes. Sauté diced onion, celery bits, and pieces of bacon together. Then combine all of these with milk and a can of tuna. It's a pretty good chowder.

The oil from canned fish can be very good for sautéing onions and other vegetables. You can also mix the oil with lemon juice and a little pepper to make a fine salad dressing.

Cooking

Fish have delicate flesh and dry out easily. Never overcook. Until you've learned how long to cook fish in a particular dish, test it constantly. The moment it flakes easily with a fork, it's done. If the fish is thick, separate the flesh deep inside and examine it. When it loses its translucency, it's done.

Get yourself a very wide spatula—they come up to 8 inches wide. There's nothing better for removing a fish from its poach-ing water without breaking it, or for turning a long fish which you're broiling or sautéing.

Burn some sugar in a pan (using disposable aluminum foil) to neutralize the odor of cooking fish.

If there's any one dish which calls for wine in the cooking, it's fish.

Add some good dry red wine and a bay leaf when you cook mackerel. They flavor it beautifully and take away the fatty taste.

If you find salt fish too salty even after you've soaked it, try using milk in the cooking.

Many an indifferent fish dish can be made into something special if you sprinkle it with grated cheese or cover with a thin layer of Swiss or Gruyére, then place it under the broiler to brown.

Mix a cold salad containing flaked fish gently, lifting the pieces with a fork so as not to macerate the tender flesh.

A nice garnish for fish and seafood is crisp watercress dipped in cold water, shaken well, then dipped in paprika and again shaken well.

Baking

The best fish for baking are fatty ones like mackerel, fresh tuna, whitefish, bluefish, shad, salmon and trout. Less fatty fish tend to dry out.

A whole fish which weighs about 4 pounds should be baked at 400° for 30 to 45 minutes.

When baking a large fish, cut shallow slits on the top every 2 inches or so. Then oil and season it.

Most fish should have a covering of oiled brown paper laid over them when you bake them. Remove this toward the end of the cooking if you want the fish browned or crisped on top.

You can transfer a baked fish to a platter easily, and also keep it from breaking during the process, if you lay the fish on buttered or oiled paper or aluminum foil extending well out in both directions before baking. After baking, raise the fish by holding the paper or foil at both ends and ease it off onto the heated platter.

Grilling and Broiling

When you're grilling fish, make the grill *very hot* and oil it very well (brush the fish with oil too) otherwise the fish will stick to the bars and break when you turn it over or remove it. Oil the fish from time to time during cooking.

Make a few light diagonal gashes through the skin about 2 inches apart on both sides of a fish before you set it to broil. This will help keep the fish flat.

You don't need to turn most fish fillets when you broil them.

Fish fillets will be less inclined to flake or break during cooking if you leave the skins on.

If you're putting fish fillets in a pan under a broiler flame, the heat of the pan will cook the undersides by the time the tops are cooked. Again, be careful not to overcook.

When you pan-broil split fish or fillets which have skin on one side, cook them skin-side down first. Then turn and finish cooking skin-side up. This will prevent the fish from falling apart.

Some cooks like to remove the skin from fish steaks before they broil them because it eliminates the fishy odor. Use a sharp-pointed knife for this.

When you broil fish steaks, just as with fillets or split fish, oil or butter the grill and heat well. Grill a fish steak under high heat to begin with, to seal the outside. Then finish cooking under moderate heat.

For delicious broiled fish, be sure that the fish is thoroughly dry before you put it in the pan or on the grill. (Use paper towels or paper napkins, pressing gently to dry.) Coat the fish if frying; or brush with a little oil, if broiling.

You can get a crunchy, cracker crumb coating on fish if you dip the fish in evaporated milk before you roll it in the cracker crumbs. Let stand about 10 minutes before frying or sautéing.

You can make a flour coating for fish crispier and lighter if you whip a little cornstarch into the flavored flour (about 2 teaspoons to ½ cup of flour).

Put a little ginger (powdered or fresh) in the oil in which you sauté fish for a zippy flavor.

When you broil fish (this is true of meat, too), add salt only after cooking. Salt pulls the moisture out of fish (or meat).

Poaching

In many dishes you can treat any white-fleshed fish fillets the same as you would crabmeat. Poach or sauté the fish gently; when cold, dice or shred. Serve with the same sauces that crabmeat recipes call for. You can also serve the diced or shredded fish hot with a sauce, or brown the fish under the broiler, just as you would crabmeat.

Because it's difficult to remove the skin from a cooked fish after it has cooled, skin it immediately after cooking or poaching, especially if you're planning to serve it cold.

Fish fillets won't curl when you poach them if you use a very sharp knife to lightly score a line down the side of the fish from which the skin has been removed.

When poaching fish, add some grated horseradish to the court bouillon (the flavored poaching liquid).

145

If you're poaching fish for no more than 4 people, use white wine and seasonings instead of water. (Poaching for more than 4 may require at least 2 bottles.)

Never discard the liquid you poach fish in. If you're not going to boil the liquid down for a sauce—or if you have more than you need—freeze it and use it for poaching fish at another time. The liquid will get more and more full-flavored, and can be used in a fish chowder or as a base for fish sauce.

If large fish such as salmon and halibut have been properly poached, their flesh should be custardlike—not raw, and not dry and stringy from overcooking.

When you poach fish, see that the liquid barely reaches the top of the fish.

The best fish to use for poaching are firm smooth-fleshed ones such as pompano, bass, striped bass, perch, red snapper, trout, salmon, halibut and swordfish.

Poach fish in a wide low pan. Cover with a piece of waxed paper with a small hole in the center, then put the pot lid on this. Bring the liquid to a boil, then turn it down to simmer. Cook the fish only until the flesh coagulates, at which time it should separate easily from the bone. Usually, cook 7 to 10 minutes for every 2 pounds of fish. For a fish weighing over 8 pounds, simmer it 5 minutes for every 2 pounds, but check by flaking and examining.

Remove fish from the poaching liquid either with a very wide spatula or with your two hands, wearing a pair of clean rubber household gloves. If you're poaching a very large fish, you may want to wrap it well in cheesecloth first. This holds it together and makes removal easier.

Fish cooked in liquid will be more resistant to breaking if slightly undercooked, then left in the liquid for about 10 minutes after the flame has been turned off. If you intend to serve the fish cold, let it cool in the cooking liquid.

Before you remove a poached hot fish mousse from its mold, let it stand in the mold 5 to 8 minutes so that it shrinks a little. You'll be able to remove it more easily.

If you add lemon juice and milk to the court bouillon or seasoned liquid in which you cook white fish such as halibut or cod, the flesh will stay white. (Never mind if it curdles.)

Sautéing and Frying

If you sauté fish in butter, use clarified butter.

Before you sauté or fry fish, always pat it thoroughly dry before you drop it into the hot fat, otherwise there'll be painful spattering (and partial steaming of the fish).

To test sautéed fish for doneness, use a toothpick to separate the flesh near the backbone. The fish is done when the flesh is no longer translucent.

If you want crisply fried fish, you must dry it thoroughly before you dip it into flour or crumbs.

When you fry fish, add salt only after cooking. Salt pulls the moisture out of fish.

If you're going to dip fish in egg before frying, try adding a little sherry to the egg.

Fish dropped into deep hot fat rises to the surface when it's done.

Vegetable fats and oils hardly absorb any fish odor, so you can often strain and reuse them in cooking fish.

Wash your hands with strong salt water, or rub them with salt and then wash, and you'll remove any fish odor they may have.

You can remove fish odor and grease from the pan in which you've cooked fish if you pour ½ cup of vinegar in the pan and boil, then wash.

FISH STOCK

See also *Soups, Stock.*

Any time you have liquid left from cooking fish, boil it down to a manageable amount, then strain and freeze, labeling the jar. Use this whenever you need a court bouillon or fish stock. You can use and reuse, since you'll be adding to it and boiling constantly. It gets richer and richer. Eventually you may want to use it as a base for a fish chowder or bouillabaisse.

147

You can enormously improve your fish chowders and soups if you use shells and bones when you prepare the fish stock. Shrimp and lobster shells and fish bones cooked in water, then strained carefully, will give you a rich stock base.

Use all the fish bones you can get your hands on. Ask your fish store to save you the carcasses of flounder, sole, haddock, etc., after the fillets have been cut from them. Fish bones make the most splendid stock imaginable. And save the remains, including bones, of any fish you serve. They're still full of flavor. If you're not ready to make stock right away, freeze the bones in a plastic bag until you are.

Save all the liquids from canned fish and seafoods. Pour them into a jar and freeze. Add later to fish stocks, or use as the base for a fish stock.

Fish stocks and soups should be made from lean fish. The skin and fat from fatty fish often give an unpleasant taste to a stock, as do fish heads. In spite of what many recipes advise, avoid them.

When you use fish stock to make fish soup or chowder, you'll have already discarded the fish and bones which have given their flavor to the liquid. Add the vegetables and cook, then add the fish, saving the most tender for last.

A fish glaze is made of rich fish stock cooked slowly for hours, until it becomes thick, jelly-like and lightly browned. Bottle and keep it in the refrigerator. With a little boiling water, you can have a rich stock or fish gravy any time.

FLAMBÉ DISHES

Be sure you avert your face from the dish when you ignite brandy or liqueur.

Here's how to ignite brandy or any other liqueur when you're making a flambé dish. First heat the brandy gently over a low flame. When it's quite warm light a match, and tilting the brandy slowly from the pan into the serving dish, apply the lighted match to the fumes close to the surface of the brandy in the dish. It will ignite readily in a running blue flame. Serve it as soon as the flame disappears.

FLOUNDER: see FISH, SOLE

FLOUR

See also *Blender, Thickeners.*

There are 3⅓ cups of all-purpose flour to 1 pound. Sifted, this will give 3¾ cups.

There are about 3 cups of cake flour to 1 pound.

1 pound of sifted cake flour makes 4½ cups.

All-purpose flour (used for pie dough, breads and some cake) is a blend of hard and soft wheats and has a high gluten content which forms an elastic framework for holding the carbon dioxide bubbles released by the yeast. Breads should be made at least partly with flour containing gluten if you want them light.

Cake flour is a finely milled soft wheat flour with a very low protein content. It produces a delicate crumbly texture.

You can't generally substitute cake flour for all-purpose, or vice versa—they have different characteristics.

Many boxed cake flours are self-rising (containing baking powder). Since most cake recipes don't call for self-rising flour, don't substitute it for regular cake flour unless you omit the baking powder called for in the recipe.

Pastry flour is made from soft winter wheat and contains less protein (gluten) than all-purpose and bread flours. It gives tenderness to pastries and cakes.

Whole wheat flour is made from the kernel of the wheat, which includes the germ and bran (or outer covering).

Whole wheat pastry flour is a soft whole wheat flour, finely ground.

Semolina is a flour made from a hard wheat called durum. It's used chiefly in making different kinds of pasta and some kinds of farina.

Gluten flour is a high-protein hard wheat flour which has had most of the starch removed from it. It's very good for bread, but hard to find.

Graham flour is a hard whole wheat flour with the bran coarsely ground.

Some flours on the market call for no sifting at all. These presifted flours are fine for cakes, cookies and gravies, but they're not as good for pastry dough because the flour grains won't adhere to one another when the shortening is added.

Whole wheat flour can be made lighter and more delicate for use in cookies and cakes if you sift it. Use the finer sifting for the cookies and cakes, and add the coarse siftings, which remain in the strainer, to the flour you use for baking bread.

Instead of sifting white flour, pour it into a screw-top jar and shake briskly before you measure out the flour. For a cake or pancake batter, measure flour into a jar, then add baking powder, salt, and the other dry ingredients. Shake and pour. Quick, and no mess.

Unbleached white flour can remain good for up to 2 years if stored well wrapped and kept fairly cool.

Store all-purpose flour in huge glass jars with wide mouths and screw tops. Shake the jar before sifting the flour. Also, measuring from a jar is easier than having to monkey around with the paper bag that flour usually comes in.

You can make a decent oat flour for baking bread by putting uncooked oats in the blender and running it until the oats are finely ground. You can also use oat flour in pancakes, muffins, and waffles.

It's very easy to measure out cake flour if the flour is stored in a large round box that oats come in. Before measuring the cake flour, shake the box up and down briskly, then give the flour a minute or two to settle. The cake flour is now sifted—it doesn't need to be put through a sifter or strainer.

Don't wash your flour sifter or strainer after each use. Bang it against a towel folded over the side of the sink and it will be perfectly clean for its next use.

The best way to dust flour onto cake and bread pans and over meats is to keep it in a giant saltshaker near the stove. You get an even distribution and no mess.

Keep a large flour shaker already mixed with seasonings such as paprika, salt, pepper, powdered garlic and pulverized herbs near your cooking area.

Flour expands when it's dissolved in a liquid and heated, hence its use as a thickener.

Always cook sauces and other mixtures containing flour for at least 10 minutes with a low flame to rid them of the raw taste which flour tends to give.

FRANKFURTERS

Read the labels on frankfurter packages. Know whether you're getting 1) meat with cereals added (this means less meat); 2) franks made with beef and pork or other meats; or 3) franks made from all beef. Know what you're paying for.

Franks won't split during cooking if you don't cook them at too high a temperature. Cook them slowly and for a long time. Don't prick them or they'll lose some of their juiciness. Remove them with tongs,

It's possible for franks to be rid of quite a lot of fat and still remain tasty. Before you sizzle them in a frying pan, put them in a pan of cold water, bring to a simmer, and cook them gently for 5 minutes. Quite a bit of fat will appear in the water. If you have to add a little vegetable oil to the frying pan, it will be healthier than the fat from the frankfurter.

We tend to forget, but years ago a frank wasn't just slapped into a roll and handed to us. The roll was *toasted* and *buttered* first. Go thou and do likewise.

FREEZER AND FREEZING

See also *Bananas, Cooking for One.*

For freezing bacon, see *Bacon.*

If you don't wrap foods absolutely airtight before you put them in the freezer they'll get "freezer burn" and dry out and lose their texture and flavor.

Some foods don't freeze well. Don't try raw tomatoes, celery, hard-boiled egg whites, fresh caviar, raw or boiled potatoes, cooked pasta, mayonnaise, custards, cream pies, meringue pie topping or liquid cream. The curd of cottage cheese breaks down when it's frozen and thawed, but this is all right if you intend to whip it or use it in cooking.

Overripe fruits and vegetables are not good for freezing, so be sure that any fruits and vegetables—from your garden or store-bought—that you intend to keep in the freezer are not too ripe.

Any fresh vegetables, fruits, herbs, etc., that you intend to freeze should be as dry as possible before you wrap them to put in the freezer.

If you're freezing food you've already cooked, store it in cans. Cover the cans with aluminum foil, label them, and stick them in the freezer. When you want to defrost a can of food, the quickest method is to stand it in a pan of water and heat it up—no worry about scorching. You can pour the contents of the can straight into a serving dish.

The waxed cardboard containers that milk and cream come in are also handy for freezing foods—especially stock, soups, etc. Wash and dry the containers before use. When you're ready to remove the frozen food, tear the carton apart and discard it.

Put a piece of waxed paper under any container placed in the freezer and the container will never stick to the freezer shelf. This is particularly good for anything that has a moist bottom, such as an ice cube tray.

Clear plastic shoe boxes are wonderful for freezer storage. Put *wrapped* meats, fish, chicken, or vegetables in them and label the side of the box that faces front. They're space-saving and can be stacked. One box can be used for small odds and ends: Throw them all in, label the box miscellaneous, and save yourself a lot of rooting around in the freezer when, for example, you want that little jar of lemon juice or that egg white you froze for future use.

If you have an electric self-cleaning oven, defrosting your freezer is a cinch. Stash all the frozen foods in the oven and keep the door closed. A self-cleaning oven is usually so well insulated that it will keep even ice cubes frozen for a couple of hours.

Don't season food which you intend to freeze. Add the seasonings after defrosting, when you're reheating. Many seasonings lose their flavors when they're frozen.

If you let frozen food thaw slowly in the refrigerator, there will be less leakage. This is particularly true of meat and fish.

Don't freeze meats, fish or chicken when their surfaces are moist. Pat them very dry before you wrap them for the freezer.

If you plan to freeze a bird, cooked or uncooked, avoid stuffing it first; stuffing tends to draw out the juices.

You should thaw a whole frozen bird before cooking, otherwise the flesh tends to be stringy. Frozen parts such as legs and breasts can be sautéed without prior thawing, but they should be cooked under a cover for the early part of the cooking.

Keep sliced or unsliced bread in the freezer. Wrap it as airtight as possible to prevent it from drying while frozen.

A whole unsliced loaf is very easy to slice when it's frozen. You can also slice a frozen loaf into thinner slices than you can at room temperature.

If you freeze baker's yeast, it will last indefinitely.

You can freeze whole containers of milk. They usually take 2 days to defrost in the refrigerator, about 6 hours at room temperature.

If you're cooking more than 2 packages of frozen vegetables at one time, use separate pans. The combined liquid they give up in cooking will be too much to evaporate before the vegetables are cooked and will tend to make them mushy.

FRITTERS

Be sure the fruits, meats and fish used for fritters are thoroughly dry before you dip them in batter, otherwise the batter won't adhere to them.

Mix fritter batter only until just smooth if you want a fine crisp crust. As with biscuit dough, overmixing causes toughness.

Fritter batter makes a good coating for larger pieces of meat, poultry and fish to be deep-fat fried.

Most fritters will benefit if you add some curry powder to the batter.

FROSTING: see ICING

FRUITCAKE
See *Cake*.

The uncooked dough for fruitcake should be very stiff.

Always bake a fruitcake in a very low oven.

Fruitcake may rise 2 or more inches during baking. Allow for this when you fill the pan.

You can keep fruitcake from burning before it's finished baking (since it must bake a long time) if you put a pan of hot water on the oven floor. (You may need to add more water before the cake is done.)

Try baking fruitcake in muffin tins. You can ice the cakes, or decorate with candied cherries or pineapple. Wrapped in waxed paper, they'll keep for weeks.

FRUIT JUICE
Fruit juices can be substituted for milk in many cake batters. If the juice is slightly acid, add ½ teaspoon of baking soda to the dry ingredients.

Save the liquids you drain from canned fruits and thicken with a little cornstarch; heat, and you have sauce for cake or pudding.

Freeze and save the juices from canned fruits until you have enough to combine with flavored or unflavored gelatin to make a dessert or salad.

Frozen juices not only taste good but also are a healthful treat for youngsters. Pour the juice into 6-ounce paper cups and put them in the freezer. They're ready to eat, popsicle style, in a few hours: Push up on the bottom of the cup to use it as a holder.

Put small cans of fruit juice in the freezer, and when they're frozen use them to pack with lunches that have to be kept cool. If packed in the morning, the cans will have served their purposes as "ice cubes" and be thawed by lunchtime.

FRUIT JUICERS
The type of hand juicer you turn a half of orange or lemon on to press out the juice should have a pointed cone, not a rounded one. You'll get more juice.

FRUITS
See also the names of individual fruits.

See also *Berries, Dried Fruits.*

Try to buy your fruits from a market where you can pick them individually. Buying fruits in ready-packed bags runs the risk of finding some of them partially spoiled, of a size you don't want, or not completely ripe.

Don't wash fruits for storing. Put them dry in the refrigerator and they'll keep longer. Wash them just before eating or using.

If it's possible, scrub all fresh fruits in warm soapy water before eating. The skins may have been sprayed with insecticides or decay-inhibitors before they were sent to market.

If you're going to add fruits to cake or pudding batters, they'll be less likely to sink if you heat them in the oven first. You can also dust them with flour before adding them to a batter.

Don't buy fruits because you like their shiny coats. These fruits are often covered with a thin coat of wax to make them more attractive. And some oranges are artificially colored. An intelligent consumer knows that true beauty is more than skin deep.

The syrup in which canned fruits are packed is often labeled light, heavy, or extra-heavy. These refer to increasing amounts of sugar in the liquid.

Cereal will get less soggy if you put the sliced fruit or berries in the bowl *first*, then cover with the cereal.

Fruits that are cut up for salad will keep their natural color if you sprinkle them well with lemon juice.

155

Dried fruits will be less sticky to chop or cut if you freeze them first. And cutting will be easier still if you heat the knife or keep dipping it in hot water. If you're using scissors, dip them in water.

Any fruit you eat, you can drink. All you need is a blender. Depending on the fruit, you can add water, milk, honey, lemon or lime juice, or anything else that appeals to you. Invent your own fruit punch.

You'll find that stewed fruits will need less sugar if you simmer the fruit for about 10 minutes before sweetening.

FRYING

("Frying" in this section means deep-fat frying.)

See also *Batter, Burns, Fats, Oil, Sautéing.*

The best fats to use for deep-fat frying are vegetable fats, salad oils, and nut and seed oils. Foods fried in olive oil taste more like olive oil than the foods themselves.

Don't use butter for deep-fat frying—it burns easily.

The pot you use for deep-fat frying should be a heavy metal one which keeps the fat at a constant temperature.

Always heat the fat for deep-fat frying before you add the food. Food put into cold fat absorbs an enormous amount.

The proper temperature for deep-fat frying is 370° to 375°.

If you don't have a fat thermometer, you can drop a 1-inch cube of bread into the hot fat; if it browns in 45 to 50 seconds, the fat is the right temperature for cooking.

If the heat is too high—above the smoking point—the food will have a bitter taste and be hard to digest. If the heat is too low, the food will absorb too much fat.

If you don't thoroughly dry uncoated foods (using paper towels) they'll develop a tough crust instead of a tender one after they've been cooked in hot fat.

Don't cut food to be deep-fat fried too thick, or the center won't cook.

Be sure all foods you fry are at room temperature. Cold foods lower the temperature of the cooking fat.

Don't put too much food in the hot fat at one time or you'll lower the temperature of the fat.

When you deep-fat fry, be sure you have enough fat in the kettle to completely cover the food.

Hot fat rises several inches when you drop food into it. Choose a pan which will allow for this.

If you invert a colander or a large strainer over a frying pan or pot whose contents spatter, steam will still be able to escape and you'll be able to avoid small painful burns.

If you cover foods after you've fried them, their steam will make them lose their crispness. They'll also get limp if you put them on a cold dish. Heat the serving dish first.

Always drain deep-fat fried foods very well before serving. Try pressing them gently between paper towels.

If the fat is the proper temperature and the food is dried well and not overcooked, deep-fat fried food soaks up much less fat than sautéed food.

Anything you dust on deep-fat fried foods (salt, sugar, spices or herbs) should be fine to the point of being powdered; fried foods won't absorb seasonings, and you don't want a gritty feel to the food.

Fats and oils used in deep-fat frying can be strained well and reused. Those you've used for fish can be used again for fish or seafood cooking (see *Fats*).

As soon as frying fat which has been used more than once gives you trouble in producing a golden crust, it's "fried out" and should be discarded.

FUDGE

If you add a little corn syrup to the other ingredients when you make fudge, the candy will be creamier.

Very few fudges which you buy in candy stores are of the proper consistency: a piece of fudge, when you bend it, should break in two, not pull like a piece of taffy. If you're making it at home, experiment with boiling times until you achieve the right kind of fudge. It should be very, very thick before you pour it out to cool.

To cool fudge, spread it about ¾ of an inch thick in the cooling pan.

After being poured, fudge should cool for at least 30 minutes before being cut.

FUNNELS
Every kitchen should have funnels of at least 4 neck sizes. Not only do jars and bottles have different sized necks, but some liquids, like soups, contain larger pieces of solids, and a wide-necked funnel does away with the painstaking transfer by spoon of these large pieces.

GADGETS

You don't need too many gadgets in the kitchen. If you know how to use it, a French chef's knife will take the place of many tools for mincing, slicing, chopping and dicing. See *Knives* for how to use a French knife.

GAME BIRDS: see BIRDS

GARLIC

Pick heads of garlic that are hard to the touch. Soft, spongy garlic has lost much of its flavor and may be partially spoiled.

The yellow, central strip of the garlic clove (the "lily") has the sharpest garlic odor and taste. Halve the garlic clove and you can remove the lily easily with the point of a knife.

As long as it stays dry, garlic keeps in the refrigerator for weeks. You can store it uncovered—its own papery covering will keep it from smelling up the interior. A good way to store garlic is in a small open container on one of the door shelves.

Like onion, garlic peels easily in hot water. If you have to peel a lot, drop it into boiling water for 30 seconds or so, then drain and peel.

When you add garlic to oil or vinegar for flavoring, as in salad dressings, if you impale each clove of garlic on a toothpick you can remove it easily later.

To make garlic oil to use later in dressings or for sautéing, let split cloves of garlic stand in oil overnight at room temperature. (You can also let garlic stand in oil for weeks; you'll get a very nicely garlicked oil, always ready at hand.)

To make garlic-flavored vinegar, put several cloves of garlic, sliced, in a bottle and cover with white or red wine vinegar. You can remove the garlic after a few weeks and you'll have a flavored vinegar to use in dressings.

If you have a mortar and pestle, use it to pound garlic to a paste and add this to dishes calling for mashed garlic. Nothing releases the oils and flavors of garlic as well.

You can also crush garlic with the broad side of a knife. This, too, will release the essential flavors.

If you object to garlic oil or juices on your fingers when you mash garlic, press or smash the clove between two thicknesses of waxed paper, using the side of a heavy knife handle. Then slide the garlic off the paper into the dish you're preparing.

Don't overcook garlic when you heat it in butter or oil. Don't let it brown—it will become bitter, and so will the oil. Instead, heat the oil or butter, then add small pieces of crushed garlic, and use this garlicked concoction as needed. The garlic flavor will transfer immediately to the hot butter or oil. You can strain out the garlic if you don't want bits of it in the hot sauce.

When you boil garlic in a soup or stock it's never as "garlicky" as it is when you sauté it or use it raw.

You'll be surprised to know that you can use huge quantities of garlic in stews, braised meats, or chicken, with a richness of taste that isn't "garlicky." *Very* lightly brown 6 to 10 cloves of garlic with a little onion and fat, then add this to your top of stove dish. It will taste splendid.

Rub the inside of a cooking pan with half a clove of garlic if you want only the slightest hint of garlic in what you're cooking.

Before you put salad in a serving bowl, squeeze the juice of 1 clove of garlic into the bowl, or put the clove through a garlic press. In either case, rub the bowl thoroughly with the juice or the pressed bits before adding the salad. The garlic will be transmitted gently to the greens without overpowering them.

Garlic that is to be removed after you've used it in cooking or flavoring brine for pickles, etc., need not be peeled first. Wash the cloves, cut them in half lengthwise, and drop them in whatever you're preparing.

You can peel a garlic clove easily if you first lay it on its side and swat it with the handle of a heavy knife.

To make a pleasant garlic oil to use on meats or to rub on a chicken before roasting, add slices of garlic to cooking oil and heat gently until the garlic begins to darken. Immediately remove from the heat and strain.

A good way to store garlic for months in the refrigerator is to peel it, put it in a small jar, and cover it with salad oil. After you've used up the garlic, use the oil for sautéing or in salad dressing.

To grow garlic greens in your kitchen window, plant separate cloves of garlic in little pots and keep the soil moist. Each clove will shoot up greens that can be cut and used like chives. As you cut the shoots off, new ones will grow. And they'll grow for months. Garlic greens have a slightly milder flavor than the cloves.

You can make your own garlic powder at much less than the cost of buying it. Remove the skin from garlic cloves, cut the cloves into slices, and dry them thoroughly at room temperature. After the garlic slices have dried, pulverize them in the blender, or cover them with a piece of plastic wrap and pound with a hammer. Or use a mortar and pestle. Bottle the powder.

If you've overindulged in garlic and have become a social problem, eat a lot of parsley. It's a great tamer.

GARLIC BREAD
Authentic garlic bread is prepared by spreading French or Italian bread which has been split or cut into slices, not quite through to the bottom, with a smooth paste of pounded garlic and salt and a coating of soft butter. Press the bread together and put it in a hot oven for 5 minutes.

GARNISHES
See also *Hors d'oeuvres*.

Garnishes are the little surface touches, edible decorations, that can make a dish look more exciting and add that special something to its color, texture, and taste. Here are some ideas for garnishing:

All-purpose Garnishes
Red or green peppers cut into thin strips or circles
Toast points, fried and toasted with paprika
Dips, thick and creamy and forced through a pastry tube
Ham slices, very thinly rolled
Eggs
Eggs, hard-boiled slices or halves
Egg yolks, hard-boiled and crumbled or pushed through a strainer
Egg whites, hard-boiled and finely minced
Fish
Anchovy strips
Oysters, smoked
Shrimp
Fruit
Banana slices, fried
Lemon wedges or slices, peeled and fluted
Melon balls
Orange sections
Orange slices, sautéed
Vegetables
Artichoke hearts or bottoms, marinated or unmarinated
Asparagus tips
Capers
Carrots, thinly sliced and notched at the edges
Celery curls
Celery stuffed with any minced or creamed mixture
Celery hearts
Chives, finely minced
Endive stalks stuffed with cheese paste
Gherkins, sliced or whole
Lettuce hearts
Mushroom caps, sautéed
Olives, black or green, halved or stuffed and sliced
Onions (small), pickled
Onion rings, fried or very thinly sliced

Parsley sprigs, fresh or deep-fat fried

Peppers (red or green), diced or cut in strips or circles

Pimiento strips or dice

Radish roses or radishes cut into thin slices

Rice, cooked and well-seasoned, then formed into small molds

Scallions (green), finely minced or sliced

Tomato (cherry) slices

Tomatoes (cherry), lightly braised in butter

Tomato slices broiled plain or covered with buttered bread crumbs

Truffles

Vegetables (even leftovers), cooked, seasoned, and blended, then forced through a pastry tube

Watercress, plain, or dipped in cold water, shaken well, dipped in paprika, and shaken again

Here are some techniques chefs use to give a touch of elegance to an ordinary dish:

Soups

Chop a handful of almonds or toss them into the blender. These can be plain almonds, with their skins on, or blanched or toasted almonds. Each has a slightly different flavor, but they all look lovely sprinkled over a soup.

Cut scallion greens very fine, crosswise, into tiny green rings to float on soups.

Serve a dollop of faintly salted whipped cream on tomato soup or any creamed soup. You can dust the dabs of cream with paprika, curry powder, or finely minced chives.

Mix grated cheese and fresh parsley together in the blender. Dust the mixture over the top of a hot soup immediately after it's been ladled into bowls.

Float very finely shredded lettuce on a clear soup.

Fish and Seafood

Serve lemon slices, naturally—or lime. Better still, cut the lemons or limes into wedges to make squeezing easier. (Have you ever tried to squeeze a slice of lemon?)

Run some mayonnaise in the blender with a handful of

165

chopped-up watercress to make the mayonnaise green and zesty. Put dollops here and there on the platter. You can also make pink mayonnaise by using a little tomato paste or ketchup.

Celery leaves, if they're bright green and fresh, are a delicious fish garnish. So is a handful of chives, finely cut, shaken from a spoon over the fish.

Cut stuffed olives in thin slices and arrange them, overlapping like fish scales, over part of the fish.

Meats and Chicken

Garnish any meat or chicken dish with tiny, white boiled onions (canned onions will do). Drain them well and heat in a little butter and honey until they're brown. They look and taste wonderful.

Throw some button mushrooms or mushroom caps into a pan with a little oil or melted butter and brown slightly. This doesn't take long if kept at a good sizzle. Sprinkle some paprika over the mushrooms and arrange them around a hot meat or chicken dish.

You can do the same with orange sections, adding a bit of sugar to the hot oil or butter to caramelize the orange pieces a little. They send up a lovely aroma.

Desserts

Whole blanched almonds, or halves of almonds, for decorating cakes or puddings are tastier when dipped halfway in melted sweet or semisweet chocolate.

GELATIN: see ASPICS AND GELATIN DISHES

GINGER: see HERBS AND SPICES

GINGERBREAD

For a dark gingerbread, mix into the batter 1 tablespoon of melted chocolate to each cup of warmed molasses called for.

GLASS BAKING DISHES: see POTS AND PANS

GLAZE

To glaze a ham, see *Ham.*

To make a meat glaze (a highly concentrated stock used in sauces and ragoûts) boil down 1 quart of rich stock to about 4 tablespoonfuls. Do this very slowly as it thickens. Store the glaze in a small bottle in the refrigerator. It lasts indefinitely and a tiny bit goes a long way. Add a teaspoonful (or less) to an ordinary gravy or soup and it won't be ordinary anymore.

You can make a fish glaze by cooking rich fish stock slowly for a long time until it becomes thick and lightly tanned. Use it for fish stock, court bouillon, chowder and sauces for fish.

GOOSE

A goose has no white meat.

A 10-pound goose will serve 6 to 8 people. Don't buy a goose weighing under 8 pounds—most of this weight will be bone.

Like duck, goose has a lot of excess fat in its body cavity. Always take this out before you cook it.

Since a goose is a very fat bird, it never needs oiling or buttering. Before you roast it, prick the skin well with a sharp-tined fork around the wings and legs to let the fat run out during cooking.

An 8- to 10-pound goose should be roasted at 325° for 1 hour on one side, then 1 hour on the other side, 1 hour on the breast and finally 1 hour on the back until the breast is well browned. Larger geese take longer roasting—about 25 minutes to the pound.

Goose is tougher than turkey or duck and should be cooked in a covered roaster. It should be uncovered toward the end of roasting to facilitate browning.

When you roast a goose, baste it every 15 minutes with a few tablespoons of boiling water to help rid it of fat. Spoon out the melted fat from the bottom of the roaster from time to time, or use a bulb-type baster to siphon it.

GRAHAM CRACKERS AND
GRAHAM CRACKER CRUST

See *Crumbs and Crumb Crusts.*

1 pound of graham crackers will yield about 4½ cups of crumbs.

If you're going to use a graham cracker crust for a pie which has to bake, refrigerate the unbaked crust until it's very cold (use a metal pie pan, not a glass one). Then pour the filling in and put the pie in the oven. If the crust is very cold, it's less likely to burn before the filling has baked.

Graham crackers quickly go limp if exposed to air. Store them in an airtight jar. You can also heat them in a 250° oven for a few minutes to make them crispier before serving.

GRAPEFRUIT

1 medium grapefruit will give you about 1 cup of juice.

Heavier grapefruit are usually juicier and have more meat.

Grapefruit, like oranges and lemons, should be open to the air during storage. Don't put them in closed bags or the skins will mildew.

If you intend to peel grapefruit, buy thick-skinned ones—they're easier to peel.

Any grapefruit can be peeled in the following way: wash the grapefruit, then cut off a slice of peel from the top and bottom. Set the grapefruit with one cut end down on a cutting board and cut the peel off in strips from top to bottom with a sharp knife.

Cut a thin slice from the rounded end of half a grapefruit and it will stay flat on a plate.

If you want to use grapefruit skins as shells for salad or fruit cups, cut the grapefruit in half, remove the pulp, and then put the skins in ice water until serving time so that they will be firm.

You can use grapefruit juice in place of vinegar in many oil and vinegar dressings.

GRAPES

Grapes are delicious when served slightly frozen. Put a bunch of seedless grapes in the freezer for about 45 minutes, then serve.

GRAVY
See *Sauces and Gravies*.

Browned flour will give a richer color and taste to gravy than white flour. Heat the flour in a dry pan over a medium flame until it becomes the color of cinnamon. You won't need any fat for this, but you should stir the flour constantly. Then add a little heated fat, stir it well and add some of the warmed liquid. This is the procedure for making a brown roux, which gives a nice color and flavor to gravies.

If you want to thicken clear gravy and have it remain clear, use potato starch, cornstarch or arrowroot. Flour makes gravy opaque.

Before you add flour or any other thickener to gravy or sauce, mix the flour first with a little cold water to form a paste, then add this to the gravy, stirring constantly. This helps to prevent lumps.

Another way to avoid lumps when mixing gravy is to use a wire whisk for stirring and beating.

If you want to make a good meat gravy, never add any liquid to the meat before it is browned (seared thoroughly to a good rich color).

You can get a dark full-bodied gravy if you gently brown as much as 1 pound of sliced onions in a little fat and then brown the meat in this. Onions—a lot of onions—are the secret to success.

If you add any meat blood to a gravy, you can keep it from curdling by mixing a small amount of lemon juice thoroughly into the gravy.

Add a couple of tablespoons of tomato paste to meat gravy. Also, ½ cup of good red wine can do no harm. Cook gently at least 20 minutes after you've added these.

Try adding a bit of instant coffee powder to a gravy for a rich brown color and a really nice addition to the flavor.

You can also give brown color to a gravy if you add a few drops of caramel (burnt sugar) to it.

Add a little sour cream to meat or chicken pan drippings for a delicious gravy.

If you want thick, low-calorie gravy, boil a lot of onions in a small amount of liquid until they are very tender. Cook them until little or no draining is necessary, then whip them in a blender or force through a sieve. You can flavor this purée in any way you like for meats, fish, chicken or vegetables.

GREEN ONIONS: see SCALLIONS

GRIDDLE
To tell when a griddle has reached the right temperature for cooking pancakes, heat it, then let a few drops of cold water fall on it. If the drops bounce and hiss, the griddle is ready.

GRIDDLECAKES: see PANCAKES

GUEST DINNERS
A trick you always discover after a catastrophe: write out your complete menu—down to the olives and celery—and put it on a part of your kitchen wall where it will stare you in the face during the last minutes of preparation. Check it before bringing your guests to the table and you won't forget a single dish you've prepared.

HAM

When you buy a cured cooked ham ask your butcher to remove the rind and all but a very thin layer of fat.

An uncooked ham should never be *boiled.* If you cover it with cold water and then cook it over a low flame, at a simmer, the flavor will stay in the ham. Simmer for about 20 minutes per pound. Slow cooking will make it tender. It's cooked enough when the little bone at the shank end is loose when you move it.

If you're going to serve a "boiled" ham cold, it will be much juicier if you let it cool in its cooking liquid.

To glaze an unbaked ham, remove the rind, leaving about ½ inch of fat over the ham. Then sprinkle sugar—granulated or brown—liberally and evenly over the surface, and put the ham in a 450° oven. The sugar will caramelize over the fat, giving a beautiful dark brown coating.

Don't cook thick ham slices too fast. Turn them several times to avoid burning and cook them until they're evenly browned on both sides. They'll remain tender and juicy.

Save the juices from sweet pickles or spiced fruits and use them to pour over ham slices which will be baked in the oven.

Canned ham is easier to slice—especially if you want thin slices—if you first chill it thoroughly.

If you love ham and eggs, save some slices from your next baked ham to fry later with eggs. You can freeze a few slices for future use. The conventional boiled ham slices which you buy are no substitute for the real thing.

Don't throw away the ham bone from a baked ham. For an excellent dish, cook it with dried lima beans and herbs or cloves.

Run very hot water for a minute or two over a can of ham before you open it and you'll find the ham will slip out easily.

173

To eliminate quite a lot of salt from thick ham slices used for sautéing, let the ham slices soak in water in the refrigerator for a day. Rinse and blot dry with paper towels before sautéing.

An uncooked, smoked ham will stay fresh longer if you wrap it in a well-wrung-out cloth that has been saturated with vinegar. Then wrap the cloth-covered ham in waxed paper and refrigerate.

Before you bake a ham, make a lengthwise slit through the rind on the underside. Place the ham, slit side down, in the baking pan. After the ham is cooked, the rind will pull off easily.

HAMBURGER

If you're interested in getting the leanest meat to use in hamburgers, ask the butcher for lean ground round. You can always add a little salad oil (it's healthier than the beef fat) when mixing so that it won't be too dry when you cook it.

Hamburger meat sold ready-prepared at low prices usually has a high fat content. But it's an unhealthy bargain because you'll eat more fat with each bite than you would eating lean meat. A good cut for hamburger is lean chuck, ground to order.

Keep hamburger meat very cold and use it as soon as possible. Any kind of ground meat deteriorates faster than whole meat.

If you're storing hamburger in the refrigerator for a day or two, flatten it so that the cold can penetrate quickly.

You can extend hamburger meat by adding many cooked vegetables and grains, ground or cut-up. But don't overdo it, or it won't taste like meat. Packaged soy bean filler sold for this purpose seems inexplicably expensive. Experiment, but keep an eye on the weight of what you're paying for. You might decide to stick with meat, or use your own kitchen-made additions.

If you have leftover cooked vegetables, blend some and mix with the raw meat before you form patties. This often makes a very juicy, tasty hamburger.

Try adding some grated raw potato to hamburger meat. This stretches the meat and also gives juicier hamburgers.

Add 1 teaspoon of aromatic bitters to 1½ pounds of ground beef before you form it into hamburgers—this is delicious.

Wet your hands before you form the patties so that the meat won't stick to them.

If you shape hamburgers lightly, with not too much pressure, they'll be juicier.

If you like a crusty hamburger, dip it in seasoned or un-seasoned flour before you put it in the hot fat.

Hamburgers will have fewer calories if you pan-fry them in a salted skillet, without any added fat. There's usually enough fat in the meat to cook them properly.

When you broil hamburgers, heat the broiling pan until very hot before you put the hamburgers on it. This will seal and keep in the juices.

You can cook hamburgers ahead of time. Undercook slightly, then wrap them individually in foil. At serving time put the foil-wrapped burgers in a very hot oven for about 5 minutes or on barbecue coals for about 2 minutes.

Add some finely diced, lightly sautéed bacon to your ham-burger mixture.

¼ cup of liquid to 2 pounds of meat is the right amount of liquid to add to hamburger meat to make it juicy for broiling.

Before you put hamburgers on a grill, coat the tops with any good spicy steak sauce or Worcestershire sauce.

To make professional-looking hamburgers (and to lessen the work), form the chopped meat into a cylinder of whatever diameter you wish. Roll the cylinder in plastic wrap or waxed paper and put it in the freezer for about an hour. Remove, un-wrap, and cut into slices as thick as you like.

HASH
The rule of thumb for hash is that there should be about ⅓ as much gravy as the amount of solid ingredients.

HAZELNUTS: see NUTS

175

HEARTS

Beef, veal and lamb hearts are delicious in stews or by themselves, but they are tough. You can cook them in a pressure cooker to tenderize them, then use in any recipe calling for stewed or braised meat. Experiment with the time needed—different kinds of hearts call for different cooking times. Try pressure-cooking for 20 minutes. You can always cook them longer if they aren't tender enough.

HERBS AND SPICES

If you're not familiar with certain herbs or spices such as cardamom, chervil, cumin, fennel, or mace, then become familiar—experiment. Take *one* of the many herbs and spices found on your market shelf and use it in the foods you usually cook. This is the best way to acquaint yourself, one at a time, with the magical flavors the rest of the world has discovered. You'll find your own favorites.

Like all plants, fresh herbs contain a great deal of water. For this reason, the same volume of the *dried* herb has more herb essence and flavor. So when you substitute dried herbs for fresh, use approximately ⅓ of the amount.

Herbs lose flavor when they get old. They rarely have a shelf life of more than 4 months. If you've had yours for some time, add a bit more than you would ordinarily to the dish you're preparing. Open the jars sniff now and then. And it's not a bad idea to note on the jar label the month and year you bought the herbs. Replace when necessary.

To freeze fresh herbs, wash and rinse them and then purée in the blender with a little water. Freeze the mixture as you would ice cubes, then store in plastic bags. You'll find these cubes fine and fresh tasting for soups, stews, or salad dressings.

You can buy a very expensive mixed spice-and-herb grind from France—or you can grind your own. Put a little of about a dozen different spices and herbs—whatever you've got on your spice shelf—in the blender, grind to a powder, and bottle. It's very good in omelets and cheese sauces—and in gravies, too.

Keep a few little jars of herbs and spices already mixed with salt and pepper near the stove.

Whenever possible, buy whole rather than ready-ground spices (allspice, cardamom, cinnamon stick, cloves, nutmeg, pepper), and grate or grind them yourself. You can often use the blender for this, or a mortar and pestle, or a pepper grinder. You'll get much more pungency and flavor.

To measure herbs, pepper, and other spices you're going to grind, do the grinding over a piece of waxed paper. Curl the paper and pour into a measuring spoon.

You can grow many fresh herbs in pots near your kitchen window or in window boxes. Plant seeds in the late winter or early spring and keep the soil just moist.

You can keep fresh herbs like dill, parsley, chives or basil in near-fresh condition if you wash them, shake them well, and put them in tightly closed glass jars in the refrigerator. (Fresh rosemary will keep in a glass of water in the kitchen for 2 weeks or more if you change the water daily.)

Practically all fresh herbs can be frozen if you wrap them airtight. Their fresh green color won't disappear if you use them straight from the freezer, without thawing.

You can dry herbs or celery leaves too if you put them in a paper bag, twist it closed and hang it up in your kitchen. Shake the bag now and then. Look into it after several days. Drying time depends on the amount of moisture in the air.

Dried herbs keep best in containers which shield them from light. Use screw-top or ground glass stopper jars and keep them away from heat. (You can use ordinary glass jars if you cover the outsides with plastic adhesive covering.)

Spices also keep best away from heat and light. Put them in covered jars in a cool place. If you have the room, keep bottled herbs—especially paprika, curry and chili powder—in the refrigerator. Their color and flavor will last longer.

Use restraint when you add herbs or spices to various dishes, especially if they're ones you haven't tried before. You'll soon

177

find out how much you like in particular dishes, but it's best to err on the light side to begin with.

Avoid too many kinds of herbs or spices in the same dish. You can often use 2 and sometimes 3, but the combination shouldn't overpower any one of them.

When you double a recipe, don't double the amount of herbs or spices. Use just a little more than called for in the original recipe.

Dried herbs and spices (unless they've been on your shelf for months and months) are more pungent than fresh, and you should use them more sparingly.

Dried herbs will bring more flavor to your food if you crush or crumble them well between your palms as you add them to your cooking. This releases the bouquet.

If you're going to add dried herbs to a sauce like mayonnaise, put them in boiling water for a minute, then strain and pat them dry with a dishtowel. They'll be greener and have more flavor.

To make a *bouquet garni* which you can remove easily from the cooking pot, wrap the herbs (usually a sprig or two of thyme, marjoram, parsley and a bay leaf, fresh or dried) in a square gauze pad—the kind you buy at drug stores—and tie it with white thread.

Another way to make an easily removable *bouquet garni* is to put the herbs in an aluminum tea holder that snaps shut.

Keep a small jar containing a mixture of salt, pepper, paprika, powdered garlic, powdered onion, or any other herbs or spices you like, in the refrigerator. This combination is handy for seasoning meat, chicken and fish. When refrigerated, it keeps indefinitely.

Try making herb-flavored butters. This can be done with fresh herbs or ones that have been parboiled for 1 minute and then drained and dried on a towel. A good mixture is 4 tablespoons of herbs (whatever kind you like) to ½ cup of butter at room temperature. You can keep these in small glasses in the coldest part of the refrigerator, or even freeze them. They're good to have on hand when you want a first-class sauce for a hot vegetable, fish or meat, without having to go to a lot of trouble at the time.

Why pay premium prices for flavored vinegars? Make your own. Use a soft white wine vinegar, add any herb whose flavor you like in a salad dressing—such as tarragon, rosemary, celery or dill seeds—and bring to a simmer. Let cool, bottle and store.

Anise

When you're using anise seeds in a cake, pudding, or other dish, crush the seeds first for maximum flavor. Do this between sheets of waxed paper with a rolling pin.

Basil

To use basil in pesto sauce, see *Sauces and Gravies*.

Use fresh basil leaves in salads.

Fresh basil will keep aromatic and green at room temperature for weeks in a glass of water. Change the water daily.

If you grow basil in your garden, dig up some of the plants in the fall and grow them inside in the kitchen in a sunny window. You can have fresh basil through much of the winter.

Caraway

Caraway seeds are marvelous in a creamed soup. Simmer a tablespoon or two of the seeds in a clear soup stock for about 15 minutes before adding the milk or cream. Strain out the seeds, discard them, and continue with the soup as you normally would. Don't cook the soup for too long after this, or you'll lose the subtle caraway flavor.

Crush caraway seeds by pounding them with a hammer covered with a dishtowel or by putting them in a blender. Add these to a meat or vegetable sauce for a nice new flavor.

Chives

To grow chives in your kitchen, buy a pot of them from the vegetable market, but transplant to a larger pot with more soil and a drainage hole at the bottom. Water only enough to keep the soil moist. They'll grow for months if you keep them in the light.

The best way to cut chives is with small kitchen scissors. Cut them off at the top of the plant and the plant will keep growing.

179

To freeze chives, wash the stems well and shake vigorously. Then put them in waxed paper, plastic wrap or a tightly capped jar and store in the freezer. They'll keep their green color if you use them without defrosting as soon as you remove them from the freezer.

Cinnamon

Put 2 or 3 sticks of cinnamon in a jar and cover with sugar. Screw the cap on tight and let stand for a few weeks. Use this sugar in cakes, tea or coffee for a very nice flavor. (You can also add vanilla pods to this.) Replace the sugar as you use it, shake the jar well, and return to the shelf.

Mix sugar and powdered cinnamon and keep the mixture in a jar (1 teaspoon of cinnamon to 2 tablespoons of sugar). Ready-made, this mixture costs three times the price of making it yourself.

Add ¼ teaspoon of cinnamon to any rich pan gravy to serve over meat, chicken, or rice. This is common in Near Eastern cookery—and should be universal.

Add cinnamon to any rice dish—not just rice pudding—for wonderful flavor.

Cloves

To give doughnuts a lovely flavor, drop 5 or 6 whole cloves in the fat you fry them in.

Coriander

Coriander is a dark-green, pungent herb that is delicious cooked in a fish or meat sauce. It is also known as Chinese parsley.

Curry

Curry powder is generally a combination of the following ground seeds and herbs: cardamom, cayenne, chili pepper, coriander, cumin, fenugreek, ginger, and turmeric.

Curry powders differ so much that the safest rule to follow is to use half the amount of curry powder or paste called for in a recipe. You can always add more to taste before serving.

You can add a little curry powder to almost any soup (especially creamed or puréed soups).

A little curry powder added to a meat or chicken gravy will

lift it to another plane. The gravy then becomes a vehicle in itself: Add some sautéed onion, diced fruit (apples or mangoes are the usual, but any will do), and pieces of chicken or meat. Heat all this up and serve with rice. It's a fine way to use leftovers. In fact, curry powder was invented for leftovers. It will go with anything: birds of any kind, fish, meat, seafood, vegetables.

And don't forget eggs: Add a little curry powder to mashed hard-boiled egg yolks when you make stuffed eggs. Add it also to omelets or to scrambled eggs.

Sauces made with curry powder become "hotter" when they stand. So, if you don't intend to eat a curried dish as soon as it's made, go a little easy on the amount of curry you use.

Spice things up a bit by adding 1 teaspoonful (or more) of curry powder to biscuit dough, bread dough, dumplings, salad dressing or cottage cheese.

Dill

To freeze fresh dill, first wash and hang it upside down to dry. Then wrap in waxed paper or plastic wrap and freeze. Use straight from the freezer.

Dry your own dill for much less than it costs to buy it dried in a jar. Cut it into small bits with scissors and then spread it on a cookie sheet covered with some paper toweling. Either let dry at room temperature (stirring now and then) for a couple of days, or put in a low, low oven. Stir from time to time. Then put in a tightly covered jar. If the oven is low enough, the dill will keep its green color.

The dill you buy to use in pickling must be mature and not young feathery dill. Ask for dill which has just gone to seed. This is most often sold dried. Young dill (the kind that's used for salads) won't give pickles the right flavor.

Use scissors to cut feathery dill tips into cream sauces served with fish or vegetables. Also add them to leafy green salads for a fresh garden flavor. Use a lot of fresh dill in a hot vegetable soup.

Pound 2 teaspoons of dill seed and mix into the dough of a white or whole wheat bread.

181

Ginger

1 tablespoon of raw ginger (bought in a fruit and vegetable or Oriental food store) equals ½ teaspoon of powdered ginger in flavoring power.

Add thin slices of candied ginger to meat, fish, and chicken dishes. It's also marvelous in curries and sweet and sour sauces such as for tongue.

Fresh ginger root isn't always easy to find, and it can be expensive. But you can grow your own in the kitchen. Place a piece of the root that contains a bud in a pot of soil. The root will send up shoots and leaves, and when the plant later becomes dormant and the shoots die off, you'll be able to dig up half a dozen or more new large roots (actually, rhizomes) to use in cooking— and to start new plants

Grate a little fresh ginger root into a salad dressing and shake well.

Mint

Fresh mint leaves are great breath sweeteners. Chew a few.

Mustard

Plant mustard seeds (the same kind you use in pickles, etc.) and grow mustard cress on your kitchen windowsill. The seeds will sprout in less than a week. Use the tiny leaves in salads, sandwiches, or any dish in which you use watercress.

To make a good prepared mustard at home, mix dry powdered mustard with enough cool water to make a smooth paste. Add a little salt and other flavorings such as turmeric if you like. Let it stand about 10 minutes to reach full flavor. Mustard prepared in this way is pungent and tasty, but unfortunately begins to lose strength after about 1 hour. Don't bother to save what's left. Make it fresh each time you want it.

Nutmeg

An average nutmeg will give about 3 teaspoons grated.

Ready-ground nutmeg is flavorful, but it doesn't have the "zing" of freshly ground. Buy nutmegs whole and grate them into batter or on top of creamed dishes and custards.

Add some grated nutmeg to puréed spinach the next time you make it.

Paprika

You can use paprika with many chicken, meat or fish recipes, as well as sprinkled on many vegetables, salads and creamed dishes. It also gives a rich color and flavor to soups, stews, and rice.

Use *plenty* of paprika when you make pot roasts. It not only adds incomparably to the taste but it also gives a beautifully colored gravy.

To make your own paprika, dice sweet red peppers, dry them thoroughly, and grind to a powder in the blender. Or cover with plastic wrap and pound with a hammer. You'll get a deliciously pungent red powder which, although not from the same variety of pepper as the commercial paprika, has all the qualities of paprika—and tastes fresher. Furthermore, you can make a mild or tangy paprika. For a mild flavor, remove all the seeds and the white pith before you dry the peppers. If you like it tangy, leave the seeds and pith in when you set the peppers to dry, and grind everything together.

Parsley

Eat the parsley that comes as a garnish with your meal. It's full of vitamins A and C—and is also a fine breath freshener.

You can keep fresh parsley green and crisp in the refrigerator for at least 2 weeks if you wash it and dry it thoroughly (roll it in a dish towel to dry). After it's clean and dry, put it in a screw-top jar and refrigerate.

A fast way to mince parsley very fine is to cut the leaves from the stems and discard the stems. Force the leaves into a tight ball, and holding the ball firmly with one hand, slice down through the ball of leaves with a sharp knife, working from the outside inward and making the slices very close together.

Use a full-leaved sprig of parsley for brushing or sprinkling flavored oil or melted butter on fish or vegetables.

Parsley freezes very well. Wash it, shake and hang to dry, then cut off the leaf heads and put them in the freezer in a covered jar or plastic container. If it has been well-dried before freezing, the parsley will crush into fine flakes if you rub the frozen leaf heads vigorously between your palms. The color and flavor keep excellently.

Parsley will chop very fine if it is thoroughly dried with a dishtowel before you cut it; otherwise the pieces will stick together and not disperse into fine flakes. See *Knives* for how to use a French chef's knife for this purpose.

You can dry finely cut parsley spread on a cookie sheet in a 200° oven. Stir from time to time until it's thoroughly dried. Then put in a tightly covered jar. If the oven is properly low, the parsley will keep its green color.

Keep a jar of dried parsley beside the stove. You'll find yourself using it in many dishes, and they'll all be the better for it.

Pepper

Buy a pepper grinder and a package of whole peppercorns. Grind pepper fresh whenever you need it. Freshly ground pepper is in a different league from ready ground.

When you buy a pepper mill try to avoid wooden ones or any which are difficult to wash. The glass or metal kinds are best. Get two, one for the table and one to keep beside the stove.

There's no appreciable difference in flavor between white and black pepper. White pepper is black pepper with its outer shell removed. It's slightly less spicy than black pepper. Use white pepper in light-colored dishes—in cream sauces, with white-fleshed fish, in chicken consommé—where you might not want flecks of black pepper to show.

Green peppercorns have a stronger flavor than white or black ones.

Rosemary

Dried rosemary tends to be a splintery herb. Try putting it in a pepper grinder, then grinding it over the dish you're cooking. It's much easier on the tongue and more pleasant to the taste buds.

Saffron

Unless the dish already contains a lot of liquid, pour about 1 tablespoon of hot, but not boiling, water over saffron before you use it to flavor or color a dish.

Tarragon

Tarragon is one of the best herbs to use with chicken. Soak 1 teaspoon of dried tarragon in ½ cup of dry white wine for ½ hour. Pour this mixture over the chicken, then cook it any way you want.

HONEY

See also *Cake*.

Try to buy raw uncooked honey in any of the many wildflower varieties. You'll find these in health food stores. Many commercial honeys are produced by sugar-fed bees and have been pasteurized. They're sweet, but don't have much flavor.

Keep honey at room temperature. It can be kept a little cooler, but the colder the temperature the more likely it is to crystallize.

If honey crystallizes, stand the jar (at room temperature) in a pan of warm-to-hot water until it liquefies.

Before you measure honey, oil the inside of the measuring cup or spoon and the honey will pour out easily, leaving no residue.

Wipe off the rim of the honey jar with a damp cloth every time you pour from it, then replace the cover. The cover will never stick.

Try substituting honey for sugar in coffee and tea, in cake batter, bread dough, and for other sugar uses. It is remarkably more delicious.

Doughs or batters containing an appreciable amount of honey should be baked at a slightly lower temperature than those containing sugar alone.

Cakes and cookies made with honey keep much longer than those made with sugar and remain pleasingly moist. You can substitute ¾ cup of honey for 1 cup of white or brown sugar in baking, but reduce the liquid in the recipe by ¼ cup for every ¾ cup of honey you use.

You can get a potful of unusual honey without having to shell out a potful of money. Slowly boil 1 cup of honey with ½ teaspoon of ground cloves. Cool the mixture before serving. It's great on waffles or ice cream.

Honey and corn syrup can be used interchangeably in baking.

HONEYDEW MELON: see MELONS

HORS D'OEUVRES
See also *Garnishes, Leftovers, Sandwiches.*

You can make remarkably good pâtés or other spreads for canapés, etc., with meat or vegetable leftovers. Put them in the blender with a little butter or oil, possibly some sour cream or cream cheese, or anything spreadable you like. Spice it up plenty. People will beg you for the recipe.

To make your own canapé crackers, cut thin-sliced white bread into rounds with a cookie cutter. Either toast the rounds lightly or butter them and cover with a topping that can be lightly broiled.

Put half a lemon or lime, cut side down, on a plate and stud it with the party picks your guests will need for spearing. This is very handy and looks pretty.

To blend the ingredients in a spread or a dip for appetizers, refrigerate the spread or dip for a couple of hours before serving.

Use cookie cutters on bologna, cheese slices, chicken loaf, sliced meats, etc., to make a fancy-looking platter of cold cuts. Grind the scraps to use in a pâté.

For dips, buy a can of tortillas instead of the usual crackers. Cut them into quarters and sauté lightly until crisp. Drain and cool—you'll have a delicious and unusual substitute for toast or crackers.

Melba toast keeps its crispness better than crackers.

Use a cookie cutter to stamp shapes from thin slices of white or brown bread.

Leftover meats, minced and mixed with a pungent sauce, often make an excellent hot hors d'oeuvre.

Most hot hors d'oeuvres can be made in advance, refrigerated or frozen, then heated in the oven or broiler before serving.

Make up and freeze small canapés. Take them out of the freezer about 2 hours before you want to serve them. (But don't freeze any containing mayonnaise—it darkens and separates. And don't use crackers—they get soggy.)

If you want to store tiny sandwiches, cover them with a thoroughly wrung-out damp dishtowel and keep them in the refrigerator. Take them out and uncover about 20 minutes before serving to enable the dampness to disappear.

HORSERADISH

Mix grated horseradish with finely minced, cooked or pickled beets. A delicious relish.

If you make your own grated horseradish (mixed with vinegar), store it in dark glass jars or in jars covered with brown paper. Horseradish tends to turn a grayish color when exposed to light.

Grated fresh horseradish mixed with applesauce is a great accompaniment to beef and pork dishes as well as cold leftover meats.

A little grated fresh horseradish is wonderful for flavoring a fish sauce. And, used sparingly, it can be added to a salad dressing, too, especially for a coleslaw or chef's salad dressing.

HOT LIQUIDS

Never pour hot liquid into a glass container without first rinsing the container well in hot water. If you have many to fill, stand the containers in a pan containing a little water and heat it on the stove. Fill them while they're still standing in the hot water.

If you're pouring hot liquid into a glass, rinse the glass well with hot water and stand a long-handled metal spoon or fork in it. This will carry the heat upward and prevent the glass (especially thick glass) from cracking.

187

ICE CREAM

Before you buy a homemade ice-cream mixer, consider that many owners feel the ice cream you buy (if it's good ice cream) tastes better than homemade, and it is a lot less expensive.

ICE CUBES

Ice cubes tend to splinter and become slightly hollow if they stay in the freezer too long. This can be avoided if you slide the trays into long plastic bags and twist the ends closed. Safe from the air, they won't lose moisture.

Plastic egg cartons can be used for ice cube trays.

You won't have trouble with ice cubes getting into the spoon when you ladle punch or sliding out the spout of a pitcher if you make the cubes giant size. Use ½- to 1-cup size plastic containers.

You can also make ice cubes in muffin pans or small empty cans. And you can get all kinds of odd shapes if you use éclair tins, ladyfinger pans, madeleine pans, etc.

If you need ice cubes for their cooling action in picnic baskets, etc., freeze water in plastic containers with covers (leave room for expansion when you fill them). If the covers fit tight, you won't have any trouble with leakage. And the melted water can be drunk.

Fold a linen towel and sew up both sides to make a "bag" in which to store ice cubes. Empty the cubes directly into the linen bag and store in the freezer until you need them. They won't stick together.

Strong lemonade frozen in ice cube trays can be used in all sorts of drinks, including iced tea.

If you want ice cubes clear and without air bubbles, boil water, cool it slightly, then pour it into ice cube trays. Cool some more, then freeze.

ICED COFFEE: see COFFEE

ICED TEA: see TEA

ICES
When making sherbet or ices, leave the mixture in the mixing bowl (with the beaters of your electric mixer, too) and put the whole thing in the freezer. In this way, when you have to beat the mixture again, there's none of the mess that usually results when it is removed from the freezer tray. Also, when both bowl and beaters are cold, whipping and thickening are quicker.

ICING
See also *Sugar*.

You can make chocolate icing with either baking chocolate or cocoa. To substitute cocoa for chocolate, use ⅓ cup of cocoa plus 1 tablespoon of melted butter for each 2 ounces of chocolate.

When you use confectioners' sugar, push it through a strainer first and you'll have no trouble with lumps. Use a wire whisk for stirring.

If you add ¼ teaspoon of baking powder to confectioners' sugar icing, the icing will stay moist instead of drying and cracking.

Remember that when you add liquid to confectioners' sugar to make an icing, it takes *very little* to thin it to spreading consistency. Add the liquid 1 teaspoonful at a time, otherwise you run the danger of needing more sugar to thicken it again. This is a terrible thing to discover when you've already put all your sugar in the bowl.

When you make any cooked icing, use a heavy pot (to forestall scorching) which is at least double the height of the ingredients before cooking to allow for rising during boiling.

When making an icing which involves boiling water and sugar

together (usually with cream of tartar) until it forms a hair when dripped from a spoon, don't stir the boiling mixture until the hair stage is reached—if you do it will crystallize.

One of the main secrets of a good icing is steady, constant and long beating.

Don't add raisins or nuts to icings until the very last moment. They tend to make it thin.

Be sure a cake is thoroughly cold before you ice it. If it's even slightly warm, the quality of the icing will be altered.

Use a metal spatula or a wide-bladed knife to ice a cake. Dip it into hot water occasionally to help spread the icing and keep it from thickening too quickly. This will also give a nice sheen to the icing.

Before you ice layer cakes, hold each layer over the sink and brush well with your hand to remove all loose crumbs—otherwise they'll mix with the icing and ruin the looks of your cake.

Before you ice a cake, cut triangles of waxed paper and arrange them, overlapping slightly, to form a circle on the cake plate. Put the first layer on this. When you've finished icing the cake, pull the pieces of paper gently and slightly sideways, from under the cake. You'll find that the cake plate will be perfectly clean with no icing smudges.

When you ice a 2-layer cake, set the bottom layer upside down and cover it with icing. Then put the second layer, right side up, on top of this. Let it set a little so the top layer will be "glued" in place. Ice the sides next and the top last. This allows you to put your hand on top of the upper layer while you ice the sides, thus holding the layers in place.

If the top layer of a cake persists in sliding when you ice it, you can "pin" it with 3 or 4 toothpicks inserted through the layers, spaced well apart. Look for them when you're serving the cake slices later.

To quickly ice a cupcake, rub off all crumbs until smooth, then swirl it around, upside down, in a pan of icing and lift with a quick flick of the wrist. (Keeping the pan of icing over warm water will keep it liquefied.)

Here's another quick icing for a cupcake: put a piece of sweet or semi-sweet chocolate on top of a hot cupcake as soon as you've removed it from the oven. Cover it with a little aluminum foil until the chocolate softens to spreading consistency. Spread quickly with a knife.

Warm the milk before you add it to confectioners' sugar and you won't have lumps.

When a cooked icing is left standing for a while, it often "sugars." If this happens, beat into it ½ teaspoon or so of strained lemon juice.

To get an icing to whip up thick, put it in the freezer until it's very cold—then whip it.

If you're making a creamy fudge icing that doesn't stiffen after beating 15 minutes, whip in a teaspoonful of confectioners' sugar and let it stand for a little while. Then continue to beat the icing. And if the icing becomes too stiff to spread, add a teaspoonful of cream and beat some more.

To put the finishing touches to an iced cake, dip a broad-bladed knife in cold water and smooth the icing over the cake. The wet blade will keep the icing from sticking to it.

You can make a pleasing and quick cake icing out of mashed bananas. Add a little soft butter, lemon juice, cream, and some confectioners' sugar to the mashed banana, and mix well.

You can make a super-quick, delicious (and fattening!) icing by beating heavy cream until it's thick, adding a little vanilla extract, and finally, enough well-sifted confectioners' sugar to make the icing easy to spread.

For a quick white glaze on sweet rolls, brush the tops before baking with an egg white that has been lightly beaten with a tablespoon of milk. Sift sugar over this. If you want a yellow glaze, mix an egg yolk with the milk and dust with sugar.

A fine peanut butter icing can be made with very little fuss. Mix peanut butter, honey, and a little butter or margarine until you get a spreadable mixture. Spread this over a hot baked cake while it's still in the pan and stick it under the broiler until the top sizzles. Then let the cake cool.

When you're icing cookies, place them on cake racks that have been set on waxed paper. Scoop up the icing that spills on the paper and return it to the icing bowl. There's no waste—and you don't have to be unduly careful about applying the icing.

The amount of icing it takes to fill and cover a 9-inch, 2-layer cake will usually cover about 2 dozen cupcakes.

If you have to cover an iced cake with plastic wrap, oil the plastic wrap lightly before you put it on the cake. This will keep the icing from clinging to the wrap when you remove it.

Store leftover icing in a plastic container in the freezer. Keep adding any leftover bits of icing until you have enough for a cake. Never mind if the colors are different—add a little sifted cocoa with a tiny bit of warm milk for blending and you have a quick chocolate icing.

A good substitute for icing is a combination of cinnamon and sugar (1 tablespoon of cinnamon mixed with ½ cup of granulated sugar). Sprinkle over cakes and cupcakes while they're hot.

Another substitute for icing is to place a lace paper doily over the top of a slightly warm cake. Sprinkle finely sifted confectioners' sugar liberally over the doily, being careful to cover mainly the little openings. Then carefully lift off the doily.

JAM AND JELLY
See also *Berries*.

Here's a swift and easy way to make "jam." Mash any kind of berries and add a little honey to them. Mix well. You can also cook berries, cherries, or other fruit with honey until thickened. Then mix well and refrigerate. Use within 3 weeks.

If you have trouble removing the paraffin layer from the top of a jar of jam, try inserting a corkscrew carefully into the center of the paraffin.

Cooking fruit in a pressure cooker for making jelly will extract a great deal more of the juice than regular top-of-stove cooking.

For some reason, fruit jellies and preserves always come out better when you make them in small amounts. So don't double a recipe.

You can tell that jelly has boiled enough if it drops thickly from a cold metal spoon or it jells on a cool plate. (Remove the cooking jelly from the flame while you're testing.)

When you pour jelly into sterilized glasses, put the glasses in a pan containing a little boiling water. They'll be less likely to crack.

Before you seal jelly jars with melted paraffin, hang a piece of sterilized string across the top of the glass, letting it rest on the jelly, but with the ends hanging over. Pour the paraffin over this. Later you'll be able to lift the layer of paraffin by pulling up on the string.

JARS AND BOTTLES
See also *Cleaning Tips*.

Before you refrigerate a jar of food that you intend to open within a week or so, loosen the cover. A cold jar can be difficult to open.

If you find it hard to remove odors from jars and bottles whose insides you can't get at easily, pour in a mixture of 1 cup of hot water to 1 tablespoon of baking soda. Let it stand for a few hours or overnight.

Don't pour very hot liquid into a glass container without first rinsing the container well in hot water. The thicker the glass, the more likely it is to crack if it hasn't been properly heated first.

Here's how to get a bottle filled with water to empty quickly: Hold the bottle upside down with two hands and make a quick, circular, sweeping motion. This forms a whirlpool inside, and the water will drain out in no time flat.

If your kitchen tools (wooden spoons, whisks, etc.) won't stand upright in a storage jar, put a handful of marbles in the bottom of the jar.

Put on a pair of rubber gloves to open a stubborn jar; it does the same job as a rubber jar opener.

If a jar is hard to open, tap the cover (not too hard) flat down against the floor. Or hold it an inch or two above the floor and drop. This works better than tapping against the side of the cover.

You can frequently open a jar whose metal cap is stuck if you turn the jar upside down and immerse the cap—*only* the cap—in near-boiling water. Hold it there for 30 seconds. The heat causes the metal to expand, often enough to let you unscrew the cap.

You can sometimes use a nutcracker to open a tightly screwed-on jar or bottle top. (If the top is plastic, cover it with a cloth before you apply the nutcracker.)

Another way to get a good grip on the screw-top of a hard-to-open jar or bottle is to wind a wide rubber band once (or a narrower rubber band several times) around the cover.

You can also get a thin, flat circular piece of rubber designed to give an excellent grip on a jar cover. These are sold at most hardware stores.

JERUSALEM ARTICHOKES
These aren't really artichokes and they don't come from Jerusalem. They're tubers of a kind of sunflower and are a delicious vegetable with a nutty flavor.

There's really no need to peel Jerusalem artichokes (they're difficult to peel when raw and almost impossible when hot). Scrub them well with a brush and soapy warm water and rinse.

But you can peel raw Jerusalem artichokes and use them sliced in salads. They taste very much like—and have the same texture as—Chinese water chestnuts.

To peel Jerusalem artichokes raw, either use a potato peeler or rub the skin off gently with a fine grater.

Jerusalem artichokes are easier to peel before they're cooked, but if you do cook them first, peel while they're hot, otherwise too much flesh comes off with the skin.

KALE

Cook kale as you would spinach (see *Spinach*), but a few minutes longer.

KETCHUP

An unopened bottle of ketchup or chili sauce will stay fresh for about 1 year. An opened bottle (which should be refrigerated) will keep its flavor and color for about 3 months.

To get ketchup to flow from a freshly opened bottle, insert the blade of a table knife a couple of inches inside and run it around the neck of the bottle. Invert, and out the ketchup will come.

Before you throw away an empty ketchup bottle, pour in a little vinegar and oil, cover, and shake. Pour the mixture into your bottle of salad dressing.

KIDNEYS

If the beef, veal, lamb or pork kidney you buy hasn't been skinned by the butcher, plunge it into boiling water, remove at once and peel off the membrane. It usually comes off easily. If you have any trouble, use nail scissors with curved blades.

You can remove the gamy flavor from beef or pork kidneys if you soak them for ½ hour in cold salted water, or blanch them quickly in salted water, drain and rinse. Then cook as your recipe directs.

Kidneys won't lose their juices if you first sauté them whole to "set" the juices, then slice and cook them lightly in sauce and serve.

KITCHEN LADDER

A low folding stepladder in the kitchen is usually just the right height to sit on—placing your feet either on the floor or on one of the steps—while you wash dishes, peel vegetables, mix batters or iron. If you do as much of your kitchen work as you can sitting, you'll be less tired at the end of the day. This takes only a few days to become a comfortable habit. Don't kick the ladder away and get up on your feet again until you've given it a chance.

KITCHEN TIMER

This is one of the handiest things in the kitchen. Set it going, carry it to where you can hear it ring, and you'll never forget you have something cooking or something in the washing machine or dryer.

KNEADING: see BREAD

KNIVES

See also *Carving, Slicing.*

Buy good knives—they'll last as long as you do.

Both carbon steel and stainless steel knives are good. Properly sharpened and cared for, they'll keep a good sharp edge.

If you don't have a really good knife sharpener, you might prefer carbon steel knives. Once well-sharpened, they generally hold their edge longer than stainless.

You can't have too sharp a knife for food preparation as long as you handle it with knowledge and respect. It's the dull knives that slip and cut.

Ask your butcher if you may bring in your knives to be sharpened from time to time, when he sends his own out. He may charge you a small fee, but it's worth it. (Wrap the knife in a newspaper or cardboard scabbard when you carry it.) With proper care your knives will stay close to razor-sharp for many months.

For general use, 3 important knives in any kitchen are a short, slender paring knife, the large heavy French chef's knife and a long narrow slicing knife (called a *tranche-lard*). The blade of this last is 9 inches or longer. When you buy a slicing knife, look for one which has a finger guard.

The best way to use a knife for general food cutting is with a sawing motion.

To use a French chef's knife for mincing (you can also slice, cut and chop, and do away with a dozen gadgets once you've learned the technique), place the knife sharp-side down over the food and hold the tip to the cutting board with your left hand (reverse hands if you're left-handed). Don't let the tip of the blade leave the board at any time. Do all the cutting at the broad end of the blade, near the handle. Use short up-and-down motions, moving the knife in a circle so that it traverses all of the food to be minced. Go back and forth in an arc until the food is as finely minced as you like. Use the same principle for slicing. Just remember to keep the tip of the knife on the board at all times.

The Chinese cleaver or kitchen knife (*choy doh*) can usually be used in the same way as a French chef's knife.

The best way to handle dirty knives (the sharp ones you use in food preparation) is to wash them at once, dry and put them away, instead of letting them wait with the rest of the dirty dishes to be washed later. They're easier to wash when they've just been used and are less likely to rust or stain.

Never wash good sharp knives in very hot water. This cuts down on the sharpness of the edge.

Don't soak knives, forks, spoons or any utensils with wooden handles. Wash and dry them immediately. Soaking will make the handles swell, warp and, in time, pull away from the metal.

Don't buy a knife sharpener that looks like a pair of wheels between which you insert the blade for sharpening. It sharpens a knife edge unevenly and in time will ruin a good knife.

Get a small steel or ceramic cylindrical knife sharpener instead. And every time you wash a knife, give it a few strokes on each side of the blade. Rinse the knife and put it away. This is how to keep your knives sharp all the time.

After you've sharpened a knife, don't use it before you've washed it; otherwise tiny bits of steel dust could get in the food.

Some of our grandmothers used this effective method to sharpen knives. There's often a rough, unglazed ring on the underside of kitchen mugs or ironstone plates, and this makes an excellent surface against which to sharpen a knife. Hold the knife at an angle, just as you would with a cylindrical knife sharpener.

A knife loses its sharp edge not from the actual cutting of food, but from contact with the cutting surface—cutting board, counter top, etc.

Fruits or other foods containing acid will blacken and discolor a carbon steel knife (and any food you cut with it immediately afterward), so wash the knife as soon as you've used it on acid-containing foods.

If you keep your knives in a drawer, make scabbards for the blades by flattening the cardboard cylinders that come with rolls of paper towels.

Onions tend to become discolored when cut with a carbon steel (as opposed to a stainless steel) knife. This won't matter for onions intended for cooking, but you might prefer to use a stainless steel knife if you're slicing onion rings for salad, for example.

You can remove the stains from carbon steel knives if you wet the blades, sprinkle with scouring powder, then rub with a wet cork. Since they have a tendency to rust, oil them lightly now and then with vegetable oil before storing.

The safest and handiest way to store knives is on one or two long magnetic knife holders, placed high on the wall.

KOHLRABI

This cabbage-related vegetable is delicious. Buy small heads—the larger ones are inclined to be woody inside.

LABELS
See also *Cans*.

Get in the habit of reading the weights and lists of ingredients on the labels of bottles, boxes and cans. This will certainly affect your buying habits for the better.

You should be interested in the drained weight, not the net weight, of most foods.

If soap and water won't scrub the labels off dishes, glasses, etc., try rubbing with nail polish remover (acetone) on a bit of rag. Lighter fluid is also good for this.

Self-adhesive labels are handy for labeling the contents of cans or jars for storage on the shelf, in the refrigerator, and in the freezer. They pull off easily, but they don't wash off.

Make labels to attach to bottles, jars and other containers (or their covers) in which you freeze food. Plastic adhesive tape can be written on, erased, and will withstand dishwashing.

LADYFINGERS
If you're making a dessert that calls for ladyfingers (such as tipsy pudding) and you want them to stand upright around a glass bowl, butter the ladyfingers very lightly on one side, and press the buttered side against the glass. Then fill the bowl with the dessert filling called for.

LAMB
See also *Liver, Meats, Mutton, Roasts*.

Lamb is meat from an animal under 1 year old. Older lamb should be classified as mutton. "Spring lamb" comes from 3- to 5-month-old animals. You can now buy this all year round. "Baby lamb" comes from an animal 6 to 8 weeks old.

The best—and most expensive—chops for broiling are rib or loin chops. Shoulder chops are cheaper but generally tougher. (Cut up, they're great for stew.) If you want to use a cheaper shoulder cut, try a "round bone" shoulder chop. Ask for it by this name, and try to get it 1 inch thick, slightly thicker than butchers usually cut it.

Buy all lamb chops at least 1 inch thick. Thinner ones won't be juicy and will be easily overdone.

Buy a leg or half a leg of lamb, and have your butcher cut it into lamb steaks. This is much cheaper than lamb chops and twice as good. The steaks broil beautifully, are tender, and will feed more people than chops. Freeze what you don't use.

The next time you buy a leg or shoulder of lamb, refrigerate for 2 or 3 days before cooking. The meat will taste much better.

Don't remove the fell (parchment-like covering) from a leg of lamb before you roast it. It keeps the juices in and helps the roast to cook more quickly.

Squeeze the juice of an entire lemon over a leg of lamb and rub it in well before putting the meat in the oven. This tenderizes the meat and adds greatly to the flavor.

Throw a tablespoon of caraway seeds into the pot the next time you cook lamb stew.

If you want lamb chops to taste just beautiful, put some rosemary in a pepper grinder, grate into a blender with some garlic, and blend into a paste. Rub this into oiled lamb chops before broiling.

When you broil lamb chops, make slashes about 1 inch apart on the fat surrounding the meat. This will keep the edges from curling.

Broil or sauté lamb chops only until the centers are pink. The chops will be juicier, more tender and have more flavor.

A 3- to 4-pound lamb roast should be roasted at 325° for about 35 minutes per pound.

Roast lamb served on the pink side, medium-rare, like lamb chops, is juicier and tastier than well-done lamb roast.

LARDING

The secret of the wonderful taste of meats served in great res-
taurants often lies with larding, the sewing of strips of fat into
the meat before cooking. These fat strips can—and often should—
be marinated in wine or brandy and herbs for 30 minutes before
you use them.

To improve their flavor and keep them from becoming dry,
lean meats are the ones which most often need larding before
roasting or braising. To lard meat, cut salt pork into long
shoelace-like strips. Thread a long larding needle with a strip and
push it through the meat. Pull the needle out the other side and
cut the pork strip flush with the meat on both sides. Do this about
every 3 inches.

If you don't want to do it yourself, your butcher can lard a
loin of veal and any cut of beef or lamb for you.

When you serve meat which has been larded, slice it diagonally, so that the larding will appear as attractive small white
dots here and there.

LEEKS

Wash leeks very carefully under cold running water to remove
the sand which lodges between the flat leaves. Trim and slice
them lengthwise. If they're very thick, slice them lengthwise in
quarters. Again hold them under cold running water to remove
the sand.

Tie leeks in bunches and cook them in boiling water, as
you would asparagus, until they're just tender. Serve with a
sauce.

For incomparable flavor, substitute leeks for onions in soups
and stews.

A leek cooked and puréed with other vegetables for the base
of a cream soup adds marvelous flavor.

Put a couple of white leek bulbs in a pot of moist dirt. They
will sprout green shoots that you can cut and use just as you
would scallions.

LEFTOVERS
See also *Blender, Hors d'oeuvres.*

When you make something using egg yolks, you're left with the whites. And when you prepare a dish using egg whites, you're left with the yolks. Make a list of recipes using egg whites and another list for those using yolks. Similarly, some recipes call for ingredients you don't use every day, and you may be left with more than you needed. Make a list of dishes using these too, so you need never throw precious food away. Examples: sour cream, coconut flakes, heavy cream, cottage cheese—to name just a few.

The greatest use for leftovers that has ever been invented is spaghetti sauce. You can start with either a basic tomato sauce or a white sauce. Chop the leftover meats, chicken, vegetables, or even fish and mix them into the sauce. Spice it up with condiments of any kind. Heat and pour over cooked pasta. What you have, friends, is a dish you'd pay a small fortune for in a good restaurant.

And sandwich fillings! Put leftovers in the blender with a little mayonnaise and jazz up the mixture with some seasoning. You'll have a delicious sandwich spread.

Don't despise leftovers. It's lunacy to throw away good food, and a little imagination is often all it takes to turn some leftovers into great dishes. Leftovers have been made into such tasty dishes by great chefs that they've been known to repeat them, using fresh materials when they've had no leftovers on hand.

Many meat, vegetable and other food remnants can be cut into small pieces, mixed with beaten eggs, milk and a dash of imagination, then baked into a soufflé; or, put through a blender and cook the purée down until it's thickened. Follow any vegetable soufflé recipe.

When you make hash out of leftovers, remember that there should be about ⅓ as much gravy as solid ingredients.

Leftover muffins can be hollowed out, filled with creamed mixtures and served hot as a luncheon dish.

Mix minced leftovers with noodles and bake.

Add minced leftovers to pancake batter.

Force puréed leftovers through a pastry bag and use as a garnish.

Crumble dry leftover cake, add some sherry to the crumbs and use this as a topping for soufflé and cream desserts.

You can mash leftover canned or baked beans, season and make them into croquettes. Dip in egg, crumbs, then deep-fat fry.

Add leftover wine to the vinegar bottle and you'll have a new supply of wine vinegar.

What's been left out? Salmagundi, covers for shirred eggs, stuffings for vegetables, sandwich spreads, spaghetti sauces, leftovers minced and mixed with rice. . . .

Batter

Leftover pancake or waffle batter can be beaten into a creamed soup or sauce or other creamed dishes. Or it can be used as the base for a cream sauce to go over vegetables, etc.

Finely cut-up leftovers make great fillings for crepes and omelets; mixed with batter, they can become fritters.

Cereal

Leftover cereal can be used as a thickener for stews, soups and gravies; it can also be combined with meats or vegetables in escalloped dishes.

Fish

Leftover cooked fish can be put through the blender and made into a pâté, just as chicken or meat can. Add mayonnaise or other moisteners, herbs, and other flavors. Use for stuffing celery or eggs, or as a canapé spread, or for fish cakes.

Meats

A substitute for hamburger in recipes: ground or chopped bits of leftover roast or steak or stew meat. The final dish will probably be better than if you'd followed the original recipe.

You can make remarkably good pâtés or spreads for canapés with meat (and vegetable) leftovers. Put the leftovers in the blender with a little butter or oil, possibly some cream cheese or mayonnaise or sour cream—anything spreadable. Spice it up plenty. People will ask for the recipe.

Use meat and vegetable leftovers in a stuffing for chicken or turkey; or for stuffing cabbage leaves, green peppers, or tomatoes.

Any leftover chicken or meat, fish too, can be ground and mixed with dumpling batter to make the tastiest dumplings ever.

Leftover meats or chicken shouldn't be cooked twice because they toughen and dry out. To serve them with a sauce, heat the sauce first, then warm the meat in the sauce until it's the right temperature.

Cut up leftover meats and vegetables and serve them in a curry sauce.

Pickle Juice

Mix the juice with oil and make a salad dressing. Usually no other flavorings are needed for this zippy dressing.

Slice fresh unwaxed cucumbers very thin and set them to marinate in the refrigerator for a couple of days in pickle juice. You'll have crisp pickle slices.

Salad Dressing

To make a delicious hamburger, mix leftover salad dressing into the meat. Leftover salad dressing is also good mixed with flaked fish or chopped hard-cooked eggs for a sandwich.

Soup

Pour the leftover soup with its solids into the blender. Add curry and other seasonings, and blend. Then heat the thickened mixture. What you have is a very tasty curry sauce to serve over rice. And although it may not be Indian, curry sauce is also great over noodles.

Throw almost any kind of leftover soup minus bones into the blender to get a sauce or gravy for vegetables or meat.

Leftover soups in any quantity can usually be used as a base for other soups. Freeze them.

Use blended leftovers as a base for a creamed soup.

Vegetables

Cut up and serve with a cream sauce flavored with curry powder.

Mince and use as a filling for stuffed eggs and stuffed peppers.

Mince and use in an omelet.

Mash and add to chopped meat for very juicy hamburgers or meat loaf. Add herbs or spices if necessary.

Make chowders and creamed vegetable soups; add to pancake batter; make fritters.

Put raw leftover onion in a tightly capped jar in the refrigerator. It keeps very well.

To rebake baked potatoes, dip them in cold water and put them in a 350° F oven for about 20 minutes. Or peel and slice and make hashed browns or mash them. Mashed baked potatoes with butter are what mashed potatoes are meant to be.

Dice, dry, and bottle leftover vegetables to use in omelets, soups, stews, and dozens of other dishes. Dried vegetable bits are not storage problems.

Don't be too wedded to printed recipes. Feel free to make substitutions when they seem sensible to you. For example, if a particular sauce recipe calls for steamed cauliflower bits and you have lots of celery on hand, use it instead. Carrots, pumpkins, squash, turnips—even potatoes—often can be used interchangeably from one recipe to another (the same is true of fowl, meats, etc.). In some cases you may have to alter cooking times a bit, but that needn't be a great hurdle. Use up what's on hand.

Pieces of uncooked vegetables such as carrots, green peppers, or onions can be frozen for future use in soups and stews. See *Vegetables*.

The midnight food snacker discovered long ago that there are mighty few hot dishes that aren't also delicious cold. If you have part of a casserole or some cooked vegetables left from a meal, you don't always have to try to pretty them up for future heating—make them part of a cold smorgasbord.

LEMONS
See also *Pies*.

6 average-sized lemons will give you a little more than 1 cup of juice.

The heavier lemons are, the juicier and meatier they are.

Lemons should be kept open to the air during storage. Don't keep them in closed bags or the skins will mildew.

Like oranges, lemons with smooth skins have more juice than rough, thick-skinned ones.

Rough-skinned lemons, however, are much easier to grate than smooth-skinned ones.

Because lemons have probably been sprayed, it's safest to scrub them very well with a brush and use hot, soapy water. Rinse and dry before you use them.

Don't strain lemon juice to use in bread, cake or cookies. Just remove the seeds. Otherwise you're throwing out the bulk of the lemon flavor.

For an even stronger lemon flavor, peel the lemon, remove the pith and pits, and blender the lemon at high speed. You have a marvelous flavoring for cakes, cookies, puddings, and sauces.

There are about 3 average lemons in 1 pound.

The rind of an average lemon gives about 1 tablespoon, grated.

The juice of an average lemon will yield about 2½ tablespoons, strained.

You can use limes in every way you do lemons.

A lemon is easier to grate when it's whole. Even if you want only juice, grate the lemon (after you've scrubbed it with soap and water and dried it) and save the particles for future use. Grate lightly so that you get only the yellow part, with its aromatic oils—the white portion tends to be bitter. Let the particles dry thoroughly, then bottle and save for future use in cakes, cookies, puddings and icings. (You can also freeze grated rind without drying it.)

A lemon which has begun to age and dry is next to impossible to grate, unless you do it this way: try thinly peeling off the outer layer, using a potato peeler. Drop the thin strips of peel into a blender and blend at high speed. You'll get small favorful flakes which you can use as you would grated peel. (You can do the same with a fresh lemon—using a blender is usually easier than using a grater.)

As far as flavor goes, lemon extract is a better substitute for lemon peel than it is for lemon juice.

Canned or bottled lemon juice never tastes as good as freshly squeezed. Furthermore, many juices are "reconstituted"—they're not canned or bottled fresh. Skip them if you want true lemon flavor in your cooking.

To get the utmost juice from lemons, heat them in a 300° oven for 5 minutes, or simmer them in boiling water for a few minutes. Remove, cool, and store in the refrigerator. You'll increase the juice yield by at least a quarter.

Another way to get more juice from a lemon is to roll it around on a hard surface, pressing hard with the palm of your hand.

It *is* possible to get juice from a dried lemon. Drop it into boiling water, remove the pan from the flame and let it stand for 5 minutes. Dry the lemon, then squeeze.

If you need only a few drops of juice, prick one end of a lemon with a fork and squeeze out the amount you need. Then put the lemon in the refrigerator—it won't dry out.

If you use a lot of lemon juice in your cooking, squeeze the juice of several lemons and store it in a small bottle in the refrigerator. The flavor lasts well for more than a week. You can also freeze it, but allow room in the bottle for expansion during freezing. If you freeze lemon juice in small bottles, it thaws quickly at room temperature. Lemon juice you freeze yourself tastes exactly like freshly squeezed lemon juice.

Whenever you see lemons on special, buy them even though you may not need them immediately. Squeeze the juice out of as many as you like and refrigerate or freeze.

Lemon juice is the master of fish. Use it any time, with any fish.

Lemon juice is a fine tenderizer or marinade for meats. Rub the juice of an entire lemon over a leg of lamb before you roast it.

Add lemon juice (¼ teaspoon or more) to a gravy containing blood from any kind of liver, and the blood won't curdle.

219

Add 1 teaspoon of lemon juice to the water in which you cook rice, and the rice will be whiter.

If you add lemon juice to the water in which you soak potatoes, the potatoes will keep their color and remain usable for several days if refrigerated.

If you rub lemon over the cut surfaces of peeled apples, avocados or the stem ends of artichokes they won't discolor.

Lemon slices are hard to handle for use at the table. Serve them cut lengthwise, in wedges.

To prevent a lemon wedge from squirting in the wrong direction, prick the flesh first with a fork, then aim and squeeze.

Cut whole raw lemon into very, very fine slivers to add to a tossed salad.

For a marvelous spread, add grated lemon peel to soft butter.

You can make a delicious lemon flavoring by covering shaved lemon peel with sugar and letting it stand until a liquid forms.

Lemon (or lime) is great for ridding cutting boards and hands of onion or garlic odors. Rub half a lemon over the surface of the board or on your hands, then rinse.

Squeeze lemon juice into ice cube compartments for freezing. When you need to add the juice of a lemon to a sauce, for example, drop in one of the frozen cubes. For a cold dish, defrost the cube before use.

After you have squeezed a lemon, instead of throwing away the lemon skin, cut it into strips and freeze. Lemon strips are handy for flavorings and in cakes, cookies, and puddings.

You can also freeze thin strips of lemon peel in ice cube trays, after pouring a little water over them. These make pretty ice cubes for many types of cold drinks.

It's easier to grate a lemon diagonally across the grater rather than up and down. The lemon will move more smoothly over the grating surface.

Strong lemonade frozen in ice cube trays can be used instead of ice cubes in all sorts of drinks including iced tea.

LETTUCE
See also *Salads and Salad Greens.*

Leaf lettuce has more vitamins A and C than head lettuce.

The best way to wash a head of lettuce (also escarole and other greens that come in heads or bunches) is to fill a large bowl or pot with cold water and pump the head of lettuce, stem side up, up and down in it. Do this in a couple of changes of water if necessary.

You can stuff lettuce leaves the same way you can cabbage leaves.

Crisp shredded lettuce can be substituted for shredded cabbage in coleslaw.

Wash wilted lettuce in cold water, shake it fairly dry, cover, and put in the refrigerator. In about 12 hours the lettuce will have freshened up surprisingly.

The leaves of refrigerated lettuce will be less likely to "rust" if you wrap the lettuce in dry paper towels before you refrigerate it.

Most lettuces make excellent hot greens, cooked as you would spinach. You have to flavor them a bit with celery salt, nutmeg, pepper and perhaps some garlic, but it can be a fine dish. Also try creamed lettuce.

Don't throw away the coarse outside lettuce leaves. Use them as greens in stews and soups.

Some finely shredded lettuce is very good added to a vegetable soup shortly before you serve it.

LIMA BEANS: see BEANS

LIMES
Limes can be used in every way lemons can. See *Lemons.*

Limes turn from dark green to pale green to yellow as they age, but this doesn't necessarily affect their quality; in fact, limes a few weeks old give more juice than dark green freshly picked ones do.

Like lemons, limes should be bought by weight. The heavier they are, the juicier and meatier they are.

Buy very green limes. These are the tart and tangy ones. Yellowish limes have less flavor.

Limes keep well in the refrigerator if you store them in a capped jar.

LIVER
See also *Chicken Livers.*

Peel the membrane off slices of liver before you sauté them and they won't curl in the cooking pan.

Lamb, mutton or pork liver will taste better, prepared any way, if you first scald the slices in boiling water for a very short time. Then drain and rinse.

For extra-tender liver (steer, calf, lamb or pork) cover the slices with milk and let them stand for about 2 hours in the refrigerator. Remove, dry thoroughly, and dip in seasoned flour or bread crumbs for sautéing or broiling.

If you need to grind uncooked liver for a particular dish, you can parboil or sauté it lightly first, then cut in pieces and put through the food grinder.

Another way to grind raw liver is to freeze it partially first. (Or, if it's already frozen, partially defrost it.) Semifrozen liver grinds without losing its juices. Cut it into strips and feed it into the grinder.

Liver of any kind easily becomes tough, so don't overcook. Brown quickly at high heat for a short time, then cook gently at low heat, also for a short time. Turn it once, but cook the second side still less. Liver should be very tender in the middle.

If you want to use the blood from any kind of liver in a sauce or gravy, add ¼ teaspoon of lemon juice and it won't curdle.

If you don't remove the fat surrounding a liver pâté, it will keep for several weeks in the refrigerator.

LOBSTER
See also *Shellfish.*

¾ pound of cooked lobster meat will give 1½ cups.

When you buy an uncooked lobster it should always be alive (moving). It's usually brownish green in color. It becomes bright red when cooked.

Every part of a lobster is edible except the intestinal vein, which runs through to the tail just under the back, and the "queen" (a little bag near the head which contains gravel). The "coral" is the roe, and should never be discarded. It's delicious. And the liver, called the "tomalley," is considered especially choice.

A live lobster is not necessarily a fresh one—it may have been kept in a tank of seawater for a week or more. The meat in such lobsters is puny. If you're in an area where lobsters are easily available, demand freshly caught ones.

To cut up a live lobster, insert a knife where the tail and body meet and cut the spinal cord. Then turn the lobster on its back and split lengthwise. Remove the intestinal vein and the sac behind the eyes.

If you buy a lobster already cooked, see that the tail is curled. This means that the lobster was alive (as it should have been) when it was boiled.

Don't buy a cooked lobster if you want to serve it in a hot dish. It will be tough and often dry if you have to cook it further.

To boil a lobster, plunge it head down into a very large pot holding several quarts of tepid water, then put the cover on. Heat the water gradually to boiling and cook for about 25 minutes. (Scientists say that a lobster feels no pain if the water is heated gradually. If you have no such qualms, plunge the lobster into several quarts of boiling water and cook for 15 minutes.)

If you're boiling lobster to be served cold, cook it for a shorter time and let cool in the cooking liquid. It will have much more flavor.

Lobster toughens and shrinks when overcooked.

Dismember and serve a boiled lobster by twisting off both claws, then the head. If you cover it with a dishtowel and do this underneath, you can avoid squirting the juices far and wide.

Then cut down the middle of the soft under shell and crack the claws with a nutcracker. The best meat is in the claws.

If you're making a sauce which contains lobster meat, first break the lobster shell into small pieces using a hammer and cook these in the sauce liquid. Strain and use the liquid. The shell gives a wonderfully rich flavor to any shellfish sauce. (The same holds true for shrimp shells.)

LOW SALT DIETS
See *Salt*.

When you use salt substitutes, add them to the food just before serving. Cooking often neutralizes their taste.

Dishes which contain little or no added salt can be made more palatable by any of the following:

judicious use of fruit juices such as pineapple, apricot, lemon or lime, particularly with vegetables and meats;

the addition of liberal amounts of paprika to chicken, fish and meats;

the addition of honey;

as your imagination directs—powdered mustard, powdered onion, almost all spices, vanilla and other flavoring extracts, diced fruits, and berries;

adding caraway seeds and a pinch of sugar to greens such as spinach;

adding a bit of sugar, honey, or an onion to the water in which you cook fresh vegetables;

the addition of nutmeg;

flavoring your food with a lemon juice and garlic combination. Lots of garlic not only makes many a dish taste better, but it's also rich in vitamin C. (And holds vampires at bay!)

natural peanut butter—ground to order with nothing but roasted peanuts—is a godsend for people on low-salt diets. You can sometimes buy this in grocery stores—check the labels.

MACARONI: see PASTA

MACAROONS

Bake macaroons on unglazed paper spread on cookie sheets. After you've baked them, put the sheets of paper on a very damp towel and remove the macaroons with a spatula as they loosen from the paper. If the bottoms are moist, set them to dry on a wire cake cooler or a dry thick towel.

When you store macaroons be sure they don't touch one another, especially if you store them covered. Wrap each one lightly in a small paper napkin, then place in the storage container.

You can use stale macaroons as a delicious flavoring for icings or as dessert toppings. Break them up, spread in a pan and toast gently for about an hour in a *very* low oven (about 200°). When they're thoroughly dry and toast-colored, take them out and let cool. Put them in a blender a little at a time or through a grinder. Store the crumbs in a tightly capped jar—they'll be good for at least a couple of months.

MANGOES

Pick mangoes which are orange-yellow to red in color and which give slightly with pressure. Green mangoes are hard, and have to ripen before you can eat them.

Slightly green mangoes should be ripened in the dark, like tomatoes. Put them in a brown paper bag. They're ripe when they develop a sweet fruity smell and become orange to red in color. (Some mangoes are ripe when they're yellow or if they develop small brown spots. You can test their ripeness by pressure.)

MAPLE SYRUP: see SYRUPS

MARBLE SLAB

If you use a marble slab for rolling pastry (which is recommended because the surface is always cool) never allow acidic foods like vinegar, lemons or tomatoes to come in contact with the surface— acid corrodes marble.

MARGARINE

Margarine is often a good and economical substitute for butter, especially if you want to cut down on animal and polysaturated fats. Look for the 100 percent corn or safflower oil margarines.

You can buy margarine either salted or sweet, just as you can butter.

Margarine is almost as tasty as butter spread on bread and in most baking. But it cannot replace the taste of warm butter in sautéing or in dishes such as butter sauce which call for the flavor of melted butter.

Try mixing a little butter with margarine when you want a butter flavor.

Like butter, margarine picks up flavors and aromas from other foods in the refrigerator. So keep it well covered.

If you like the texture and easy spreadability of whipped margarine, it's very easy to make—and cheap. Let a stick of regular margarine come to room temperature, then whip it to lightness with an electric beater. Add 3 tablespoons of salad oil, 1 at a time, and whip everything up well. With a rubber spatula, transfer the mixture to a small bowl, cover tightly, and refrigerate. This also increases the volume of the original stick of margarine.

If you're out of regular margarine and absolutely have to use whipped margarine in baking, weigh it—don't go by volume.

MARINADE

Prepare a marinating sauce for meat, fish, or chicken the day before you need it. This allows the flavors to blend and enhance one another.

There are two easy ways of marinating. One is to put the meat in a very large screw-top jar along with the marinade. Screw on the lid and let stand, inverting the jar from time to time.

The other method is to put the meat and the marinade in a large plastic bag that you can twist-tie closed. Put the bag in a bowl and turn it now and then.

Most marinating is best if done at room temperature, except in very hot weather when you may need to set the bowl in the refrigerator for a few hours.

The larger the piece of meat, the longer the marinating time that is required. A leg of lamb or a large beef roast will benefit if marinated for a couple of days.

If the piece of meat to be marinated is very large, prick it with a sharp fork here and there to allow the marinade to penetrate the meat.

If you're marinating meat in a bowl, be sure the marinade covers the meat at least halfway. And turn the meat every few hours.

You can use almost any salad dressing made with flavored oil and vinegar, lemon or lime as a marinade for ripe olives, fresh or canned mushrooms, and many vegetables (if you blanch them first), including cauliflowerets, green or yellow beans, green or red sweet peppers, and onions. Let them marinate in the dressing for a day or so.

MARSHMALLOWS
16 marshmallows weigh about 4 ounces.

Store marshmallows in an airtight container in the freezer to keep them from drying out.

Marshmallows are easier to cut if you freeze them.

To cut marshmallows, use scissors dipped in water.

MAYONNAISE
See also *Blender*.

Don't think of mayonnaise as just a dressing for salads, potatoes and cole slaw. It's a sauce in its own right—served warm

229

over vegetables, or cold with fish, seafood or chicken. Flavor it with many kinds of herbs and spices.

An unopened jar of mayonnaise will stay in good condition for about 8 months; opened (and refrigerated, of course), for from 4 to 6 months.

Mix mayonnaise with some yogurt to make a zippy dressing.

You can also mix sour cream with mayonnaise to make a very smooth and delicate dressing. Mix well.

Here are three ways to add variety to mayonnaise: Mix ground watercress or feathery dill into it for green mayonnaise; a bit of tomato paste for pink mayonnaise; and a little turmeric and a dash of curry powder for a tasty yellow mayonnaise.

Make your own mayonnaise. It's easy, cheaper than bought mayonnaise, and free of preservatives. More important, it's delicious, far better than bought mayonnaise, which tends to taste somewhat harsh and on the sharp side, possibly because there's too much vinegar in it and vinegar is high in acidity. But the mayonnaise you make yourself can be extremely delicate, and less expensive. Many cookbooks contain recipes for making mayonnaise, and if you have a blender, it's a cinch. One hint: The best vinegar to use is rice wine vinegar, which can be bought at many supermarkets. It's also available at Oriental grocery stores and gourmet shops.

Here are some tips for making good mayonnaise:

be sure the eggs and oil are at room temperature;
use only fresh eggs;
don't use too much salt;
beat the egg yolks for mayonnaise in a warmed bowl and add
    the oil in tiny quantities, beating as you go, so that you won't
    have to worry about the ingredients separating;
adding too much oil too quickly will also prevent the mixture
    from thickening. If this does happen put the container in the
    freezer for about half an hour. Then take it out and beat fren-
    ziedly or put it in the blender until it's thick. You can then
    begin to add more oil slowly;

use lemon or lime juice in place of some or all of the vinegar for
    less pungency;
add a few crushed mint leaves or some minced watercress to the
    mixture before refrigerating.

Everyone is afraid of curdling mayonnaise while they're mixing it. Properly made, this shouldn't happen. But here are several corrective measures if your homemade mayonnaise does start
to curdle:

add 1 teaspoon of prepared mustard to a hot dry bowl, then add
    1 tablespoon of the curdled mayonnaise. Beat with a whisk
    until the mixture is smooth and thick. Continue adding 1 tea-
    spoon of mayonnaise at a time, beating well after each addi-
    tion. The trick here is to add the curdled mayonnaise by single
    teaspoonfuls;
put an egg yolk in a bowl and gradually beat the mayonnaise
    into it;
beat the curdled mayonnaise briskly with an electric beater or
    blender and add a small amount of sweet cream, with a pinch
    of sugar.

After you've made mayonnaise, mix in 1 tablespoon of boiling water and it will be less likely to separate in the refrigerator.
(It *won't* separate unless you keep it too cold.)

2 tablespoons of warmed, very finely mashed potato mixed into
a pint of homemade mayonnaise will also help to keep the emulsion stable.

To make a mayonnaise which is stiff and holds its shape (such
as for coating eggs and fish) soften 1 tablespoon of unflavored
gelatin in ⅓ cup of cold liquid (a mixture of stock, some wine, a
little lemon juice perhaps), then heat this until the gelatin dis-
solves. Cool, then beat gradually into 1½ cups of mayonnaise and
chill the mixture until the gelatin sets. (You can also pipe this
mixture through a pastry bag for garnishing a dish.)

Any opened jar of mayonnaise and all mayonnaise made at
home must be refrigerated.

Store mayonnaise in the least cold section of the refrigerator —high up or on the door shelf. (Store-bought mayonnaise should not separate unless frozen.)

You can't freeze mayonnaise because the contents will separate.

If you're going to store any mixture containing mayonnaise, omit the mayonnaise during the mixing but cover the surface of the mixture with it. Refrigerate. This will keep the mixture from discoloring or drying out while it's stored. Just before serving mix well.

If you find mayonnaise too thick for a particular use, try thinning it with sour cream or yogurt. (You can also thin it with sweet cream, of course, though this dilutes its flavor. It becomes very delicate.)

If for some reason the mayonnaise you make doesn't thicken properly, you can always beat an equal amount of commercial mayonnaise into it, put it in a jar, and refrigerate. Most store-bought mayonnaises can stand a bit of thinning and all of them benefit by being made more delicate.

MEASURING

Here are some workable equivalents: 3 teaspoons equal 1 tablespoon; 4 tablespoons equal ¼ cup; and 5 tablespoons plus 2 teaspoons equal ⅓ cup.

Weights are more dependable than measures and also easier to work with when you're measuring foods such as solid fats.

If you have favorite recipes you hate to slip up on, or if you want to perfect a particular one, convert the measurements to weights. You'll come out with more uniform results. A cup of flour will vary in volume, depending on how you pack it, but once you've determined the correct weight of flour you need in a recipe—and stick to it—you won't have to worry about the result each time you use that recipe.

Keep a set of measuring spoons (held together by a ring) in each canister of flour, sugar or salt that you use. Put them back in the canister after each use to avoid washing each time.

Invest in a kitchen scale, preferably one which measures by gram weight. Metric measurement is on the way.

Get in the habit of putting the container into which you're measuring something over the sink in order to avoid a mess if anything spills.

An ounce of liquid equals 2 tablespoons.

The little plastic measuring cups that come with cans of ground coffee hold exactly 2 level tablespoonfuls.

To measure flour or sugar from a container into a cup, set the cup on a piece of waxed paper. Later you can easily pour the overflow back into the original container.

If a recipe calls for shortening plus honey, molasses, or syrup, measure the shortening first. Then use the same measuring cup, without washing, for the liquid sweetening. It will roll right out of the cup when you pour.

Suppose your recipe calls for ½ cup of solid shortening. The easiest way to measure it is to fill half the cup with cold water first, then spoon the shortening into this, pressing down until the water reaches the whole-cup level. For a ⅓ cup of shortening, fill the cup ⅔ full of water, etc.

MEATBALLS

Form raw meatballs around a cube of cheese—any kind of cheese—mozzarella, American, whatever you have on hand. Cook the meatballs as you usually do and they'll have soft, creamy centers.

MEAT BASTER

You can buy a meat baster with a needle attachment, for injecting liquids—oil, wine, vinegar or spiced liquids—into roasts or turkey. This is a wonderful kitchen device. (A medical hypodermic syringe with a broad-gauge needle will do as well.)

MEAT GLAZE: see GLAZE

MEAT GRINDER

To keep a grinder from slipping, put a piece of sandpaper sand-side down on the surface you stand the grinder on.

If you want to grind uncooked liver, you have to parboil or sauté it lightly first, then cut it in pieces and feed these into the grinder. It isn't possible to grind raw liver without its getting mushy and losing its juices unless it is frozen.

When you grind crackers with meat for a meat loaf, add the crackers both first and last to prevent the meat from sticking to the grinder.

If you grind pork at home, be sure to scrub the grinder afterward with a brush and scalding suds. Then boil it to be on the safe side.

MEAT LOAF

See also *Hamburger, Meat Grinder.*

Meat loaf tastes much better if you make it from a combination of ground beef, pork and veal.

If you want a meat loaf to retain most of its juiciness, use coarsely ground meat, ground only once. If you add vegetables to the meat loaf, chop them coarsely and then mix with the meat. In other words, avoid mincing any ingredients too fine.

Add some grated raw potato to meat loaf mixtures. The meat goes farther, stays moist inside and the potato helps hold it together.

A little cream, evaporated milk or vegetable juice mixed into a meat loaf will make it more tender and juicy.

Sprinkle the top of a meat loaf with water and rub it well before you put the loaf in the oven. It will be less likely to crack during baking.

Cover a meat loaf with a light tomato sauce before you bake it and you'll get a crisp, shiny crust.

Let a meat loaf rest in its pan out of the oven for 10 minutes before you serve it. It will be firmer and easier to slice.

A little grated raw winter squash or pumpkin is a fine extender for a meat loaf.

Substitute wine (white, red, or rosé) for the liquid called for in your meat loaf recipe.

When you put a meat loaf mixture in its baking pan, be sure to press the meat down firmly (use the flat of your hand) so no air holes are left at the bottom.

If you're using bread crumbs in a meat loaf, you're better off using soft crumbs rather than the fine dry ones used for breading. Your meat loaf will be moist and delicate.

If you want meat loaf to cook faster than usual, fashion it into individual-sized loaves. Or cook it in cupcake tins.

If you want to remove an entire meat loaf in one piece from the loaf pan, butter or oil the pan first and then put a wide strip of aluminum foil down the length of the pan, with an inch or so of the foil overhanging at each end. Butter or oil the surface of the foil too, then fill and bake as usual. Let the meat loaf stand for 10 minutes after removal from the oven. Loosen it from the sides of the pan with a knife and invert the pan over a plate. The whole loaf should come out neatly. If you're careful, you can turn the meat loaf again, top side up, onto another plate.

MEATS
See also *Bacon, Beef, Beef Cuts, Braising, Broiling, Garlic, Ham, Hamburger, Hearts, Kidneys, Lamb, Leftovers, Liver, Meat Loaf, Mutton, Pork, Roasts, Steak, Stew, Sweetbreads, Tongue, Veal, Wine.*

Study the meat charts in your cookbooks and learn from which part of the animal a particular cut comes. You should learn to recognize a cut at sight. Your butcher will be glad to help you. In the meantime, see *Beef Cuts.*

The more exercise a muscle gets, the more flavorful it is. Since exercise also tends to make muscle tough, the most flavorful cuts are generally those which require long cooking, such as pot roasts, braises and stews. But proper aging tenderizes meat, thus the loin in beef, for example, produces very flavorful and tender meat.

Unless you freeze them, you should use certain meats—sweetbreads, tripe, brains, liver and kidneys—very shortly after or, if possible, the same day you buy them.

You can store steaks and large cuts of meat in the refrigerator for 2 or 3 days. Their flavor and tenderness will improve if you first squeeze some lemon juice over them.

If you must store or refrigerate ground meat for more than a day, flatten it so that the cold can penetrate it quickly. Ground meat deteriorates rapidly.

If you have to slice meat into very thin strips, as for sukiyaki, partially freeze the meat first and you'll find it much easier to cut.

When you slice raw meat for any dish, cut it against the grain and the meat will be tender. This is especially important if you're slicing meat in thin strips.

Remove meats from the refrigerator about 1 hour before you cook them.

You don't need a special mallet if you want to flatten pieces of meat. Place the meat between sheets of waxed paper and hammer it with the underside of a small heavy frying pan.

Most dishes calling for ground or chopped meat, such as meatballs, meat loaves or patties, taste better if you use a combination of beef, pork and veal. If you include pork, don't serve it rare.

½ pound of ground meat equals about 1 cup.

If you have to store meat in the refrigerator a bit longer than you usually would, dust all the surfaces of the meat well with ground white or black pepper. Wipe the pepper off with a damp cloth when you're ready to prepare the meat.

Before you put any kind of meat in a grinder, cut it into pieces and freeze the pieces for about 30 minutes. This cuts down on stringiness when you grind the meat.

Some commercial meat tenderizers contain salt or monosodium glutamate. Since sodium draws the juices out of meat, it's not a good idea to use these products. Read the labels before you buy.

The tannin in tea is a remarkably good meat tenderizer. If you've bought a tough cut of meat that you're going to use for stew, cook it in a little strong tea for 10 or 15 minutes, turning it now and then before you put it in the stewpot. Flavor the tea with a little salt, pepper, garlic, or any seasoning you like and pour it into the stewpot. It will contribute very nicely to the gravy.

Squeeze or rub the juice of a papaya over a tough cut of meat. The enzymes are an excellent meat tenderizer.

There are other ways to tenderize a tough (and therefore usually inexpensive) cut of meat: Marinate it; braise it (cook in a little liquid, slowly, for a long time); pound it with a heavy instrument, a pot cover, or a special mallet; serve it sliced across the grain of the fiber.

A large roast of any kind should always be removed from the refrigerator at least 2 hours (3 is better) before being cooked.

Cooking

You should always brown meats for stews or ragoûts before you put them in any liquid. Pat the pieces very dry with a towel, heat fat to bubbling in a heavy pot, then place the pieces of meat in the fat so that the pieces don't touch one another. Only after this, when the meat has browned well on all sides, add vegetables and liquids.

Here's a method for quick browning: add 1 level teaspoon of sugar to hot fat in a heavy pot, stir until it becomes dark, then sear pieces of well-dried meat in this, turning frequently. You'll get a beautiful mahogany color, with very little discernible sweetness.

A piece of tough meat can become very tender if you boil it for 10 minutes, then simmer for 1 hour or more, depending on its size. Flavor it plentifully during cooking.

When your recipe calls for adding water to meat, substitute consommé, broth, stock, vegetable juices, wine, beer or diluted gravy. *But* use as little liquid as possible when you cook meats. Little liquid and very low heat will always give you tasty meat which is internally juicy. If you use this method, allow plenty of time—usually several hours. Check now and then for liquid and only add if you must. Keep testing for doneness. (This is true for both top of stove and oven cooking.)

A meat stew cooks even better in the oven—at about 350°—than on top of the stove. Be sure you cover the pot with a good heavy lid and check it now and then for liquid.

Meats which you intend to broil or roast won't lose as much moisture if you rub or brush the outsides with flavored or un-flavored oil before and several times during cooking. Oil forms a seal which prevents meats from losing their juices.

Make up a combination of herbs, spices and other dry flavorings. Store in a small jar and use them to add to meat loaves and stews and to rub into meats and chicken. Keep the jar at the side of your stove.

Meats will shrink less during browning if you start the browning slowly.

Roast all meats in a slow oven to prevent them from shrinking and losing their juices.

Once a cut of beef is halfway roasted (after the outside has become well-sealed by the heat and oils), baste it with a red wine. Burgundy is especially good for this.

When grilling or broiling meat, the longer you cook it the tougher it gets.

When you prepare a leg of lamb for roasting, make tiny gashes here and there in the fat. Press a small piece of garlic into each gash. The roast will taste heavenly.

Leftover bits of pickled, corned, or smoked meats can be used as you would use crumbled bacon. Chop coarsely, and sauté in any fat or oil until crisp. These are lovely in omelets, salads, or spreads of any kind.

MEAT THERMOMETER

Before you insert a glass-stemmed meat thermometer into a piece of meat, make a hole for it with a skewer or you may break the point.

Insert the thermometer through the fat side of the meat, being careful not to touch bone. Bone conducts heat faster and you'll get a false reading of the meat's temperature.

MELONS

A honeydew melon, if bought too green, will never ripen properly. Avoid any that are green, hard, and smooth.

A ripe and ready-to-eat honeydew melon has a light-yellow, velvety-feeling skin with a slight softening at the blossom end.

A ripe casaba melon is yellow in color (not greenish) and the blossom end should be a little soft when pressed.

Unripe muskmelons (cantaloupes) will never get very sweet.

Here are the best ways to tell when a muskmelon is ripe: The surface netting should be coarse-looking and grayish and the scar at the stem end should be sunken in a bit. Also, there should be a slight softness at the blossom end, and a sweet fragrance.

A ripe muskmelon will keep its sweetness if it's chilled as soon as possible after being picked.

An ice-cream scoop is great for removing the seeds neatly and cleanly from the cut halves of melons.

Don't buy a watermelon if one side is pale green or whitish—a sign that it was picked too green. It will never develop into a tasty melon.

Want to eat a slice of watermelon without washing your face? Make cuts an inch or so apart down the slice as far as the white part of the rind. Spread the ends of the slice apart and each "finger" of the melon will stand up for easy eating.

Shake a watermelon to test for ripeness—you should hear a slight rattling inside. If you knock it with your knuckles, it should give off a faint echo. If it sounds hard and dull, it's not ripe. Look at the stem end. The stem should be dark green and the immediate surrounding area dark green, almost black. (A light green stem area suggests an unripe melon.)

It's hard to test a Spanish melon for ripeness because its rind is so hard that it resists pressure. Look for a yellow, not too white, underside.

Melons taste best when they're *thoroughly* chilled. Since it takes a long time for cold to penetrate to the center, put a melon in the refrigerator at least 2 days before you serve it.

Once a melon is cut, it absorbs odor from other foods easily. Wrap or cover it tightly before storing in the refrigerator.

MERINGUES
See also *Egg Whites.*

There's no substitute for an electric mixer when it comes to whipping meringues. Whipping by hand makes you feel that your arm will drop off.

Egg whites for meringues should always be at room temperature.

Add a pinch of baking soda to egg whites before you whip them. They'll whip higher and firmer.

Any fat (including the slightest drop of egg yolk) will prevent egg whites from whipping into the stiffness required for a meringue.

Never add sugar to egg whites until you've beaten the whites into firm peaks. You'll end up with a marshmallow-like sauce which will never become firm.

For a thicker, denser meringue, use ⅔ cup of sugar to 3 egg whites.

Don't beat solids such as nutmeats into a meringue—they tend to liquefy it. Instead fold or cut them in lightly.

When you add chopped nuts to meringue batter, don't chop them too fine. If you do, you release too much of the oil, and this interferes with the proper consistency of the meringue. (It won't bake to a dry flakiness.)

Always bake meringues on cookie sheets greased with a solid vegetable shortening or fat—whether or not your recipe suggests this. Let them cool before you remove them and they'll come off easily. Remove meringue cookies from a cookie sheet with a moistened metal pancake turner.

You can also bake meringue cookies on bakers' paper sold in houseware or cooking supply stores. (Peel the paper off when the cookies have cooled slightly but are still a little warm.)

When you bake meringue shells, always grease the pan well

with a solid vegetable shortening. Have your oven very low—as low as 200°—and bake the shells for 1 hour or more (depending on their thickness) until they are a pale tan in color.

To test a baked meringue shell for doneness, flick it with your finger. If done it will give forth a dry hollow sound.

Instead of smoothing meringue over a pie, tart or cake, spread it roughly, making mounds and peaks. This looks more interesting and also browns attractively.

When you've finished spreading meringue over a pie, be sure you've spread it to the edges. Don't leave any space between the meringue and the sides of the pie or else the meringue may become watery at the edges.

If there are "tears" on the meringue topping you've browned in the oven, the sugar probably did not dissolve completely. To avoid this use smaller amounts of sugar at a time, and whip well between additions.

If you cut a meringue-topped pie with a greased or buttered knife the meringue won't tear as you slice through it.

Meringue-topped pies should always be cooled at room temperature—not in the refrigerator. And keep them away from drafts, otherwise you're likely to get "tears" in the meringue. Once cooled, refrigerate.

Dip a knife blade in water and use it to smooth or shape meringues before you bake them.

To give a delectable, thin, crispy surface to a meringue topping for a pie, lightly shake some sifted confectioners' sugar over the top of the meringue before you set it in the oven to brown.

If you've made a meringue that won't thicken because you either added the sugar too soon or because a bit of egg yolk might have escaped into the whites when you were separating the eggs, you've at least got a marshmallow sauce. Add a little almond extract and use what you have as a sauce for cake, or pudding, or ice cream. (You might like it enough to purposely add sugar to the egg whites too soon so you can get that velvety smooth sauce again.)

241

^^

METRICS

See also *Temperatures*.

If you're working with traditional recipes which use ingredients measured by ounces, cups, or tablespoons, you can easily convert them to their metric equivalents. There's no need to toss out your favorite tried-and-true recipes because you can no longer buy a traditional measuring cup or a set of measuring spoons based on the 4-ounce system of volume measurement.

Here are approximate metric equivalents for most kitchen measures, which are exact enough to use with complete success in any recipe.

1 quart	.946 liter (approximately 1 liter)
1 pint	½ liter
1 cup	¼ liter
1 ounce	28 grams
1 pound	450 grams
2.2 pounds	1 kilogram

Here are metric weight equivalents for the most commonly used foods, given in amounts commonly used in recipes.

1 cup apples, chopped or sliced	150 grams
1 cup beans, green or yellow string	165 grams
1 cup (8 ounces) beef, ground, uncooked	240 grams
½ cup butter or margarine (1 stick)	115 grams
1 cup carrots, raw, chopped	120 grams
1 cup cheese, grated	130 grams
1 cup chicken, cooked, cubed	250 grams
1 oz. (1 square) chocolate, baking	30 grams
½ cup chocolate bits	95 grams
½ cup cocoa	35 grams
1 cup cream, heavy	230 grams
1 cup flour	120 grams
½ cup ketchup	135 grams
¼ cup lemon juice	60 grams
1 cup macaroni, raw	125 grams
½ cup mayonnaise	110 grams

1 cup meats, cooked, cubed or chopped	150 grams
1 cup milk, fresh	240 grams
1 cup milk, evaporated	255 grams
½ cup milk, powdered	60 grams
1 cup mushrooms, fresh, chopped	100 grams
½ cup nutmeats, chopped	65 grams
½ cup oil	105 grams
1 cup onions, chopped	150 grams
1 cup peas, fresh	180 grams
1 cup potatoes, raw, chopped or grated	200 grams
1 cup rice, raw	200 grams
1 cup sugar, brown, well packed	210 grams
1 cup sugar, granulated white	245 grams
1 cup sugar, confectioners'	130 grams
1 cup tomato sauce	230 grams
1 cup tomatoes, canned, drained	280 grams
1 cup tomatoes, chopped	220 grams
½ cup tuna, canned, drained	120 grams
½ cup vinegar	115 grams
1 cup water	220 grams
½ cup wine	110 grams
1 cup yogurt	230 grams

MILK

If you're not in the habit of using much milk, you still don't have to worry about part of it going sour. Divide each quart of milk into thirds. Keep ⅓ in the refrigerator, and pour the rest into small containers (⅔ full) and freeze. Each container will defrost in about 4 hours at room temperature and can be used like fresh milk.

If milk does begin to go a bit sour, no need to throw it out. Don't drink it, but it's safe to use in cooking. Use it right away in cake batter or cookie dough (add ½ teaspoon of baking soda to your flour), or in pancake batter. Or use it in recipes calling for buttermilk in a cooked dish.

"Scalded" milk is milk that has been heated until bubbles form a ring around the top. Heat no more than this, or you'll have boiled milk.

If you don't want skin to form while you're heating milk, first rinse the pan with water, then cover it while heating. You can also beat the milk while it's heating.

When you add milk to flour mixtures, mixed vegetables or anything containing starch, warm the milk first and it will have less tendency to form lumps.

When you make a cream of tomato soup which contains milk or cream you can prevent curdling if you add the tomato to the milk, rather than vice versa, or first add a little flour to the milk, beating it in well.

Before you scald milk, rinse the pan with water. This will prevent the milk from scorching and sticking to the sides of the pan.

You can scald milk over boiling water in the top of a double boiler without having to worry about scorching. The milk is scalded when a skin forms on top.

As a substitute for cream in coffee, milk will have a richer taste if you scald and then strain it hot into the coffee.

You can freeze whole containers of milk. They usually take 2 days in the refrigerator or about 6 hours at room temperature to defrost completely.

Powdered, Skimmed and Evaporated Milk

Most powdered milks are of the instant variety and give little trouble when you mix them with water, unless the water is ice cold. One of the quickest and least messy ways to mix powdered milk is to pour a quart of water in a large screw-top jar, add the powder, screw the cap on and shake well. Put it in the refrigerator until cold and you have a quart of good drinkable milk, which you can also use in cooking.

When you're measuring skimmed milk powder, don't pack it down in the measuring cup; spoon it in lightly.

Dry (powdered) milk, if very well wrapped, will stay fresh for a couple of years.

To whip powdered milk for a pretty fair whipped topping, add equal parts of powdered skimmed milk and ice water and whip with an electric mixer at highest speed, as though you were beating egg whites. After 3 or 4 minutes, the mixture should stand up in peaks. Add a little vanilla and beat again. Then add sugar to taste, beating well.

Skimmed milk (or skimmed milk powder mixed with water according to the directions on the box) contains all of the nutrients of whole milk except fat and vitamin D. It can be healthfully and economically drunk by everyone, including people on low cholesterol diets.

If you don't like 100 percent skimmed milk for drinking, mix a quart of milk made from skimmed milk powder with a quart of whole milk. You get 2 quarts of good-tasting milk at very little more than the price of one. Of course you can dilute whole milk with skimmed in any ratio you like, and you'll still be able to save calories and money.

Canned skimmed milk, undiluted, is a good low-calorie substitute for cream in cooking and sauces.

When heating skimmed milk, first rinse the pan to prevent scorching. And don't use too thin a pan. Without fat to form a coating, milk solids burn easily.

To whip evaporated milk, pour it into a freezing tray and freeze for about ½ hour until particles of ice begin to form around the edges. Remove the milk from the freezer, pour it into a chilled bowl and whip it briskly with a chilled electric beater until it thickens. Then sweeten to taste.

Another way to whip evaporated milk is to heat it just to the scalding point, then add gelatin which has been softened in cold water (1 cup of evaporated milk calls for ½ teaspoon of unflavored gelatin softened in 2 teaspoons of cold water) and stir until the gelatin is dissolved in the hot milk. Pour everything into a bowl and chill. Beat with a cold beater until stiff and then sweeten.

Sour Milk and Buttermilk

To make good sour milk for cooking and baking using evaporated milk, mix ½ cup of evaporated milk with ½ cup of lukewarm water, add 1 tablespoon of soft white vinegar and let the mixture stand for ½ hour at room temperature.

You can also make good sour milk from regular milk by adding 2 teaspoons of lemon juice or soft white vinegar to 1 cup of milk or cream at room temperature. Then mix and let the mixture stand for ½ hour.

If you need sour milk or buttermilk for a recipe and you don't have any, use equal parts of yogurt and regular or canned evaporated milk to make up the amount of sour milk or buttermilk called for.

You can substitute buttermilk for sour milk in any recipe.

You can often substitute sour milk or buttermilk for sweet milk in cake or cookie batters if you add ½ to 1 teaspoon of baking soda to the dry ingredients. The resulting cakes and cookies are exceptionally tender.

You can extend 1 quart of cultured buttermilk into 4 quarts. To make each quart, add 1 cup of buttermilk to 3 cups of lukewarm skimmed milk. Add ¼ teaspoon of salt and mix well. Let the milk stand at room temperature for 1 day, lightly covered, then refrigerate.

MINT: see HERBS AND SPICES

MOLASSES
See also *Cake, Gingerbread.*

If a pie filling contains molasses, use a deep-dish pan or even a cake pan to bake the pie in. Molasses usually bubbles high during baking and might run over. To be safer still, set the pan on a cookie sheet.

Heat 3 parts molasses to 1 part butter for a very tasty spread for pancakes and waffles. This saves on butter as well as syrup.

1⅓ cups of molasses weigh 1 pound.

Oil the inside of a measuring cup or measuring spoon before you fill it with molasses and it will pour out neatly, leaving no residue.

In a batter containing molasses, use 1 teaspoon of baking soda to each cup of molasses. Add the baking soda to the dry ingredients.

In sweetening power, 1 cup of molasses is equal to ¾ cup of granulated sugar. If you use molasses in place of sugar in a recipe calling for sugar, decrease the amount of other liquid by 2½ fluid ounces for every cup of molasses. (And don't forget the baking soda.)

Add a little melted chocolate to the batter of a molasses cake or cookies to give a nice color and flavor.

MOLDED DISHES: see ASPICS AND GELATIN DISHES

MOUSSE

See also *Aspics and Gelatin Dishes, Fish.*

If you're making a chicken, meat or fish mousse to be served cold, you can use the same recipe as you would for any hot mousse, as long as you add 1 tablespoon of gelatin (which has been dissolved first in a little cold water). Chill the mousse thoroughly before serving. (A cold chicken, meat or fish mousse is nicest when it's covered with a clear aspic.)

Before you remove a poached hot fish mousse from its mold, let it stand 5 to 8 minutes so that it shrinks a little and becomes easier to remove.

Turn a cold mousse out on a cold serving plate 1 or 2 hours before serving time, then put it in the freezer for 15 minutes to reset any softening. Refrigerate until it's time to bring to the table. It will be ready whenever you want it, and you won't have to worry about melting.

MUFFINS

See also *Biscuits.*

Never beat muffin batter. Stir the ingredients only until you see no more dry flour—the dough is supposed to be lumpy. If

247

you continue mixing, you'll have tough dry muffins which won't rise properly.

Put ¼ to ½ cup of some whole grain cereal in the blender and grind to a fine flour to use in place of an equal amount of the white flour when you make muffins.

You can make wonderful muffins using yogurt. Substitute the same amount of yogurt for the liquid called for in the recipe. Add about ¼ teaspoon of baking soda to the dry ingredients, mix, and bake as usual. You'll have deliciously fragrant muffins.

When you make yogurt muffins, use any commercial yogurt-fruit mixture. Stir the contents well so the fruit is evenly distributed. You'll end up with tender, fruit-flavored muffins.

Make muffins with a surprise inside. Pour only half the batter into the muffin tins. Place in each a piece of apple, or a pitted cooked prune, or a piece of canned pineapple, or any fruit you have on hand. Pour the rest of the batter on top and bake.

With only one batch of muffin batter, you can end up with several kinds of muffins. Add chopped walnuts or pecans to 1 cup of the batter; add bits of fruit, like chopped dates, to another; put some cinnamon in another part of the batch, etc.

Sweet muffins for dessert are a tasty, healthful, and quick substitute for cake. You can cut the muffins in half, frost them, and make miniature layer cakes.

Whip up a batch of unsweetened muffins to serve instead of bread not only for breakfast, but for dinner, too.

It's not necessary to grease the entire inner surface of muffin tins, only the bottoms.

Fill muffin cups about ⅔ full.

Muffins, which bake best in a somewhat humid atmosphere, do better in electric ovens than in gas ones (see *Ovens*). If you're baking muffins in a gas oven, leave one of the muffin cups empty and instead of filling it with batter, pour hot water into it. Then bake. The muffins won't scorch during baking.

Bake muffins in a preheated oven. They need a sudden blast of hot air to rise to their maximum.

For a crunchy, sugary crust on muffins, sprinkle a little white or brown sugar over them before baking.

If you have trouble getting muffins out of the pan because the bottoms stick, place the pan while it's still hot on a wet towel for about 30 seconds. Then it will be easier to remove the muffins.

If you break apart muffins just baked and they show elongated holes running up to the top, you've probably overmixed the batter. Remember next time to mix the ingredients *only* until everything is moistened—no longer.

Hollow out leftover muffins, heat, and fill with a creamed mixture of any kind. A great luncheon dish.

To reheat muffins that have hardened, set a pan of boiling water in the heated oven before you put in the muffins. They'll become nicely softened.

You can bake muffins (as well as small cakes) in small buttered or oiled flat cans such as tuna fish cans. And if you remove both the tops and bottoms of the cans, you can use the rings to bake English muffins in. (English muffins are actually cooked on a greased griddle on top of the stove. See recipes for English muffins or crumpets.)

If you're going to freeze English muffins, cut or tear them apart, stack the halves one on top of the other, the cut sides up, in a long plastic bag. In this way, the halves won't stick to one another.

MUSHROOMS

A 4-ounce can of sliced mushrooms, drained, will give you about ¾ cup.

Read the labels before you buy fresh packaged mushrooms. Some brands have been sprayed with sodium bisulfide to keep them white. Sodium bisulfide may not be harmful, but when the sprayed mushrooms start to age they become slimy-looking, unlike mushrooms in their natural state.

Older and somewhat darker mushrooms are more flavorful than white, freshly picked ones. Mushrooms lose moisture as they stand, and their flavor intensifies.

Don't wash fresh mushrooms before you store them in the refrigerator. Like berries, they should be handled as little as possible until you're ready to use them. If your refrigerator is properly cold and the mushrooms are dry, they should keep well for more than a week. When it comes to storing mushrooms, moisture is their enemy.

Braised, stewed, or sautéed mushrooms are delicious beyond belief when you mix a little thick whipped cream into their juices and then combine with the mushrooms.

½ pound of fresh mushrooms will give about 2½ cups, sliced; 2 cups, coarsely chopped.

If you plan to serve mushrooms as a vegetable, count on 1 pound of mushrooms for every 3 people.

When you wash mushrooms, quickly pat them dry with a towel. Don't leave them in water long—they are very absorbent and a waterlogged mushroom is a sad thing to work with.

If you come across a bargain in fresh mushrooms—vegetable stores sometimes offer specials when a bumper crop of mushrooms comes in—buy 2 or 3 pounds. You can either freeze or dry them.

Mushrooms freeze very well. Wash them quickly and dry. Put them, sliced or unsliced, in a plastic bag and freeze. Use them without defrosting. They'll taste exactly like fresh mushrooms in any cooked dish.

To dry mushrooms, wash them swiftly, then cut in half lengthwise and string them with a needle and thread. Hang them up clothesline fashion, leaving space between the halves for the air to circulate. They'll dry in about 2 days, depending on the humidity. When they're thoroughly dry, put them in containers and keep them on a shelf. They need not be refrigerated.

You can rehydrate dried mushrooms by soaking them for about 1 hour in water or stock.

Don't peel firm white mushrooms. Just wash and dry them. Dark mushrooms, or those not in the pink of condition, should be peeled to make them look more appetizing. (Save the peelings for soups, stocks and gravies.)

White mushrooms will keep their color if you sprinkle them with lemon juice or steam them in milk or butter in the top of a double boiler for 15 minutes before using.

You can use very firm white raw, sliced mushrooms in salads.

If a recipe calls for mushroom caps, save the stems, just as you save peelings. Freeze or dry them and add them to the stock pot. (They give a marvelous flavor to any meat, chicken, fish, or egg dish, especially omelets.)

You can slice mushroom caps in an egg slicer.

Cooking

If you want to sauté finely chopped fresh mushrooms, they must be very dry before you add them to the sizzling butter. Bunch all the pieces together in the center of a dishtowel or a man's large handkerchief, then twist until you've squeezed out as much juice as you can.

If you want to sauté canned mushrooms, drain them (saving the liquid for the stock pot) and dry them well with a dishtowel before you add them to the hot pan to brown.

If you do not dry mushrooms thoroughly before cooking, or if you sauté too many at one time, they'll release so much moisture that they'll steam instead of brown.

Keeping the fat very hot and shaking the pan from time to time prevents steam from building up when you sauté mushrooms.

You can buy many kinds of dried mushrooms. Polish dried mushrooms have a full rich flavor and are especially good in barley and meat soups. Chinese mushrooms are very meaty and are delicious in stews and mixed vegetables. Japanese mushrooms are slightly crispy, even when cooked. To cook, simmer Polish mushrooms for 15 minutes, Chinese and Japanese mushrooms for about ½ hour. (Save all mushroom water for soups and gravies or for cooking vegetables.)

For a marvelous low-calorie vegetable, bake large whole mushroom caps on a cookie sheet for ½ hour at 300°, open side up, with nothing but a little salt sprinkled over them. A pool of liquor will form naturally inside each cap, keeping them moist.

Drain 1 or 2 cans of button mushrooms, then marinate for

3 or more days in a mixture of well-seasoned oil and vinegar. You can have superb marinated mushrooms at half the cost of those you'd buy.

MUSKMELON: see MELONS

MUSSELS
Like clams and oysters, mussels should be used only if they're tightly closed. Discard opened ones which won't close on handling or which float when placed in water.

Scrub mussels under cold water with a stiff brush or a plastic-mesh scrubber. (Wear rubber household gloves, since some of the shells may be sharp.) If the shells are very slimy, scrub them with a little dry mustard first. Pull out the "beard."

Before you cook mussels, examine each one carefully. If one seems unusually heavy or makes a slushy sound when shaken close to your ear, it is probably filled with mud or small stones. One such mussel in a potful will ruin the whole batch.

Like all shellfish, mussels toughen quickly when you cook them. Cook them covered in boiling seasoned water, wine or broth over a high flame, shaking every couple of minutes. They should open in 5 or 6 minutes. Remove them the moment the shells open. Strain the liquid very well to remove the sand.

MUSTARD
See *Herbs and Spices.*

Dijon-type mustards are stronger than the general run of mustards most frequently found on grocery store shelves.

MUTTON
See also *Lamb.*

Real mutton is hard to find and generally expensive in most American markets because of low demand, and the high demand for lamb. Mutton is tougher and has a gamier flavor than lamb, but prepared right it can be delicious. It usually benefits from soaking and tenderizing in a marinade and should be cooked longer and at lower heat than lamb.

Much of the strong flavor of mutton comes from the outside fat. Either remove part of this or rub the meat and fat well with lemon juice before cooking. If you're boiling mutton, add lemon quarters to the cooking water.

NASTURTIUM
Did you know that nasturtiums, members of the cress family, are edible and that the leaves and flowers are wonderful in salad?

NOODLES: see PASTA

NUTMEG: see HERBS AND SPICES

NUTS
See also *Oats, Peanut Butter.*

Buy nuts in the shell if you can, for breads, cakes, or just plain eating. They taste much better than shelled nuts and cost a great deal less. Nuts in the shell are in their natural state. Shelled nuts often have been chemically treated before packaging.

Nuts in the shell, if kept cool and dry, will last a year. If shelled, they should be kept cold and will stay reasonably fresh for 6 months. They will stay freshest if kept in the freezer.

Put ¼ cup or so of any kind of nuts in the blender, grind to a rather coarse powder, and add to cookie batter. Use a little less flour than the recipe calls for. Whoever eats these cookies is in for a delight.

If you have some shelled nuts—not enough to use in a cake—grind or chop them and add to ground meat for hamburgers or meat loaf. Nuts are a delicious meat extender and more nutritious than bread crumbs.

If you have a cake or cookie recipe that calls for nuts and you don't have any on hand, try using any crisp, small-grained dry cereal.

If you're going to add whole or large pieces of nuts to cake or pudding batter, heat the nuts in the oven a little first, and they won't be as likely to sink.

You can make interesting nut butters of all sorts in the blender—cashew, peanut, pecan, walnut, etc. You may have to add a little oil after you've ground the nuts as fine as possible because home blenders are not as powerful as commercial grinders, but the result is great. You might also want to add a little honey and perhaps a bit of salt, but it's not absolutely necessary.

The oil in shelled nuts won't become rancid as fast if you store the nuts in airtight containers in a cool dark place.

Keep opened cans or jars of nuts in the refrigerator and they'll stay fresh longer.

Here's a quick way to crack and shell hazelnuts, pecans or walnuts: put 20 or so in a plastic bag and twist it closed. Put the bag on a hard surface and hit the nuts gently with a hammer until they're well cracked. Then shake the bag vigorously. Most of the nutmeats will come free of their shells. The plastic bag helps cut down on mess.

You can use a blender to grind nuts, but it tends to release more of the oil. For drier ground nuts use a food or nut grinder.

Most nuts can be blanched and skinned by soaking them in boiling water until the skins wrinkle. The skins should then slip off easily. If they don't, a quick rinse in cold water usually helps.

Nuts are more easily sliced and shredded when they're warm.

If you're adding nuts to a sweet filling, as for a cake, blend them into the filling quickly and gently. If you mix them with too much vigor there's the danger that they'll liquefy the filling.

Spread finely ground nuts across the bottom crust of any pie which is to have a moist filling. They will keep the crust from becoming gummy.

Almonds

1 pound of almonds with their shells on will give 1 cup shelled, 1¼ cups chopped, and 1½ cups of ground almonds.

4 ounces of shelled almonds will give about ¾ cup of whole, chopped, slivered or ground almonds.

The way to skin and blanch almonds is to shell them, then put them in a saucepan and cover with boiling water. Let them simmer for 1 minute. If you drain them and then press between your fingers at one end, they'll pop out of their skins.

After you've skinned blanched almonds, dry them for 5 minutes in a 350° oven.

To toast skinned almonds, spread them in a pan and bake at 350° for 10 minutes, or until the almonds are tanned. Stir now and then so they'll toast evenly without burning.

When you use almonds in cooking, add ¼ teaspoon of almond extract as well. You'll get a richer almond flavoring.

Turkey and chicken have an affinity for almonds. Add toasted almonds to the stuffings and sauces which accompany them and to creamed or curried chicken or turkey.

Garnish a creamed soup or a chicken soup with chopped blanched toasted almonds.

Almonds used in cakes or other desserts will have much more flavor if you brown them first. Use the oven or a pan on top of the stove—stir and watch the almonds carefully.

You can substitute very finely ground almonds for almond extract in cakes, cookies, icings, etc. Two tablespoons of finely ground almond powder will give you the almond flavoring of approximately ¼ teaspoon of the extract.

Almonds are more easily slivered or sliced while they're hot. Split almonds immediately after you've skinned them, while they're still hot and wet. Hold the almond against the cutting board, the flat sides between your thumb and forefinger, and cut them in half lengthwise with a sharp knife. If you want slivered almonds, cut each half lengthwise into 3 or 4 thin strips.

Don't blanch almonds you intend to serve salted because they taste better with their skins on. To prepare salted almonds, use a tablespoon of butter or oil to every cup of almonds. Melt the butter (or heat the oil) over moderate heat in a large skillet, and add the almonds when the butter or oil begins to bubble. Mix with a wooden spoon as they heat. When they begin to smell toasty, remove with a slotted spoon and sprinkle with salt and maybe a little curry powder.

Brazil Nuts

There are about 40 unshelled Brazil nuts to the pound, which gives approximately 2 cups of coarsely chopped nutmeats.

To remove Brazil nuts from their shells, put them on a tray in a 400° oven for about 20 minutes. Then remove them from the oven, let them cool and crack them lengthwise.

Brazil nuts shell very easily if you put them in the freezer for 6 hours before you open them.

Chestnuts

1 pound of shelled cooked chestnuts will give you 1 cup of purée.

Roasted chestnuts have a nuttier flavor and are drier and creamier than boiled ones, but boiled chestnuts are easier to prepare.

If you're going to boil chestnuts, the best way to shell them is to make a single slash with a short knife down both the flat and the rounded sides of the nut. Then put the chestnuts in a pot of cold water, bring to a boil, cover it and boil for 5 minutes. Take the pot off the flame and, as soon as you can handle them, peel the chestnuts. The inner skins will usually come off with the outer. Those that don't come off can be returned to the boiling water for another 1 or 2 minutes. Once you've shelled them, continue cooking in any way.

You can make mashed boiled chestnuts extra-light if, after you've removed the shells, you simmer them in milk for about 5 minutes before mashing.

You can also buy dried shelled chestnuts in Chinese or Italian food shops. Cover them with boiling water (or stock, if using them in stuffing or as a vegetable) and simmer until they soften. If you are using them in a dessert, you can simmer and let them cool in milk.

To roast chestnuts, prepare them as you would for boiling— cutting a slit down the round and flat sides of each one. (Chestnuts roasted in the oven must have at least one slit or else they are likely to explode in the heat.) Then lay them flat in a pan and sprinkle ¼ cup water over them. Put them in a pre-heated 450°

oven for 20 minutes. Peel as soon as they're cool enough to handle. The inner skin usually comes off with the shell.

To "pan roast" chestnuts, prepare them as directed above, then put them in a hot skillet containing 3 to 4 teaspoons of oil. Cover and shake the pan frequently over medium-high heat for about 10 minutes. Drain off the oil and let the nuts cool slightly. You can easily remove any inner skin which may adhere to the nut by scraping slightly with a knife.

Whether you boil or roast chestnuts, the time to peel them is while they're hot.

Hazelnuts

Cultivated hazelnuts are often called filberts. To improve their flavor, toast them lightly in a 400° oven before using.

Pecans

1 pound of pecans with the shells on will give about 1¼ cups chopped.

1 pound of pecan meats will give you about 4½ cups.

You can remove the shells from pecans if you boil them for 15 minutes, then drain and let them stand until they're cold. Crack them end to end with a nutcracker.

For a marvelous ice-cream or pudding topping, combine chopped pecans with honey.

Walnuts

1 pound of walnut meats will give you about 4½ cups.

Walnuts in the shell will last well for about 6 months.

Shelled walnuts will keep well at room temperature for about a month or in the refrigerator for about 3 months. After this they will begin to develop a slightly bitter flavor. If they're airtight, you can keep them in the freezer indefinitely.

Walnuts make a very nice garnish for many dishes. First soak them several hours in salted water, then pat them dry.

For a marvelous ice-cream or pudding topping combine chopped walnuts with honey.

OATS

Don't buy oats for long storage. They have a relatively high fat content and in time the fat becomes bitter. Use them within 3 months.

To substitute oats for nuts in cookies, mix the uncooked oats with a little butter and brown lightly in the oven. They're crispy and tasty.

If you start "quick oats" in cold water, you'll never have lumps.

OIL

See *Fats and Oils*.

2 cups of oil weigh about 15 ounces.

The finest olive oil is very pale yellow. It comes from the first pressing of the olives and is more expensive than oil from the second and third pressings. These are progressively darker and greener in color. They also have a heavier flavor. If you use dark olive oil, dilute it with some plain salad oil.

You can have a delicious change of flavor in cooking oils if you try some of the nut oils sold in health food shops. Also try toasted sesame oil which you can buy in Oriental food stores. It's nut-brown and wonderfully flavored. Add 1 teaspoon or less to any oil you use for sautéing.

Some oils may cloud if you refrigerate them, but they'll clear after they're brought back to room temperature.

Add a liberal pinch of any dried herb or combination of herbs to a small bottle of oil and store it for use in salad dressings. You can use garlic (see *Garlic*), cloves—lots of things—for flavoring oils. Experiment. With flavored oils on hand you can mix fine salad dressings in no time. Use them when sautéing, too.

Buy an atomizer (with a glass or plastic rod) and fill it with flavored oil. Keep it near the stove and use it to spray oil on roasting chicken or grilled fish. This is much handier to use than a pastry brush.

If you substitute oil for solid fat in baking, use less than the amount of shortening called for. For example, if the recipe calls for ½ cup of solid shortening, use ⅓ cup of oil.

Never heat oil in a covered pan.

Never heat oil to the smoking point. It's dangerous—it may ignite—and it gives a bitter taste to food. (It will also irritate your eyes.)

Don't use olive oil for deep-fat frying. It will overpower the flavor of the food cooked in it.

When you use oil to fry or sauté, add a tiny bit of butter or other solid fat. This will help to brown and add flavor to the food.

OKRA
1 cup or more of sliced okra cooked with the vegetables in a soup will give you a good tasty thickener. Vary the amount of okra to taste.

You can pickle whole fresh okra just as you do small cucumbers.

OLIVE OIL: see OIL

OLIVES
The most common olives available in stores are green Spanish olives packed in brine. They come with pits, pitted, and pitted and stuffed with either pimientos, almonds or anchovies. Spanish olives are rather tough and totally impermeable to other flavorings. They can't be marinated. You must use them as they are.

Ripe olives can be either black or green. Black ones are very tender and rather delicate in flavor. Green ones (not Spanish olives) are meaty yet still delicate and wonderful marinated, especially when soaked in a vinaigrette dressing for a few days.

Greek and Italian black olives come marinated in flavored oil. Some are also available partially dried and salted. There are many varieties of these wrinkled black olives.

OMELETS
See also *Eggs*.

Eggs for omelets should always be at room temperature.

3 eggs are generally considered a good number for an omelet. (Omelets of this size should be made in a pan whose diameter is 7 inches.)

For a tender creamy omelet mix the eggs only enough to blend the whites and the yolks.

If you add ¼ teaspoon of baking powder or cornstarch to the eggs for an omelet it will be lighter and puffier.

To make an omelet you can use the traditional French tin-lined copper pan, but a small cast-iron skillet is also excellent.

To prepare an omelet pan, fill it ¾ full of vegetable oil and let it stand on a very low flame for 20 minutes. Pour out the oil, wipe the pan well with paper toweling, and you have a pan which will turn out fine omelets if they're properly made. After each use wipe the pan well with paper toweling and coarse salt, if you need some abrasive action, or oil, if you need some liquid, and hang it up until it's time to use again. Don't use soap on the pan because it will remove the oils which have slightly seeped into the pores of the metal. An omelet will never stick in a properly prepared and maintained pan.

An omelet is one of the few dishes which should be cooked at high heat, because it should be cooked *quickly*.

To make a French omelet, pour lightly combined eggs into 1 teaspoon of butter which has reached the bubbling stage and is pale brown in color. Don't have the flame too low. When the eggs begin to congeal at the edges, draw the edges in toward the center with the flat side of the blade of a table knife, allowing the liquid egg to flow behind it. Continue around the pan in this way until the top is moist but not liquid. With a spatula, turn the omelet half toward the center of the pan, shaking the pan lightly in the same direction to help in turning. It should end up just about folded in half. Slide the omelet off onto a warm plate. The center should be moist, the whole very delicate.

Eggs served as a main dish are a bargain when you compare their cost with that of meat. For example, make a main dish of a 2-egg omelet per person. Fill the omelets with pieces of leftover meat, chicken, or vegetables, in fact anything you have on hand. To make a filled omelet, beat the eggs with a little water or milk, add pepper and powdered garlic, then pour into a hot greased pan as you would any omelet. After the eggs have lost most of their runniness, pour the filling, which should be heated separately, on top. With a spatula, roll half the omelet over on top of the filling, heat for 15 seconds, and ease out of the pan onto a warm plate. With potatoes and salad on the side, you've got a filling and healthful meal.

For another delicious omelet, add a well-rounded teaspoon of sour cream for each egg you use. Whip well into the eggs.

For an interesting omelet variation, have ready a sauce of some kind—a white sauce seasoned any way you like, or a gravy with chopped vegetables or bits of meat in it. Make the omelet as usual and after it's done pour the sauce over it, then pop it under the broiler for about 1 minute. As soon as the sauce sizzles and begins to brown, ease the omelet onto a plate and serve right away.

If you prefer an American omelet—light, but cooked on both sides unlike the French rolled omelet—flip it over in the pan after the first side is cooked, then slide it quickly onto a warm plate. (To flip an omelet without using a spatula, see *Crêpes.*)

To see if an omelet is done, touch it with the tip of your finger. If the egg doesn't cling to your finger, the omelet is ready to be eaten.

Just before you serve an omelet, give it a quick dab with a piece of butter.

If you use water on a prepared omelet pan, oil it before you put it away.

ONIONS

See also *Scallions*.

1 small onion, finely chopped, will give you ¼ cup.

Onions that show a bit of green spear growing out of them should be used at once, otherwise they will spoil.

If you have an onion that's begun to sprout, put it in a pot with a drainage hole, fill the pot with soil—the onion should be only about half-covered—water it well, and set the pot in the light. Keep the surface moderately moist. The onion will grow lots of green sprouts. Snip just as you would chives or scallions. The sprouts will continue to grow for weeks (very nice in the wintertime), and you'll always have some nippy greens at hand for soups, salads, and a multitude of other uses.

½ pound of onions will give about 2 cups sliced or chopped.

The large Spanish (golden) onions are the best kind to buy when a dish calls for lots of onions. There's less work in peeling and slicing a large onion than several small ones. Spanish onions are also sweeter, and are very good as a vegetable.

White onions have a softer flavor than any others and are more delicate. They're best for a dish like creamed onions. They're also more perishable than other types. Keep them dry and refrigerated until you use them.

Red (Italian) onions usually have a lighter flavor and are not as tear-inducing as the yellow-skinned ones when you slice them. They're fine for serving raw in salads or on top of hamburgers, but they turn an unattractive blue-brown in cooking so use them raw.

Store onions where air can circulate around them—hanging in your kitchen in a string bag—they'll keep longer.

Keep 1 or 2 onions in the refrigerator, replacing as you use them. If you slice or chop an onion when it's cold, you'll weep less. Refrigerated onions will keep fairly well if they're protected from dampness.

You can peel an onion easily if you hold it under warm or hot running water. A wet onion is easier to peel than a dry one.

269

Cut a tiny slice from the top and bottom ends of an onion before you peel it, and the skin will come off more easily.

If you have a lot of onions to peel, cover them with very hot water for a few minutes and the skins will slip off easily.

Don't leave brown or yellow onion skins in the sink. They stain some kinds of porcelain. (Household bleach usually removes such stains, but bleach often dulls the outer porcelain finish of a sink.)

If you need only part of an onion, don't peel it before cutting. The unused portion will keep better in the refrigerator if the skin is still on.

An onion won't slip when you're slicing it if you cut it in half from top to bottom, then lay the cut-side down on the cutting board and slice in whatever thickness you want.

You can dice an onion into uniform pieces if you slice it as directed above, then hold all the slices together and turn the half-onion as a unit. Cut it in strips again at right angles to the first set of cuts.

To chop, slice or mince onions in no time at all, use a French chef's knife (see *Knives*).

A partially frozen onion is easy to slice and chop and—best of all—causes no tears.

Onions tend to discolor when cut with a carbon steel (as opposed to stainless steel) knife. This won't matter for onions intended for cooking, but you might prefer to use a stainless knife if you're slicing onion rings for salad, for example.

If you need to cut an onion in whole round slices, hang on to the tail end of the onion as you cut. After each slice, turn the onion slightly on the cutting board before you cut the next slice. This will minimize the tendency to cut on the bias.

If a recipe calls for chopped onion as an ingredient, reduce the amount called for and grate it instead. You get more of an onion flavor and it's easier to distribute.

Anything you cook with onions will need less liquid than when cooked without. Onions contain a great deal of moisture.

If you're adding onions to a stock that will later be strained and the vegetables discarded, don't bother to peel the onions. Just wash them and cut them up. The same is true of garlic. Save yourself work.

You can squeeze half an onion—with the skin on—just as you would half an orange, to get the juice.

To get a small amount of onion juice from a cut onion, sprinkle a little salt on the cut surface, then scrape with a knife or spoon to get the juice.

Many onions need taming. If they're too strong to serve in salads or for a sandwich, cut into rings and soak in cool water for 1 hour or in tepid water that has been sweetened with a little sugar (about 1 teaspoon to a measuring cup of water) for 1 hour. Particularly virulent onions should be covered with boiling water for 1 minute, then drained and soaked in ice water.

You can keep cut onions for several days in the refrigerator if you put them in a screw-top jar (to keep the odor in). Don't store them in plastic containers because the odor will permeate the plastic.

If you chop onions and then freeze them in a plastic bag they'll keep for months. Cook them without defrosting. (This is a good thing to do with half a leftover onion.)

Cooking

If you're cooking whole onions, cut a cross in the root ends and they won't be as likely to burst.

If your onions are very strong and you want to serve them boiled, cover them first with boiling water and boil 2 minutes, then drain. (Some cooks do this a second time.) Cover then again with fresh water and finish cooking. The resulting onions are very sweet and pleasant.

If they're not cooked to mushiness, boiled onions can be made firm for stuffing if you drop them gently into ice water as soon as they're cooked. (But it's important not to overcook them in the first place.)

Put slices of onions in a low oven and heat them until they're a golden brown and absolutely dry. Bottle, refrigerate and use these for future stews, soups and sauces. They'll give a richer taste and a more beautiful color than plain onions.

Most dishes calling for onions are immensely improved if you sauté the onions lightly first in oil or butter. This is especially true if onions are to be added to a stew or casserole.

A little honey added to the butter in which you sauté onions will make a really out-of-the-ordinary dish. (Don't put the onions in until the butter and honey mixture begins to sizzle.)

You can dip damp onion rings in flour, let them dry on a dishtowel and fry them in hot fat. This makes crisp rings.

There is a shortcut to making French-fried onion rings. Dry the rings well on paper towels, then dip them in prepared pancake batter and fry quickly in hot fat.

For a low-calorie sauce (for either vegetables, meat, fish or the base of a salad dressing) boil onions in a little water until they're very soft, drain them well and then either put them in a blender or press them through a sieve. Flavor them in any way you like. This is a splendid thick base you can do a dozen things with.

You can rid your hands of the smell of onions by rubbing them well with salt or vinegar, rinsing with cold water and then washing with soap and warm water.

ORANGES

1 dozen oranges will give you about 4 cups of juice.

Pale oranges, or even those showing some green, are just as good inside as those that are bright orange in color.

Oranges, like grapefruit and lemons, should be open to the air during storage. Don't put them in closed bags or the skins will mildew.

Oranges with very rough surfaces are thick-skinned and generally have less juice and meat inside. But they're preferable if you want orange sections.

Whole oranges can be peeled quickly and their sections separated cleanly without white membrane clinging, if you cover them with boiling water and let them stand for 5 minutes. Then pour off the water, cool the fruit, and peel.

The juicier the orange, the heavier it is. If you buy oranges by the dozen, compare values by weighing different-priced ones by threes. Buy the heaviest ones.

Thin-skinned oranges are usually the juiciest.

Thick-skinned oranges are the easiest to peel, but the following method can be used for any orange (or grapefruit): wash the fruit, cut off a slice of peel from the top and the bottom, then set the orange on a cutting board cut end down. With a sharp knife cut off the peel in strips from top to bottom.

Before you squeeze oranges for juice, wash and dry them, then grate the rind all around. Dry the grated rind in a low oven or on a warm radiator, and store in small jars. This will remain aromatic for months, ready for flavoring cakes, cookies, icings, custards and puddings. (You can also freeze grated rind without drying it.)

Use orange juice instead of (or in addition to) wine when you cook fish.

Julienned orange peel makes a nice garnish for fish. Parboil it slightly.

Instead of throwing away orange skins, cut into strips and freeze them. The strips are very handy for flavoring all kinds of desserts.

Orange juice that comes in cartons is of two kinds: plain, refrigerated orange juice; or reconstituted, which means the juice has been dehydrated, mixed with water, and become juice again. The second kind is often somewhat cheaper.

If you make orange juice from frozen concentrate, you'll get a tastier glass of juice if you squeeze some fresh orange juice into each glass, then fill the remainder of the glass with the reconstituted juice.

OVENS
See also *Baking, Energy Savers, Temperatures.*

Some basic oven temperature equivalents you should know are:

	Fahrenheit	Celsius (metric)
Low oven	250°	121°
Moderate oven	350°	177°
Hot oven	450°	232°
Broil	550°	288°

Temperatures from 250° to 325° constitute a low oven, 325° to 400° a moderate oven, 400° to 450° a hot oven, and 450° to 550° a very hot oven.

Be sure you know whether your oven gauge is accurate. Test it with a good oven thermometer. It may need adjusting by a stove man or handyman. You can't bake or roast with predictability if you can't rely on your heat gauge.

With the possible exception of some breads, put all foods to be baked or roasted in a preheated oven. The quick heat helps to seal in the juices.

If your oven racks stick, clean them thoroughly using a wire brush and then coat the sliding portions lightly with petroleum jelly.

If you use aluminum foil in the oven, don't cover the rack or bottom completely or you'll interfere with the proper distribution of heat.

A gas oven with a pilot light can be a fine dryer for glassware. Put the washed glasses in and leave with just the pilot going. They'll come out crystal clear.

You can also dry washed pots and pans in a gas oven with a pilot light.

An electric self-cleaning oven can make defrosting your freezer a cinch. Stash all the frozen foods in the oven and keep the door closed. A self-cleaning electric oven is usually so well insulated that it will even keep ice cubes frozen for 2 hours. With the frozen foods safely packed away, you can defrost your freezer without worrying about them.

To reduce the heat in your oven quickly for a special purpose, put in a large pan of cold water.

OYSTER PLANT
See also *Vegetables*.

Oyster plant is also called salsify.

Oyster plant darkens quickly when you peel it. Immediately after peeling, drop it into water with a little lemon juice or vinegar (2 tablespoons to 1 quart of water).

Oyster plant takes a long time to cook until tender—1 hour or more. Most recipes for oyster plant assume you've already boiled it to tenderness before you start following the recipe.

OYSTERS
See *Shellfish*.

Depending on their size, there are 40 to 60 shucked oysters in 1 quart.

If you're using oysters in their shells, buy only those which are tightly closed and which do not float when placed in water. Oysters bought already shucked should be in clear (or only slightly cloudy) liquor. This shows that they've been only recently opened.

If you're buying oysters for frying, buy them in their shells—freshly opened oysters hold together better than the ones sold already opened in containers. (You can also have your fish man open the oysters for you while you wait.) Freshly opened oysters also hold a crumb or cornmeal coating better.

It's easy to open an oyster if you take an old-fashioned beer can opener and insert the point under the hinge at the top of the oyster, then push down hard.

Another way to open oysters is to set them in a moderate oven only long enough for the shells to open slightly. Remove and pry the shells open with a knife.

Some cooks like to remove the slippery coating of an oyster before they fry or broil them. You can do this by poaching them quickly (1 minute or less) in their own liquor. A batter coating adheres better to a lightly poached oyster.

When you poach opened oysters in their own liquor or in milk, cook them only until the edges (gills) curl or until the oysters are plump.

Oysters toughen quickly—they should rarely be cooked more than 2 minutes.

Sprinkle a little nutmeg over a bowl of oyster stew before you serve it.

PANADA

A panada is a white-flour thickener which is used to thicken soup. Put 2 tablespoons of melted butter or oil in a pan and add ¼ cup of flour. Mix well until the flour is smooth. Then add 8 table-spoons of cool water and cook, stirring until the mixture leaves the sides of the pan. You can spread this out and let it cool. Use any part of this in place of flour in a sauce or soup. It will never taste floury.

PANCAKES

See also *Blender*.

The rule for light, tender pancakes is the same as for biscuits and muffins: Stir the batter only until the ingredients are evenly mixed, no more.

For perfectly round pancakes, let the batter pour straight down from the tip of a large spoon. The batter will make a circle all by itself.

A pancake is ready to be turned when it's puffed and the top surface is evenly covered with small bubbles. With an average batter, this takes about 2 minutes on the first side and 1 minute on the other. Never turn a pancake more than once—this tough-ens it.

The less liquid you use in pancake batter, the heavier and more dense the pancakes will be.

When you add eggs to pancake batter, separate them and mix the yolks in first. When everything else has been mixed, beat the whites and fold them in at the end. This will give you a lighter and more tender pancake.

For very delicate pancakes, use sour milk or buttermilk instead of sweet milk, adding a pinch of baking soda to the batter.

PANCAKES

For very tender pancakes, prepare the batter the night before, omitting the baking powder. Add this in the morning, then cook.

If you like well-browned pancakes, add 1 teaspoon of molasses to the batter.

You can use regular pancake batter to make dessert pancakes by adding 3 to 4 tablespoons of sugar—preferably fine sugar—to the dry ingredients.

When making dessert pancakes from regular pancake batter, you can substitute orange juice for the milk, and add some grated orange rind to the batter.

Add finely minced banana or almost any minced food to pancake batter. This is a good way to use leftovers.

You have to grease the pancake griddle well for the first batch of pancakes, but usually not for later ones, especially if your batter contains 2 or more tablespoons of shortening.

To tell when an oiled or greased skillet is hot enough to use, let a couple of drops of water fall on the heated pan. If they bounce up on contact with the hot surface, you can begin cooking your pancakes.

The best way to measure pancake batter is to dip a ¼ cup measure in the batter and then pour the contents in the skillet.

If you have any trouble with the griddle sticking between batches, rub the hot griddle with salt tied in a piece of gauze.

If you have to keep pancakes warm for a while before you serve them, put them in a low oven between folds of a dishtowel and they won't become soggy.

You can freeze pancakes once they've cooled by stacking them, separated by squares of waxed paper, and putting them in a plastic bag. To reheat, lay the frozen pancakes flat on a cookie sheet in a 350° oven.

If your pancake recipe calls for melted butter, be sure the milk and eggs are at room temperature before the butter is added, otherwise it will harden.

Substitute other kinds of flour for half of the white flour called for in your recipe. Use buckwheat flour or fine cornmeal or rice flour, etc. You can make a flour by putting cereals in the blender.

You'll have wonderful tasting pancakes, and more healthful ones, too.

You can substitute vegetable oil for butter or margarine in pancakes, but the cooked pancake is likely to be a little less brown.

Use orange juice or some other fruit juice instead of milk. Add ¼ teaspoon of baking soda to the flour.

Dip bread slices in leftover pancake batter, then sauté as you would French toast. Marvelous with cinnamon and sugar, jam, preserves, or syrup.

PAPAYA

Papayas are ripe for eating when the skin is a deep yellow or orange and the flesh is slightly soft to pressure.

Squeeze or rub the juice of a papaya over a tough cut of meat. It contains enzymes that are an excellent meat tenderizer.

PAPRIKA: see HERBS AND SPICES

PARSLEY: see HERBS AND SPICES

PARSNIPS

Parsnips are tender and sweet. They should be used as a vegetable in their own right, as well as in stews and soups. You can treat them as you do carrots, except that they require a shorter cooking time.

PASTA

See also *Sauces and Gravies, Storage Tips.*

1 pound of noodles, cooked, will give you about 9 cups.

1 average portion of spaghetti and spaghettini, when served as a main dish, weighs about 140 grams (5 ounces) uncooked, or the amount that, when tightly bunched together and held upright, will cover the surface of a nickel.

8 ounces of pasta—spaghetti, macaroni or noodles—will serve 3 or 4 people.

Raw pasta should be smooth and shiny. If it's dusty and brittle or crumbly, it's not fresh.

Pasta doubles in volume when it's cooked.

When you boil pasta of any kind, add 1 teaspoon of salt to the water. The cooked pasta should taste very faintly salty.

Add 1 tablespoon of vegetable oil to the water in which you cook pasta. This helps prevent the pasta from sticking together or to the pot and also keeps the pot from boiling over when the water rises during cooking.

When you cook pasta, immerse it gradually into rapidly boiling water so as not to disturb the temperature of the water. The pasta will cook more evenly.

If you have to cook pasta a great deal ahead of time, undercook very slightly, drain and rinse it in cold water. Completely cover it with fresh cold water and let stand in the refrigerator until serving. Then drain it again and cover with boiling salted water. Let it stand until it's thoroughly hot. Drain and serve.

If cooked pasta has to stand a short time before being served, drain it and add some melted butter or oil. Mix gently. This will prevent it from sticking together.

There's a very old joke about how to tell when spaghetti is done: Throw a handful against the wall and if it sticks, it's done. But why ruin the kitchen wall? Wind a strand from the cooking pot onto a fork, then pinch the doubled or tripled strand between your fingers. There should be a slight—but very slight—resistance before you pinch the strand into separate pieces. If it seems hard in the middle, keep the spaghetti cooking a bit longer. But you don't want it mushy, so watch it.

What does *al dente* mean? It means firm to the teeth.

If you're worried about overcooking spaghetti or other pasta (or if you have to cook it ahead of time), boil it to the point where it's still somewhat tough, take the pot from the heat, and let it stand quietly, covered. It will slowly absorb more water and become a little softer—never mushy. When you're ready to eat, heat the pasta quickly only until it's hot, then drain and serve.

Don't rinse pasta after you've boiled it. I don't know how such an idea ever got started.

Cooked, well-drained spaghetti can be pressed over the bottom and sides of a pie pan, and filled with any creamed chicken, fish, meat, or vegetable, or with a cheese filling. Bake it. The pasta bakes into a nice crust.

PASTRY: see PIES

PASTRY BAG

Before you use a canvas pastry bag, wet it thoroughly, then wring out just as thoroughly. Twist dry in a dishtowel, then fill.

Before you put filling into a pastry bag, turn the large open end down to form a wide cuff. Then unroll the cuff as you fill the bag, making it narrower and narrower.

When you spoon filling into a pastry bag, be sure you push it down to the bottom so that you leave no air spaces.

To prevent the filling from oozing out the top, don't fill a pastry bag too full. Leave room at the top end to twist it closed.

To use a pastry bag, always apply pressure from the top, twisting the top end more and more as the bag empties.

For a quick, no-mess, disposable pastry bag, put icing, etc., in a clean plastic bag, the kind you store food in. Twist the bag closed, snip a tiny piece off a bottom corner and squeeze.

PASTRY BRUSH

A 1-inch nylon or bristle paintbrush makes a fine pastry brush.

PASTRY DOUGH

See also *Graham Crackers and Graham Cracker Crust, Pie.*

Use pastry flour or all-purpose flour for pie dough. Don't use cake flour, it's too soft and the grains won't form a proper crust when they're mixed with shortening.

For a light pastry, add 1 pinch of baking powder to the flour when you mix pie dough.

Lard or solid vegetable shortening gives a more tender crust than butter or margarine. If you like a buttery flavor in a pie crust, use a proportion of ⅓ butter to ⅔ other shortening.

If you want an extremely flaky pastry, measure the flour and fat and refrigerate both in the bowl for at least an hour before you begin mixing.

If you want an especially tender crust for a pie, add half the shortening to the flour first and cut it to the consistency of coarse cornmeal. Then add the rest of the shortening and cut quickly to the size of small beans. Add the ice water and mix quickly.

Some cooks feel it's not absolutely necessary for anything but the water to be iced when you put together a pastry dough, but the water *must* be iced.

Too much water toughens pastry crust and makes it more likely to shrink. Too little causes it to break apart. A little practice in making pastry dough will enable you to feel when you have added the right amount of water.

You can make your pie crust flakier if you include 1 tablespoon of cold orange juice or lemon juice as part of the liquid.

If you want a crust which won't absorb moisture (for juicy pies) substitute 1 egg yolk for 1 tablespoon of water in the dough. (Mix the yolk with the water and let it chill before using.)

For tart shells, you may want to use some sugar in the pastry dough. The more sugar you mix into a crust, the harder it is to roll and hold its shape, but the crust will be much more delicate when it's baked.

Avoid overmixing pastry dough. Throw the ingredients together only long enough for them to adhere roughly into a ball. The less handling of the dough, the flakier the crust.

The reason you should handle pastry dough as little as possible is that you don't want the fat to melt. Avoid using your hands directly when you mix. Tenderness and flakiness depend on finely cut *cold* fat mixed with flour so avoid too much handling once you've added the ice water.

Slightly chilled dough handles more easily than dough at room temperature, so refrigerate it for ½ hour before rolling.

Make a little more pastry dough than you think you'll need. It's easier to roll out and spread in the pie plate without having to stretch it to fit here and there. You can always freeze and save any extra dough to combine with a future crust.

If you haven't a marble slab, an enamel tabletop or a large enamel tray is a very good surface to roll pastry dough on because the surface tends to stay cool.

You can store pastry dough wrapped in plastic wrap in the refrigerator for 3 or 4 days. But it's better to line the pie tin first, then wrap it in plastic wrap and store. You can also freeze the already lined pie tin. It will keep for months if it's airtight.

When you roll pastry dough for a circular pie, start it from the center and move out. Turn, and continue until you have a circle with a diameter 2 inches greater than that of the pan.

Never attempt to mix pastry dough in a hot kitchen. The success of pastry depends on all the ingredients remaining as cold as possible for as long as possible until baked.

For a flaky pie pastry, add a teaspoon of vinegar or lemon juice to the water when you mix.

Ordinary pie pastry tends to become monotonous. Give it some character by adding ingredients to improve the flavor and texture. If the pastry is for a meat or chicken pie, use a little curry powder in the mix, or a tablespoon of sesame seeds. Use any additions—cinnamon, chili powder, ginger—that seem to you to go with the filling.

A pie shell made (and refrigerated) the day before it's baked will be crispier after baking.

Most cookie dough makes dandy pie pastry, especially for open-faced tarts, etc. Knead the dough a little, roll it out thin, and fit it into the pie pan as you would pastry dough.

When you put dough in a pie tin to bake a shell, spread it somewhat loosely without stretching across the bottom. Press down with your fingers, then put a patch of dough on any tightly stretched spots, and press again.

You can make small pie, tart or patty shells by inverting muffin tins and fitting pastry dough on the outsides. Prick the dough all over so it won't shrink back from the pan. Let them cool after baking, then lift carefully.

It's better to let a frozen pie crust thaw unwrapped before you fill and bake it. Otherwise the inner surface may remain raw and moist.

If you freeze an unbaked pie shell in a Pyrex pan, let the pan come close to room temperature before you fill the crust and bake it. Otherwise the pan may crack when put in a hot oven.

Prick a pastry shell all over with the tines of a fork before you put it in the oven. This will prevent large blisters caused by steam forming on the underside of the dough.

The reason for baking pastry in a hot oven is to make it light. It rises and bakes quickly in the high heat.

When you divide a ball of pastry dough for rolling the top and bottom crusts, put a little more dough into the portion for the top crust. You can press, stretch, and patch the bottom crust once it's in the pan because it's going to be filled, but be sure the top crust is ample enough to cover the pie smoothly.

Pastry for the top and bottom crusts of a 9-inch pie pan should be about 11 inches in diameter.

To transfer the circle of pastry dough from the rolling surface to the pie pan without stretching or tearing it, flour the rolling pin well and drape the pastry circle loosely over it. Have the pie pan close by so you can lift the dough immediately into it.

Another method of getting a circle of pastry dough neatly into the pie pan—after you've rolled it out—is to roll the dough very lightly into a cylinder, tilt the pan so you can roll the cylinder into it, then unroll the dough.

After you've placed the bottom crust in the pie pan, the crust is less likely to shrink if you let it stand for about 5 minutes before you fill it or handle it in any way.

Roll leftover pie pastry into strips, give them a light coating of butter, honey, or jam, dust with cinnamon, and bake. Utterly delicious!

PÂTÉ: see BLENDER, HORS D'OEUVRES, LEFTOVERS, LIVER

PATTY SHELLS

To make patty shells, take an unsliced loaf of bread and cut it into thick, 2-inch slices. Hollow out the centers of the slices, being careful not to break through to the other side. Then either fry them in deep fat until they're golden—and drain them well—or toast them in the oven until they're crisp and brown. Fill them with the filling of your choice.

PEACHES

There are 4 to 6 fresh peaches in 1 pound.

A pound of peaches, sliced, will give you about 2 cups.

Peaches spoil rapidly if they're bruised. Be sure to handle carefully when packing or storing.

Peaches that are hard and show a lot of green on their skins will never ripen properly. Avoid them.

Peaches will ripen in a brown paper bag if you put an apple in with them. The apple releases a natural gas (ethylene) that aids in ripening. This is the same gas, by the way, that causes tomatoes to ripen.

To slow down the ripening of peaches, refrigerate them.

To make spiced peaches at much less than the cost of buying them, simmer canned whole peaches (or apricots) with cloves and a little real maple syrup and brandy added to the canned juice.

Very firm peaches can be peeled with a potato peeler.

A good way to peel peaches is to bring a pot of water to a boil, turn the flame off, drop the peaches in the water, let them stand for about 3 minutes and then drain them. Peel the peaches with a firm downward pull.

Dried peaches double in bulk when they're cooked.

When you buy canned peaches, look for those whose labels list the drained weight instead of net weight. You're more interested in the weight of the peaches than in the liquid or syrup.

PEANUT BUTTER

See also *Nuts*.

1 pound of peanut butter will give 1¾ cups.

Although most store-bought peanut butter is homogenized, some of the oil may still rise to the top of the jar if it stands undisturbed on a shelf for a long time. To prevent this, store the jar upside down.

For a real treat, try peanut butter made from nothing but peanuts ground to order. (Most health food stores and some grocery stores have the proper grinding machine for this.) This kind of peanut butter contains no added fats, stabilizers, or sweeteners.

Peanut butter is a good—and relatively inexpensive source— of protein. It does not have the protein quality found in meat, but it has more than other commonly eaten vegetable products.

An unopened jar of peanut butter will stay in good condition from 6 months to 1 year. Once opened, it should be refrigerated. It will remain in top condition for 3 months.

Refrigerating peanut butter slows down the possible growth of molds or bacteria, and helps to prevent the oils from becoming rancid.

To make peanut butter in a blender, grind the nuts as fine as possible and then add a little oil. Home blenders are not as powerful as commercial grinders, but the result is very good indeed. (You can also make other interesting nut butters; see *Nuts*.)

Stir 1 tablespoon of strong hot coffee into 2 tablespoons of crunchy peanut butter. Mix this combination into softened vanilla ice cream and put it in the freezer for an hour or so. This could be what the gods on Mount Olympus ate for dessert.

For a change in peanut butter sandwiches, try mixing pure unsweetened peanut butter—the natural kind that has no added sugar, salt, or oils—with some honey.

Beat a couple of tablespoons of creamy peanut butter into a white or golden cake batter, then bake as usual.

Peanut butter is great in soup! Add it to chicken stock with a little butter-and-flour thickener and some light cream. Add sautéed onions if you like. (This is a famous Southern soup.)

Peanut butter is a legitimate ingredient in a meat sauce. Mix it with soy sauce, lemon juice, a bit of sugar or honey, a little hot sauce if you like your sauces hot, and just enough boiling water to give it the consistency you want. Good on chicken, too.

Spread peanut butter on a slice of bread, add slices of bananas, top it with another slice of bread. This is known as a Paradise Sandwich.

Cucumber slices spread over a layer of peanut butter also make a delicious sandwich.

PEARS

If a pear is soft at the base of the stem, use it right away—it won't keep.

When you peel pears for cooking, treat them like apples. To keep them from discoloring, as soon as they're peeled, drop them into water containing 1 tablespoon of lemon juice.

Firm Bosc pears are good baking pears. Bake just as you do apples.

When you buy canned pears, look for those whose labels list the drained weight instead of net weight. You're more interested in the weight of the pears than you are in the liquid or syrup.

PEAS

1 pound of medium peas in the pod will give about 1 cup cooked, or 2 to 3 servings.

When you buy fresh peas, look for plump bright green pods with a slightly velvety feel to them. Avoid pale green or yellowish pods—the peas inside will be starchy, not sweet.

If you're using frozen peas, you can separate the peas from one another in the package if you hit the package hard against a tabletop on all four corners before you open it.

There's a quick way of soaking whole dried peas: boil them for 2 minutes, then take the pot off the heat, cover and let soak for 1 hour. Then they're ready for cooking.

Undercook peas. They should be a little crisp to the teeth when you serve them.

When you cook fresh peas, bring the liquid (you need very little) to a boil. Then add the peas and cover the pot. If you raise the lid occasionally and don't overcook the peas, they'll keep their color.

Never use baking soda to keep peas green while cooking. It keeps them green, but destroys their taste and vitamins.

Chicken stock is one of the best liquids to cook peas in. It is also an excellent base for cream of pea soup, which can be made using either fresh or frozen peas puréed in the blender.

1 pound of dry split peas, cooked, will give you about 5 cups.

Wash the pods of peas before you shell them. After shelling, throw the pods into your stock or soup pot. Cook for 30 minutes and remove them. They'll add a nice flavor.

If you like fresh cooked peas slightly sweet, cook them with a few of the empty pods, then remove the pods before serving.

PECANS: see NUTS

PEPPER: see HERBS AND SPICES

PEPPERS

Red peppers are green peppers that have ripened.

Many green peppers have very little flavor. Try to pick ones that show a little yellow or even some red on them. These peppers are on their way to developing a taste.

To peel a green pepper (for antipasto, marinated peppers, etc.), wash and dry firm peppers, broil them on a rack about 5 inches from the heat for about 10 minutes, or until the skins begin to wrinkle and brown. Turn them now and then. Let cool, then hold them under cold water. The skin will peel off easily.

Green or sweet red peppers don't keep well, so don't buy them too far in advance.

If you're going to stuff peppers, try cutting them in half crosswise instead of lengthwise, then you can place the halves upright in cupcake tins before you fill and bake them. They're easier to handle and hold their shape better when cooked.

PERSIMMONS

You can remove much of the astringency from a persimmon if you wrap it airtight with an apple for 24 hours.

An unripe persimmon is full of tannic acid and will give you a long-lasting dose of mouth pucker! So be sure the persimmon is ripe before you bite into it. A ripe persimmon is soft, with a yellow to dark-orange skin color. The flesh itself is bright orange. To ripen persimmons, seal them at room temperature in a plastic bag with a couple of ripe apples. Refrigerate them when they're ripe.

A ripe persimmon is one fruit that gets sweeter when kept in the cold. So keep them in your refrigerator.

To purée persimmon pulp for a fruit sauce, add about 1½ teaspoons of lemon juice to each cup of pulp to prevent discoloration.

Put a persimmon in the freezer for about 6 hours. Cut it in half and serve it. It's like a sherbet.

PICKLES

When you buy cucumbers for pickling, be sure you avoid the large green ones which usually have a wax coating. It's impossible to get the wax off. Ask for pickling cucumbers.

If you're making pickles, use plain, not iodized, salt, or you'll get an unpleasant flavor in the pickles. Coarse salt is preferable to table salt. For some reason, it gives a better flavor to the brine.

When you're making pickles of any kind, use whole—not ground—spices and herbs. Ground spices "muddy" the pickling liquid and also darken the pickles.

The leftover juice from sweet pickles is great for soaking dried vegetable flakes (carrots, celery, onions, pepper, etc.). After the flakes have marinated in the juice for a couple of days, use in salads and canapé mixtures.

The juice from canned pickles can be mixed with oil and used as a salad dressing. It's also very good for making a sweet-and-sour meat gravy.

PIE

See also *Berries, Cream or Custard Desserts, Crumbs and Crumb Crusts, Graham Crackers and Graham Cracker Crust, Meringues, Pastry Dough.*

Fillings

If a pie filling contains molasses, use a deep-dish pan or even a cake pan to bake the pie in. Molasses usually bubbles high during baking and might run over. To be safer still, set the pan on a cookie sheet.

One way to avoid a runny filling and a soggy crust in a custard pie is to be sure that both the cooked pastry shell and the custard are cool before you fill the shell.

To see if a baked custard pie is done, insert a knife blade near the edge of the pie (not in the middle). If the knife comes out clean, the custard's done. The middle part of a baked custard pie firms during cooling.

For a variation of the traditional lemon custard pie that calls for lemon juice, slice the lemon paper-thin and include the slices with the lemon juice This makes a marvelous pie. You can also cut the lemon slices into thin strips—this makes cutting the pie wedges a bit easier.

A couple of tablespoons of honey added to the pumpkin filling when you're preparing a pumpkin pie will give an attractive shiny glaze on the pie after it's baked.

You will need 4 cups of fresh berries to make a 9-inch pie.

Juices in a berry pie are likely to run under the bottom crust during baking, but you can keep the crust from sticking to the pan if you grease the pie pan and dust it with flour before setting in the bottom crust.

If you like to serve cheese with apple pie, try baking the cheese *into* the pie. Spread grated Cheddar over the bottom crust before you add the filling. Or sprinkle the cheese over the top of the pie before the last 15 minutes of baking.

Pies, especially fruit pies, are more delicious if you stick them in the oven and give them a good warming just before you serve them.

To get a glaze on your fruit pies or tarts, brush the surface with heated corn syrup as soon as you've taken them from the oven.

The fillings of many pie recipes can be baked as is, without a crust. Many can be cut into wedges and served; others can be treated as hot puddings, served with a spoon, and topped with anything that seems appropriate to you.

If the apples for your apple pie turn out to be on the dry side, mix the pieces lightly with a half-and-half mixture of lemon juice and water before you put them in the pie shell. Use enough to moisten the apples well. You can also sprinkle a little sugar over the apples before putting on the top crust.

Crusts

If you want a pie to have a well-browned bottom crust, bake it in a dark metal pie pan.

To give a pie a lovely color when baked, melt 1 tablespoon of butter in 2 tablespoons of milk and brush the top of the unbaked pie with this.

If you want a shiny, brittle crust on a pie, paint the surface of the top crust with a mixture of 1 whole egg beaten with 1 teaspoon of water before you bake the pie.

Soggy bottom crusts are the bane of a pie maker's existence. To avoid them sprinkle fine bread crumbs or finely ground nuts over the unbaked bottom crust before adding a juicy filling. This also helps to tighten up a very juicy filling.

You can also brush the bottom crust with lightly beaten egg white and let it dry completely before you fill it, or make a mixture of ¼ cup flour and ¼ cup sugar and dust this over the bottom crust before adding the filling.

If you're making a filled pie of any kind to bake later, keep the pastry shell and the filling separate until you're ready to bake. The bottom crust will become gummy if it stands unbaked already filled and baking usually won't save it completely.

You can make the sides of the top crust stick to the bottom crust if you moisten the rim of the bottom crust after you've filled the pie, then put on the top crust and pinch the edges together all around the rim.

If you want a pie with a glossy top crust, brush it with milk or unbeaten egg white before you put it in the oven to bake.

Dip a pastry brush in cream and "paint" the top of the pie crust before you bake it—it will brown beautifully.

Brush the top crust of an unbaked pie with a little milk, dot with 1 tablespoon of shortening, and sprinkle with a mixture of 1 tablespoon of sugar, 3 tablespoons of flour, ½ teaspoon each of cinnamon and grated lemon or orange rind. This will give you a nice crisp, crumbly topping when baked.

To get a flaky crust on a pie, spread the crust with ½ teaspoon of soft shortening mixed with 1½ teaspoons of soft butter. Dust the crust with flour and sprinkle with a little water, then bake.

To easily remove the wedges of a pie made with graham cracker crust, butter the inside of the pie pan very well before you press the crumbs into it.

A graham cracker pie crust is less likely to crumble when you cut it if you hold the pie pan in warm water for 30 seconds, about halfway up the side, just before you're ready to serve.

Baking

Bake a filled 2-crust pie at 425° for 30 to 45 minutes.

Bake a custard pie at 450° for 15 minutes or at 350° for 25 to 30 minutes.

You should generally put a pie in the center of the oven to bake.

It's better to bake a pie in a tin from which the outside shininess has worn off. A completely new pie tin tends to overcook the bottom. If you have new ones, use them for other baking or roasting until they've dulled.

If your pies tend to burn around the rims when you bake them, cut 2-inch strips of aluminum foil and bend these over the rim all around the pie before you bake it. When you peel the foil off after baking, the rim will be nicely browned.

Frozen pies seem particularly prone to burn around the rims. If you let a frozen unbaked pie shell thaw before you bake it, you'll get a better pie.

You can keep an empty pie shell from buckling and blistering during baking if you prick it all over with a fork, then fill it ⅔ full with small dried beans or raw rice. These help hold the dough down as it bakes and pricking enables any steam which forms to escape.

You can prevent a juicy pie from boiling over in the oven if you prick the top crust all over with a fork before you bake it. Better yet, push a few pieces of raw macaroni through the top crust—these will allow the steam to escape during baking. (This method is better than the first since it will keep the juices from rising and spoiling the looks of the top crust.)

If the juices from a berry pie still seem likely to boil over during baking, either spread a large square of aluminum foil under the pie pan or put the pie pan in a larger pan before you put it in the oven. The under pan will catch the overflow and save the floor of your oven.

If for some reason the juices from a pie *do* boil over onto the oven floor, sprinkle salt over the drippings to prevent them from smoking.

If the top crust of your pie seems to be browning too quickly, you can cover it with oiled or buttered brown paper and lower the oven heat slightly. You may want to remove the paper for the last few minutes of baking.

A pecan pie sometimes browns too quickly on top. If you see this happening, reduce the oven heat 25 degrees, leaving the oven door open so the lower temperature is reached quickly. You may even want to reduce the heat another 25 degrees in the same manner, if in another 10 minutes the pie still seems to be browning too fast.

Open-faced fruit pies or tarts look nice (and the fruits won't dry out) if you pour a fruit glaze over the top. Boil fruit juice until it's thick and jelly-like, then spoon this over the pie after it's baked.

French tart tins are pie tins with removable sides. They come in many sizes and are good if you want to remove an entire pie without damaging the side crust. To remove the pie from a tart tin, put the tin on an inverted bowl whose diameter is a little smaller than the tart pan. Push gently down on the sides to release the pie.

Cut a meringue-topped pie with a greased knife and the meringue won't stick to the knife.

PIE CRUST: see PASTRY DOUGH

PIE SHELLS: see PIE

PIMIENTOS
The unused portion of a can or jar of pimientos will last longer, without spoiling, if you drain the pimientos well and cover them with salad oil. Store in the refrigerator.

PINEAPPLE
1 pineapple, cubed, will give you about 2½ cups.

If a pineapple hasn't ripened on the tree, it never will. It may get softer, but it won't get sweeter. Test for ripeness by pulling out one of the center top leaves. The leaf will come out easily if the fruit is ripe. Also, a ripe pineapple will smell sweet and fruity, and the sharp outer coat will have lost all green color.

If one side of a pineapple is very much lighter in color than the rest of the rind, avoid it—it will be dry inside.

To get fancy pineapple strips for a special fruit dessert, cut the fresh pineapple into spears and put them in a jar. Cover the spears with raspberry juice (this can be the juice from frozen raspberries) and let them stand in the refrigerator for 24 hours. They'll be a beautiful color, and taste gorgeous.

Wash the knife thoroughly after you've cut the rind from a pineapple and before you slice it. Pineapple rind contains a mouth irritant that causes a burning sensation in some people—and a residue of the irritant may cling to the knife.

Always keep cut pineapple very well covered in the refrigerator. Dairy products quickly absorb pineapple odor.

PLASTIC DISHES
If you need to clean stains from plastic dishes, rub them well with baking soda as you would if you were using a scouring powder.

You can use bleach to remove tea, coffee and juice stains, but bleach ruins the finish of some plastic dishes.

PLUMS

If you have to peel plums, treat them as you would tomatoes. Plunge them into boiling water for a short time until the skin cracks and they'll peel easily.

If fresh plums are brownish on one side, they're likely to have a poor flavor.

POACHING

See also *Eggs, Fish.*

When you poach, try to use very little liquid, just enough to cover the food. Always poach at a simmer.

POMEGRANATES

Cut a pomegranate in half and juice it like an orange—it's divine.

POPCORN

If you want popcorn to pop like mad, pour the kernels into a strainer, wash in cold water and drain well, then pour the kernels into the popper.

You can add an interesting and surprisingly delicate flavor to popcorn if you add ½ peeled clove of garlic to the melted salted butter you serve on popcorn.

POPOVERS

Be sure that all the ingredients for the popover batter are at room temperature.

It's essential to sift the flour before you measure it when you make popovers because the ratio of flour to other ingredients is very important.

Popovers more than double when they're baked. Fill the cups only about ½ full.

Popovers sometimes collapse if the oven door is opened during the first ½ hour of baking, so try to keep it shut.

A popover is done when it has "popped" (risen very high) and is beautifully brown and shiny on the outside.

After you've baked them make a small slit in the top of each popover to allow the steam to escape, otherwise they'll become soggy inside.

If you can't serve them right away, you can leave popovers in a closed oven for 10 minutes or so after you've slit the tops and turned off the heat. But don't let them cool while they're still in the pans or the bottoms will become soggy.

Popovers can be frozen after they're baked. To defrost put them still frozen in a paper bag in a preheated 425° oven for about 5 minutes.

PORK

See also *Liver, Meats, Roasts.*

Butchers are not allowed to grind raw pork in the same machine in which they grind other meats. Unless your butcher has a separate grinder for pork alone, or you buy your pork at a pork store, you may have to grind pork in your own meat grinder. Be sure to scrub the grinder afterward with a brush and scalding suds and then boil it to be on the safe side.

Most ground meat dishes like meatballs or meat loaf taste much better if some ground pork is included. But this means you can't serve them rare.

Buy pork chops about 1 inch thick. Thinner ones tend to dry out during the fairly prolonged cooking pork requires.

To test pork chops for doneness, prick them with a sharp-tined fork. If the juice which rises is clear and untinged with pink they're done.

A 3- to 4-pound fresh pork roast should be baked at 350° for 35 to 40 minutes per pound.

Cooked pork is at its best when it's lightly pink, never rarer. A meat thermometer is the most reliable guide for determining the inner temperature of a roast, which should be about 185°.

You'll find a pork roast juicier and much more tender if you brown it on top of the stove and then cook it in the oven in a heavy covered pot instead of roasting it uncovered.

POTATOES

See also *Frying, Potato Salad, Sautéing, Sweet Potatoes and Yams.*

1 pound of potatoes will give about 3½ cups, sliced or diced.

If you have room, store potatoes in the refrigerator to inhibit the growth of "eyes." Be sure to keep them dry.

You'll find that potatoes with tough and wrinkled skins are easier to peel if you soak them in cold water for ½ hour.

Raw potatoes won't discolor as you peel them if you drop them into water. You can also rub oil on your palms and roll each peeled well-dried potato in your hands so a thin covering of oil adheres to the surface.

Potatoes that are partly green, or have green spots on them, are often bitter.

Some potatoes have a hollow, darkish center when you cut them open. (There's no way to tell from the outside.) Such a condition is more likely to occur in very large, mature potatoes.

Potatoes stored in the refrigerator become somewhat sweeter than potatoes kept in a warmer place or at room temperature.

To freeze raw, unpeeled potatoes, wrap them individually, airtight. When you need them, let them defrost at room temperature, then peel. (They peel easily.) They're fine for boiling and mashing.

Potatoes with a good starch content (mealy ones) are best for boiling and baking. To test whether the potatoes are of the proper variety, cut one in half crosswise and rub the two halves against each other briskly. If the potato has plenty of starch, it will produce a frothy juice as you rub it.

Potatoes eaten with their skins on have more nutrients than other starches traditionally served with a meal: white bread, rice, noodles. The only exception is dried beans, which are right up there with potatoes. But potatoes eaten without their skins are at about the same level as the other three starches.

If you're going to eat potatoes with their skins, scrub the potatoes very well before cooking. Many potatoes are sprayed with a chemical to keep the "eyes" from sprouting. This chemical is soluble in water. (To be safest, scrub potatoes with a brush and soapy water, and rinse well.)

Potatoes cooked whole lose fewer nutrients than those cut up.

Potatoes cooked with their skins on are very easy to peel while hot.

When baking or boiling potatoes, choose those that are as close to the same size as possible. They'll all be cooked to the same degree at the same time.

Baked

A medium to large potato should generally be baked at 400° for 50 to 60 minutes.

Idaho potatoes are probably the best potatoes for baking. They have a mealy consistency and their tough skins bake to a nice crispness. Long Island and Maine (Ketahdin) are somewhat similar to Idaho, and can generally be found later in the year. Russets are also good for baking.

If you use new potatoes for baking, you generally have to cook them longer because they contain more moisture.

Long and slow baking will give you a drier, mealier potato, regardless of the kind of potato.

You can shorten the baking time of a potato if you remove a very thick slice from each end (after you've scrubbed it well) and oil the cut ends slightly before setting the potato in the oven.

You can shorten the baking time for potatoes if you run a long heavy nail lengthwise through each potato before you put it in the oven. The nail carries the heat quickly to the center of the potato.

You can also save time in baking potatoes if you cook them first for 10 minutes in boiling salted water. (You can also boil them in water to which a little sugar has been added and when they're baked they'll have a faint delicious sweetness.)

It's not necessary to peel potatoes before you cook them with roasts. They're more nutritious with their skins on. Just scrub them well, dry and rub them between your palms with a small amount of fat before putting them in the roasting pan. This will soften their skins while they cook.

If you cover a potato with aluminum foil before you bake it, it will be steamed and won't have a real baked potato flavor.

If you bake potatoes in the same pan with roasting meat they'll absorb the flavor of the meat. But wait until about 40 minutes before the roast is done so that the potatoes won't get overdone and fall apart.

You can also bake potatoes in cupcake or muffin tins. They're easy to put in and remove from the oven.

If you like your baked potatoes mealy and dry inside, prick them with a fork at both ends before putting them in the oven. This lets the steam escape.

To avoid sogginess in a baked potato, pierce it or cut a lengthwise gash in it with a sharp knife as soon as you've removed it from the oven.

A leftover baked potato can be rebaked if you dip it in water, then put it in a 350° oven for about 20 minutes.

If your oven gives out, you can still "bake" potatoes on top of the stove. Wrap in aluminum foil, place each one on a burner over the lowest possible flame and turn it every 15 minutes or so, so that all sides have a chance to lie against the flame. Remember the two ends as well. The whole process takes from 45 to 50 minutes. Remove the foil and test after 45 minutes with a fork or cake tester. When they're done, remove the foil entirely so that the shell won't become soggy. These are really very good!

If you like a sour cream topping on your baked potato but would like to ease up on the fats and calories, use cottage cheese. Put it in the blender and whip to smoothness. If you want to thin the cottage cheese, whip in a tiny bit of milk. Add garlic or onion and some pepper, if you like.

Another great topping for a baked potato that steers clear of sour cream is yogurt mixed with chopped chives or finely minced fresh mint.

To freeze baked stuffed potatoes, wrap them individually in aluminum foil. Put them, still wrapped and frozen, in a moderate oven for about 25 minutes just before you're ready to eat them. Open and test to see if they're thawed and hot—they may need 5 or so minutes more.

Boiled

1 pound of potatoes will cook to about 2 cups, mashed.

Add a little oil to the water in which you boil potatoes to keep a gummy ring from forming and adhering to the top of the pot.

If you put a little honey in the water when you boil potatoes they'll have a very pleasant flavor.

Try putting a small piece of uncooked bacon or smoky sausage in the water when you boil potatoes. The flavor of the meat will be absorbed by the potatoes.

Potatoes boiled with their skins on peel easily while they're still hot. If you boil potatoes for cold potato salad, don't wait until they cool to peel them.

If you do have to peel cold cooked potatoes, it will be easier if you wet them first.

If you're boiling potatoes for mashing, cook them only until a fork easily pierces them. Don't let them get waterlogged.

When you boil potatoes (to serve boiled, or for potato salad), add some pepper, onion, and a bay leaf to the cooking water. Or drop in a chicken bouillon cube. Any of these will greatly improve the flavor.

Boiled potatoes always become soggy if you put them in a covered dish. You can, however, keep them warm by putting them in a dish and covering them with a napkin.

Because some potatoes contain less moisture than others, you may find it necessary when mashing boiled potatoes to add a fair amount of liquid—milk, cream, or some of the potato water—to bring them to proper fluffiness.

When you boil potatoes for mashing, mix some of the hot potato water with powdered milk and a little butter or oil. Add this to the hot potatoes as you mash for a more flavorful and nutritious dish.

Mashed

Before you mash potatoes, drain well and put them in a pot over a flame, then shake the pot (or put the pot in a low oven) until the potatoes are dry. This will make them creamier when they're mashed.

If you add a little scalded milk or cream to mashed potatoes and beat it in very well, the potatoes will be very white and creamy. But adding cold milk or cream to mashed potatoes will mat them down.

If you add ½ teaspoon of baking powder to mashed potatoes and then whip them with an electric beater, the potatoes will be light and fluffy.

You can mash potatoes ahead of time and reheat them if you brush the top with a little melted butter after they're first mashed to prevent a crust from forming. Then when you're ready to serve, whip them with an electric mixer and heat in a well-covered double boiler.

If you want to pipe seasoned mashed potatoes through a pastry tube to garnish a dish, add 1 whole egg plus 1 egg yolk for each pound of potatoes and they'll hold their shape better.

If you beat some heavy cream, whipped and lightly salted, into mashed potatoes, they become absolutely heavenly.

To mash potatoes that have become waterlogged from over-cooking, drain them well, beat with an electric beater, adding dry skimmed milk powder as you beat. Use as much powder as is necessary to make a bowl of light, airy potatoes.

The best mashed potatoes in the world are made from *baked* potatoes. Bake them as you usually do, scoop out the lovely steaming interior, add some hot milk or cream and possibly some butter as you beat. (Don't throw away those crispy skins—eat them while you work in the kitchen.)

Sautéing, Frying, and Escalloping

Sauté potatoes in a large pan filled with hot fat, some of which should be solid fat. Dry the lengths of potato thoroughly with a dishtowel before you drop them into the fat. This prevents the temperature of the fat from dropping drastically. It also helps to prevent painful spattering.

While sautéing, shake the pan so that the potatoes move around until they develop a protective coating which will keep them from sticking to the pan. Shake the pan every few minutes until they're done. Try to avoid using spoons and forks, which tend to break or crush the potatoes.

Don't make French fries (or any other kind of fried potatoes) until just before you want to serve them. They always get soggy when they stand—in or out of the oven.

Don't put too many pieces of potato in the frying basket at one time. This will not only lower the temperature of the fat, but will also make the potatoes absorb too much of it.

When you make escalloped potatoes, don't fill the baking pan more than three-fourths full, otherwise it's likely to boil over in the oven.

If you want to prevent the milk from curdling when you bake escalloped potatoes without flour, first add only half the milk called for and bake in a low to moderate oven. Add the remaining milk gradually while baking.

If you're using mashed potatoes to make fried potato pancakes, regardless of what the recipe says, first flour them on the outside. They won't stick to the pan and will brown nicely.

After you've grated potatoes (as for potato pancakes) sprinkle them with lemon juice or flour to prevent them from turning dark.

Add some grated raw potatoes to hamburger or meat loaf. This makes the meat go farther and stay moister. It also helps hold the meat together.

Grate raw potatoes into soup and simmer for a few minutes if you need a thickener.

Save the water in which you've cooked potatoes and use it in yeast dough. This makes the most wonderful bread and rolls.

Don't sauté too many potato pieces at one time. They tend to steam and stick together.

To make hashed brown potatoes brown quickly, wash, peel, dry, and slice the potatoes. Then dredge them lightly in a bowl of flour. Shake off the flour, put the slices into hot fat in a skillet, and sauté as usual.

While you're pan-frying potatoes, sauté in another pan some well-drained sauerkraut until it's very lightly browned. Add the sauerkraut to the fried potatoes with a little pepper. Mix well, heat some more, and serve. Wonderful!

A potato cutter used for making french fries can be used to make diced potatoes, too. Slice the potatoes first, as for french fries, then cut the potato sticks at right angles into cubes so the dice will be uniform in size.

POTATO CHIPS

For a nice garlic flavor, put a peeled clove of garlic in a container with potato chips and let it remain there for several hours.

You can use potato chip crumbs to roll croquettes or for many dishes requiring bread crumbs or flour. Run over a bag of potato chips with a rolling pin until the crumbs are as fine as you want them.

POTATO PEELER

Use a potato peeler for peeling cucumbers, eggplant, beets, squash, carrots, apples, firm peaches, turnips, parsnips, and pumpkins, and for cutting cheese into strips, vegetables into curls for garnishes, and chocolate bars into strips and curlicues.

POTATO SALAD

See also *Potatoes*.

Don't use Idaho baking potatoes for potato salad. They're too mealy and break easily. If you can, use new potatoes which are generally firmer.

Add a little mustard to the mayonnaise you put in potato salad.

The French serve potato salad at room temperature but dress it while it's hot, as the Germans do, so that the potatoes readily absorb the good flavors in the dressing.

POTATO STARCH

Potato starch and potato flour are the same thing. Like arrow-root and cornstarch, they thicken a sauce without making it opaque.

POT HOLDERS

Give away those pretty crocheted pot holders you bought at the church fair and buy yourself a few heavy quilted lined ones or sturdy oven mitts. A pot holder is something which is meant to keep your hands from getting burned when you heft a turkey in its roasting pan from the oven.

Pot holders thick enough to really protect your hands from the extreme heat of very hot pot handles are hard to find. If you know how to knit, you can make great pot holders out of odds and ends of yarn. The trick is to use a fairly thin needle and to purl both sides. This will give you thick, usable pot holders.

Don't grab a towel to use in place of a pot holder. The ends may catch fire.

POT LIDS

Use aluminum foil to make a temporary lid for any pot which lacks a cover. You can punch a small hole in it if you want a little steam to escape.

When you remove the lid from any cooking pot, be sure you open it outward, away from you, to avoid a sudden burst of painful steam in your face.

You can often use a pot lid to extinguish flames when food happens to catch fire. This closes off the oxygen supply and usu-ally suffices to put out small cooking fires.

POT ROASTS: see BEEF, MEATS, PRESSURE COOKER, ROASTS

POTS AND PANS

See also *Pressure Cooker.*

See *Omelets* for omelet pans.

When you measure a pot or pan for size, measure across the top, not the bottom. This is the standard way of naming pot size by inches.

Heavy metal pots and pans, either cast iron or enamel on iron, are best for most cooking. They distribute the heat well, won't dent and are less likely to scorch food. (But get in the habit of using two hands to lift them to avoid trouble with your wrists.) Thin-bottomed pans are good for nothing but boiling water.

Food chemists say that cooking foods in cast-iron pots or pans adds valuable iron to the diet.

Plain cast-iron pots do discolor some foods—artichokes, and anything containing egg yolks, for instance. But enamel-covered cast iron won't give you this problem.

When you buy Teflon-lined pans, try to get ones which are steel, club aluminum, or glass (for baking). Ordinary aluminum buckles in time. (Unfortunately, most of the Teflon-lined pans you see in stores seem to be made of thin aluminum.)

Shiny new metal bread pans won't brown the sides and bottom of bread, cake and pie as well as old or glass ones. If you have new tins, put them empty in the oven at 350° and bake until they've lost their sheen or use them for cooking other things until they're not shiny anymore. Don't knock yourself out to scrub all the baking stains off them.

If you bake bread in glass loaf pans, the oven should be 25° lower than when you bake bread in metal pans.

If you need a deep cake pan and only have the regulation 2-inch-high ones, cut a strip of heavy brown paper (from a paper bag) about 4 inches wide, butter it and stand it around the inside of your buttered and floured cake pan. When you pour the batter in the strip will stay in place and you'll have a 4-inch-deep pan.

The best way to loosen a cake baked in a Teflon-lined pan is to use a plastic knife or spatula rather than anything metal; you'll be less likely to injure the lining.

Unless you intend to boil liquid in it, always grease or oil the inside of any pan, enamel covered as well as metal or glass, before you use it. Whether you're going to sauté, stew or braise, food will be less likely to stick to an oiled pan or pot.

Teflon or similar plastic coating on a pan lets you sauté food without added fat. This is possible because the coating makes use of whatever fat is in the food itself. An egg, for example, contains some fat in the yolk; meat, chicken and fish likewise contain enough fat in themselves to sauté more or less successfully in Teflon pans. But foods containing practically no fat (onions, for instance) won't have a sautéed flavor, though they may cook without sticking. For such foods a tiny amount of fat or oil or a light greasing of the pan is a good idea.

Teflon-lined pans are great for reheating foods. Cooked rice, for example, may be reheated as it is (covered, with maybe a tiny bit of liquid added, and stirred from time to time) and it won't stick or burn if you use a low to moderate flame.

Put 1 teaspoon of salt in the water in the bottom of a double boiler, and it will transmit more heat to the food in the upper section.

Turn all pot and pan handles away from you toward the rear of the stove so you won't knock against them while you're cooking. Make a habit of this so that it comes naturally when you set a pot on the stove.

Remember not to set a hot glass dish on a very cold surface or in cold water, or vice versa. This often causes even Pyrex pans to crack.

As soon as you've emptied a pot, fill it with water if you haven't time to wash it immediately. This will make cleaning much easier later.

Don't use steel wool on enameled pots. If any abrasive action is still needed after you have soaked the pot in soapy water overnight, use a mild powdered cleanser and a sponge or a homemade pot scraper (see *Pot Scraper*). You can also try rubbing *lightly* with a plastic pot scraper.

Wash the inside of a Teflon-lined pan with a sponge or cloth and soap and water, never any abrasive. You can scour the metal underside with anything you like.

If you haven't any copper cleaner, you can clean copper-bottomed pots and other copper kitchen utensils with toothpaste and a damp cloth.

Generally speaking, the thicker the metal of a pot, the more even is the distribution of heat.

Before you buy any pan, pick it up to check the weight. Check, especially, to see if the handle is comfortable for you.

If you use an electric range, be sure your pots and pans have absolutely flat bottoms. This ensures that no heat is lost between the burner and the pot.

To season a cast-iron pot, rub the inside generously with cooking oil (use a paper towel). Then set the pot in a low to moderate oven (300° to 325° F) for an hour. Turn the heat off and let the pot stand for several hours or overnight. Remove it and wipe it well. It will stay in tip-top condition if you give the inside a wipe with a little oil every now and then, after you've washed it.

Use a permanent marker to label the outsides of pots, casseroles, etc., whose capacity you can't always remember. You will save a lot of time when you need to know if a particular pot or casserole has the capacity the recipe calls for.

If you need a cover for a pie plate or a low baking dish and your pot lids don't fit, try inverting a pot or skillet over the top.

Foods cook more quickly in a covered pan. Water also comes to a boil faster if the pot or kettle has a cover.

It's almost instinct to rap a spoon or fork against the edge of a pot to dislodge food you've been stirring. But be warned: If the pot is enamel covered, it will eventually crack and splinter.

Salt and a little lemon juice will usually remove burned stains from the outside of enamel pots.

If your stove is electric, try to match the size of the pot to the size of the burner when you cook.

Cool a hot pot down a little before you pour very cold water on it. The reaction may not be as dramatic as with glass, but metals can be damaged by sudden profound changes in temperature.

If the tin lining of a copper pan begins to wear through, you must have it relined. Acid foods cooked on a copper surface can be harmful when eaten.

If the inside of an aluminum pan darkens, heat a little vinegar and water in it. Or cook something that is high in acid, and the discoloration will disappear.

For some top-of-stove cooking, use a slightly larger pot than usual for mixtures that require stirring. The contents will be less likely to overflow during boiling. And for soups and stews, the stirring can be more thorough.

Always lift the cover of a cooking pot with the opening turned away from you so you won't get a burst of steam in your face.

To line casseroles or pots and pans that are going into the oven, turn them over and fit aluminum foil over the bottom. Turn the top side up and place the formed piece of foil inside. It will fit in quite neatly.

Always rinse out a pan before you pour any liquid into it for heating. This will keep the liquid (milk or broth, for instance) from scorching the sides of the pan as it heats.

You'll have an easy time cleaning casseroles and pans if you simply fill them with cold water and let them soak overnight.

You can eliminate most of the burned flavor caused by scorching if you immediately set the scorched pan in a little cool water or on a cold wet towel before you turn the contents (without scraping) into another pan.

Turn a cooking pot now and then, whether it's on a burner or in the oven, to equalize the heat. Many people don't think of this, but if you use this technique, it is less likely that the bottom of a pot will overheat in any one spot.

POT SCRAPER

Take 3 old nylon stockings and make knots throughout each of them as close together as you can. Wad them and stuff into the toe of another stocking, knotting this firmly so that they make a fairly hard lump. Cut off the remainder of the stocking. You have a scratchless pot scraper which is as good as most of the ones you buy.

POULTRY: see BIRDS, CHICKEN, DUCK, GOOSE, TURKEY

PRESSURE COOKER
See also *Hearts, Tongue.*

Cooking in a pressure cooker saves time and fuel.

To tenderize tough meats in very little time in a pressure cooker you don't need much water but you do have to pay strict attention to time.

To prevent possible clogging of the steam outlet, don't fill a pressure cooker more than two-thirds full.

Use a pressure cooker to cook chicken backs, wings, and necks for soup or to boil the carcass of any fowl to softness. Chicken bones cooked with water for an hour to a soft chalklike consistency can be safely fed to a dog (after straining the stock for your own use). It's very rich in protein.

There are a few foods which you shouldn't cook in a pressure cooker—those which have a tendency to bubble up and spatter when you cook them in an ordinary pot, such as pasta, split peas, cranberries and applesauce, because there's always the possibility they'll plug up the air vent which must be kept clear to release normal excess pressure.

When you've finished cooking in a pressure cooker, always wait for the pressure to subside completely before you remove the lid. You'll know that the pressure has subsided when the hissing stops. Running cold water over the closed pot will bring this about quickly.

Among the many wonderful uses of a pressure cooker is cooking a beef heart. Inexpensive, as beef goes, and when cooked to tenderness—which a pressure cooker does very well—a beef heart has as much flavor as a pot roast. Delicious!

Pressure cookers were made for pot roasts. The toughest meat comes out tender, sweet, and juicy. Although the less expensive cuts of meat are generally tougher, the tougher meats actually have more flavor. And with a pressure cooker the problem of toughness is taken care of. So pressure-cook inexpensive cuts and you'll save money and time.

The same holds true for fowl. Tough old hens and roosters are a lot less expensive per pound than younger ones. If you know how to use pressure-cooking methods, you can make a marvelous dish of chicken stew to feed a large family for relatively little cost.

Pressure cookers are ideal for making good old-fashioned steamed puddings—plum, mincemeat, apple, molasses puddings, etc.

If you are a jelly maker, you ought to know that cooking fruit in a pressure cooker extracts a quarter more of the juice than top-of-stove cooking does.

Rice cooks in about 8 minutes in a pressure cooker. If you're cooking it for rice pudding, increase the cooking time by a couple of minutes so the rice will come out soft and creamy, the way it *should* be for a pudding.

The pressure cooker is great for making soup stocks. If there's one thing that usually needs a lot of time to cook in order to develop flavor, it's stock. But why cook bones and meat and vegetable scraps for hours on top of the stove to extract all their goodness when you can accomplish the same thing in an hour with a pressure cooker?

PRUNES

There are 2½ cups of uncooked prunes in 1 pound. Cooked and pitted, there are 4½ cups in 1 pound.

The next time you cook prunes use some honey in the water, or add a few slices of lemon. For a richer syrup, use prune juice in place of some of the water.

To stuff prunes, soften them first by pouring boiling water over them and let stand away from the heat until the water cools. Drain, pit, and stuff.

PUDDINGS
See also *Pressure Cooker*.

To keep a skin from forming on top of a boiled pudding made with cornstarch, which includes butterscotch, chocolate, or vanilla puddings, set a piece of waxed paper flat against the surface of the pudding before you chill it.

A baked rice pudding will be softer and creamier if you set the baking dish in a pan holding about an inch of hot water. Then bake.

When you're cooling a boiled rice pudding, stir it now and then to prevent the rice from sinking to the bottom.

Use inexpensive short-grain rice to make a baked or boiled rice pudding. The rice will absorb the milk more quickly if you cook the rice first in rapidly boiling water for 5 minutes, then drain. Proceed with the pudding as usual.

A bread pudding will taste much better if you serve it warm with a little warmed maple syrup poured over it. Or try it with a caramel sauce.

Substitute chocolate chips or chopped dates for raisins in bread pudding.

When you're using packaged pudding mix, always add the pudding powder to the milk, not vice versa. Mix with a wire whisk and you won't get lumps.

Another way to avoid lumps is to pour the milk into a large screw-top jar, add the powder, screw the top on tightly, shake briskly, then pour the mixture into the saucepan and cook.

Any packaged pudding which requires cooking can be made more nutritious if you add 1 egg or 2 egg yolks and an extra ⅓ cup of milk. Follow cooking directions, but keep the mixture just below the boiling point.

Don't cook puddings in pots which are too thin—the bottom is likely to burn.

Always rinse a pot thoroughly with water before you cook a pudding in it on top of the stove.

When you're cooking a pudding on top of the stove, don't stir it continually. This will keep it from reaching a boil and the bottom may scorch.

Most cornstarch puddings (including packaged puddings) will unmold when cold if you run a knife blade around the inside of the mold and invert it. To be really safe, oil the mold lightly before you pour the pudding in.

For a quick sauce to serve over dessert pudding or plain cake, cook a package of vanilla pudding according to directions, add 2 tablespoons of rum and cook again until the liquid has thickened slightly. Pour while it's hot.

PUMPKIN

Don't throw away the seeds you've scooped out of a pumpkin. They're very good to eat if you dry them in a low oven, then salt and continue toasting until they're light and tan colored.

To remove strings from cooked mashed pumpkin, beat with an electric mixer and you'll find that the strings will adhere to the beaters.

If any pumpkin blossoms come your way, eat them. Wash, drain well, dip in batter and fry in deep fat. You can use them as an unusual meat garnish or with butter, syrup or honey as a breakfast dish.

Any winter squash (Hubbard, acorn or butternut) can be used in place of pumpkin in any pumpkin recipe.

Peel and seed a pumpkin, cut it into chunks, then slice it thin, and dry it in a very low oven. When dried, the slices can be ground into flour in the blender. This is marvelous to use as part of the white or whole wheat flour in muffins, bread, etc.

You can make pumpkin soup the same way you make potato soup. It cooks even more quickly. (Add a little milk at the end, but don't boil the soup.)

Why not cook and serve pumpkins as a vegetable? They're as good as squash and can be served in the same way.

QUICHE

You don't have to make a traditional pastry crust for a quiche. Instead, remove the crusts from very thin slices of white bread and press the bread firmly into a well-buttered pie or quiche pan. Fill in any cracks with soft bread crumbs. Cover with your quiche filling and bake.

RADISHES

To make radish roses, cut the peel down from the top in thin narrow strips, almost but not quite to the bottom of the radish, then put the radishes in ice water and they'll open.

RAISINS

See also *Dried Fruits.*

There are 3 cups of raisins in 1 pound.

Raisins, as an ingredient in cakes or puddings, will usually benefit by plumping first: Pour a warmed liquid over them and simmer for about 5 minutes. The liquid can be water, wine, any liquor, or fruit juice. Drain, and use the raisin liquid, if possible, in place of an equal amount of liquid called for in the recipe.

If raisins seem too dry to use in breads, cakes or puddings, steam them in a sieve over boiling water or blanch them quickly with boiling water and drain.

Raisins are easier to chop if you freeze them first.

If raisins in an opened box are beginning to dry out, pour them into a jar and cover them with any fruit-flavored brandy or liqueur. They'll keep indefinitely and are wonderful to use in desserts or dessert sauces. Drained well, they'll give a lift to your homemade raisin bread, too.

RASPBERRIES: see BERRIES

RECIPES

Always assemble all the ingredients of a recipe before you get down to work. This saves time and footwork, and it's a good way to discover if you're out of something essential before you're halfway through your preparations.

REHEATING
When you're cooking a meat or vegetable dish that you intend to reheat before serving, remember it should be slightly underdone at the end of the first cooking.

RHUBARB
1 pound of diced rhubarb will give you about 3½ cups; 1 pound cooked, 2 cups.

To make a 9-inch pie, you will need 6 cups of diced rhubarb.

The young, early season rhubarb is the best to use when making pie. The more mature stalks are inclined to be tough and stringy in a pie. Use them for stewing.

RICE
See also *Puddings*

1 cup of uncooked rice weighs ½ pound.

1 cup of uncooked white rice gives about 3 cups cooked.

1 cup of uncooked brown rice gives about 2½ cups cooked.

Wild rice (really a grass, not a rice) triples in bulk when it's cooked.

Converted (precooked) rice has a texture all its own which some people like, but it won't cook down to a cream if you want to use it in puddings or desserts.

Try buying imported Italian rice. It has a waxy surface which keeps the long grains separated and gives them a very nice texture.

Since long grain rice is more expensive than short grain, it makes sense to buy the short grain if you're making croquettes or puddings.

You should rinse wild rice many times, then soak it for 15 minutes before cooking. It requires longer cooking than white or brown rice.

If kept well wrapped or in tightly closed jars, white rice can be stored safely for a couple of years.

If you want to substitute converted rice for regular raw white rice, use ⅔ cup of the converted for each ½ cup of the regular.

Cooking

Rice cooks better in low wide pots than in high narrow ones.

If your cover doesn't fit tightly enough, you can make a good seal by cutting a piece of waxed paper slightly larger than the pot. Then punch a very small hole in the center and put the waxed paper over the pot. Set the lid on this when cooking.

To get a light fluffy rice, wash the uncooked rice thoroughly in cold water—perhaps 3 times—to remove excess starch before cooking. Some cooks boil rice first in a large amount of water (like spaghetti) until it just begins to get tender. Then they drain, rinsing in hot water to remove the remnants of the floury covering, and continue cooking. Such rice is never gummy.

To make rice lighter and fluffier, add 1 teaspoon of lemon juice to the cooking water.

If you like a nut-flavored rice, brown the uncooked rice in hot butter or oil in a heavy skillet, stirring constantly until pale brown in color. Then cook according to the absorption method (see below).

Add a little white wine, Marsala or sherry to uncooked rice which has been stirred into some melted butter in a skillet, then add your liquid and cook. You'll get superb rice.

For richly flavored rice, use liquids other than water in cooking. Try bouillon, stock, vegetable juices or any other flavored liquids.

Keep some of your cooking liquid simmering beside the cooking rice in case you need to add more liquid to the pot. Adding cold liquid will make the rice soggy.

The absorption method is a very good way to cook rice. Place washed rice in a low pot with a tightly fitting cover. Add boiling liquid in the ratio of a little more than 2 parts liquid to 1 part rice. Cover at once and set the pot over a *very* low flame until all the liquid has been absorbed.

If you cook rice by the absorption method, you'll get a better seal if you moisten the rim of the pan and the rim of the cover, then press the cover on, turning slightly.

Never stir rice which you're cooking by the absorption method.

The less the grains move, the less chance the rice will become gummy.

Instead of placing a pot of rice on top of the stove, you can put it covered in a 350° oven for about 25 minutes, or until all the liquid has been absorbed.

To get a light, separate-grained rice, moisten raw rice in a little hot butter or oil and stir it over the fire until the rice whitens. Add some well-seasoned liquid of any kind until it is twice the height of the rice. Cover tightly and cook in a 350° oven for about 20 minutes or until the liquid has been absorbed.

When you cook rice for rice pudding, parboil it first (bring it to a boil in a lot of water and let stand for 5 minutes), then drain, rinse with cold water and cook as your pudding recipe directs. The result will be a much creamier pudding than most recipes give you.

If you must stir cooked rice, use a fork, with a fluffing motion.

For a dry rice, toss it lightly after it's cooked and put it uncovered in a warm oven for about 5 minutes.

If you pour hot rice into a cold dish, the part which touches the dish will develop a gummy texture. For this reason serve rice in a heated bowl or platter.

You can freeze leftover rice or store it in the refrigerator for several days. When you're ready to use it cover with boiling liquid and let stand a short time. If the rice is frozen, you may have to simmer it for 1 or 2 minutes. This won't give you first-class rice as far as texture goes, but you can certainly use it in many dishes.

Here's a good use for leftover rice: rinse with hot water, drain and dry well with a dishtowel to separate the grains, then add the rice to pancake, waffle or muffin batter.

Brown rice takes somewhat longer to cook and absorbs more water than white rice, although the cooking method is the same. Allow an extra 10 to 15 minutes if you're substituting brown for white.

Any rice dish (not just rice pudding) will have a greatly enhanced flavor if you add a little cinnamon at the beginning of cooking.

A way to test rice to see if it's done is to press a grain between your thumb and forefinger—you should feel no hard center.

Rice cooks in about 8 minutes in a pressure cooker. If you're cooking it for rice pudding, increase the cooking time by a couple of minutes and the rice will come out soft and creamy, the way it *should* be for rice pudding.

Water left over from cooking rice is good to use when making gravy. The gravy will need less thickening.

ROASTS

If you order a boned roast, ask your butcher to give you the bones separately so that you can use them in soups and gravies.

To prevent overdrying and to insure tenderness, buy a roast which weighs at least 4 pounds.

Always leave a coating of fat on a roast. If it doesn't have one, have your butcher lard it or cover it with fat yourself. It bastes and flavors the meat and prevents it from drying out.

A roast with the bone in takes less time to cook than a boned and rolled roast because the bone carries the heat to the inside of the meat faster.

A small roast requires more minutes per pound in cooking than a large one but less total cooking time.

A frozen roast that has been defrosted requires ⅓ less cooking time than one that is put into the oven frozen.

A 3- to 4-pound beef roast should be cooked in a 300° oven, 20 minutes to the pound, if you like it rare. For a well-done roast of the same size, cook it at 325° for 30 minutes per pound.

Too hot an oven will overbrown large meat roasts before they cook properly inside.

Always place a roast in a preheated oven. This helps seal in the juices quickly.

Whenever possible, turn a roast several times while roasting. Baste frequently using a long-handled spoon, adding liquid only as necessary and a little at a time or you'll steam the meat.

Try to develop the same feel test for roasting beef as for broiling (see *Broiling*). Once you've mastered this you won't need meat thermometers or clock-watching.

Remove a large roast of any kind from the oven when it's done and keep warm for about 15 minutes before carving. You'll lose less juice.

Don't add salt to a roast until shortly before serving. Salt coaxes the juices out of meats, and unless you're making soup or stock you'll want the juices inside the meat.

If you're making a pot roast, always sear the meat in a little fat at high heat, turning until all the sides are well browned. *Then* add your liquid. This seals in the juices and guarantees good flavor.

Try substituting beer for water or stock in a pot roast. About ½ can mixed with a little tomato paste or purée will give a magnificent gravy.

ROLLS

See also *Bread*.

If you're using a bread recipe to make rolls, use less flour than the recipe calls for. In fact, keep the dough as soft as you can while still being able to handle it. You'll get much better rolls.

If you have trouble pinching off the right amount of dough to make yeast rolls a uniform size, weigh each dab of dough instead of relying on size. After you've divided the dough into equal-weight pieces, roll them and place on a baking sheet. This is much easier and faster than going by appearances.

Poppy seeds will stay on rolls if you brush the tops with unbeaten egg white, sprinkle on the seeds and bake.

If you want a beautiful amber crust on rolls, dissolve 2 bouillon cubes in ¼ cup boiling water and brush the rolls with this liquid before putting them in the oven.

If you like a hard crust on rolls, put a pan of boiling water on the floor of the oven during baking or bake them longer at a slightly lower temperature.

Yeast rolls should be baked in a 400° oven for 15 to 25 minutes.

Remove rolls from the pans or baking sheets as soon as you take them out of the oven. Cool on a wire rack. If you don't do this the bottoms will get soggy.

You can reheat cold rolls by plunging them quickly into cold water, then heating them to crispness in a hot oven. Serve immediately. They're as good as new. (You can't do this more than once—they'll get hard.)

When you prepare rolls for a guest dinner, you can save time by baking them several days ahead of time and freezing. Heat in the oven just before serving. They'll be nearly as good as fresh-baked.

ROSEMARY: see HERBS AND SPICES

ROTISSERIE BROILING: see BROILING

ROUX
See also *Thickeners*.

A roux is a mixture of flour and fat cooked together slowly until the flour has lost its raw taste and has expanded so that it can combine with liquid. This is used as a thickener for sauces for fish, meat, vegetables and chicken.

A white roux usually uses butter (often clarified if the sauce is a delicate one) as the fat which is cooked with the flour. This is the thickener used for béchamel, velouté and other white sauces. It also thickens cream soups and soufflés.

To make a brown roux (a thickener for brown sauces and meat and game gravies) heat the flour in a dry pan over a medium flame, stirring constantly until it becomes the color of cinnamon. Add a little heated fat, stir well and then add some of the warmed liquid. Cook on a low flame, then add this to the sauce or gravy.

RUBBER HOUSEHOLD GLOVES
Rubber gloves for use in the kitchen should be as long as possible—halfway up to the elbow, at least. No wet wrists.

Always dust the inside of rubber gloves with talcum powder

before putting them on. If you don't, each time you remove them you'll stretch the rubber. And in time tiny, invisible holes will let the water in.

Cut a large square or round patch from a worn-out rubber glove to drape over the lid of a hard-to-open jar. It will give you a good grip.

Rubber gloves, quite apart from their usual use in dishwashing, are indispensable for handling hot vegetables like baked potatoes or any hard-to-handle foods such as artichokes or pineapples.

Use heavy rubber gloves for picking up and turning a whole hot chicken, roast or turkey.

RUTABAGA: see TURNIPS

SAFFRON: see HERBS AND SPICES

SALAD BOWLS

Because metal sometimes imparts a slightly unpleasant flavor to fruits and vegetables, avoid metal bowls when mixing or serving salads. China, glass, or prepared wooden bowls are best.

To season an unfinished wooden salad bowl, rub inside and outside with salad oil until the surfaces can absorb no more. Let stand overnight. Then wipe dry and use. Bowls prepared in this way can be washed like any other bowl, but not soaked. Give them an occasional oil rubbing a few times a year.

Particularly in hot weather, try chilling the large salad bowl and individual serving plates as well as the salad before bringing them to the table. Your guests will be in for a crisp surprise.

SALAD DRESSING

See also *Blender, Oil.*

A mixture of equal parts olive oil and vegetable oil makes a good oil to use in a salad dressing. This is an especially good mixture if you're using a cheaper grade of olive oil which is pungent in taste and smell.

Use very little, if any, salt in a salad dressing. It interferes with the taste of herbs. And an unsalted salad is a welcome relief when it's part of a highly flavored meal.

If a salad dressing isn't sharp enough for your taste, add a little prepared or powdered mustard or a touch of horseradish rather than more vinegar.

If you need a sour cream substitute for a salad dressing, add a little lemon juice or vinegar to sweet cream and let it stand at room temperature for 1 hour.

Use jellied consommé as a base for a low-calorie salad dressing. Add any herbs or flavorings you like, including a very small amount of oil and some vinegar. Keep it very cold and shake well before serving.

Moisten a salad with dressing—don't douse it. When you've added the dressing and tossed the salad, there should be very little liquid at the bottom of the salad bowl. If there's a pool of dressing, switch the salad to another dish.

The secret of a fine salad dressing—one that isn't unduly sharp—lies in the vinegar. Don't use distilled or cider vinegar. Even many of the red wine vinegars are a bit too caustic. Look for rice wine vinegar, a soft white vinegar that's just right for most cooking uses. You'll find it in Chinese or Japanese food sections of some supermarkets.

It's not always necessary to mix a dressing before you pour it on the salad. Be sure the greens are well drained and on the dry side, then pour on olive oil or salad oil and toss to coat the leaves. Pour off any excess. Then add a little vinegar (flavored or unflavored) or lemon juice. Most salads need little else.

Make an interesting low-calorie salad dressing by using tomato juice in place of the oil and vinegar. Add herbs of your choice, a little garlic or onion, and pepper. Mix in the blender.

A cooked salad dressing is less likely to curdle if you chill the vinegar and stir the beaten eggs into it before you put the pan on the heat. (It's best to make a cooked dressing in a double boiler, over hot water.)

Grate a little fresh ginger root into a salad dressing and shake well.

Use the juice from a jar of pickles (plus oil) to make a really tasty salad dressing.

The oil from canned fish, mixed with lemon juice and a little pepper, makes a wonderful salad dressing.

For a slightly out-of-the-ordinary salad dressing, try any of these: sour cream or yogurt mixtures; sweet and sour dressing (tomato and brown sugar); mustard sauce; horseradish sauce; soy sauce.

Add a small piece of boiled potato, very well mashed, to salad dressing. It helps to form an emulsion that holds the ingredients together.

You can use practically any salad dressing as a marinade for such foods as ripe olives, mushrooms, and most vegetables (if you blanch them first)—cauliflowerets, green or red sweet peppers, small onions, green beans, etc. Marinate in the dressing for a day or so in the refrigerator.

To make delicious hamburger, mix leftover salad dressing in it. Leftover salad dressing is also good mixed with flaked fish or chopped hard-cooked eggs for sandwiches.

SALADS AND SALAD GREENS
See also *Croutons, Lettuce.*

Try using any of the following greens and vegetables in salads: fresh green celery leaves, raw firm white sliced mushroom caps, raw baby spinach leaves (particularly the tender inside leaves from a clump of fresh spinach), nasturtium leaves and flowers (if you have them in your garden or window box, see *Nasturtium),* sweet white onion slices which have been blanched and chilled, raw leaves of young beets or raw lemon cut into very, very fine slivers.

Iceberg and Simpson lettuce, the most familiar crunchy kind, actually have more texture than flavor. Try Boston, Bibb or butterhead. These are tender, and have much more taste. Also try romaine lettuce (if the ribs seem too tough for salad, cut them out with two lengthwise slashes down each leaf and use only the leafy portion), chicory (curly endive), escarole and young endive shoots. Another marvelous tasting but hard to find salad green is arugula.

Don't wash greens before you refrigerate them unless you're going to use them the same day. They keep better cold when the leaves are dry.

To store watercress, wash it, then stand upright in a glass of cold water. Wrap it (and the glass) in a plastic bag and refrigerate. Fresh cress will keep for about 1 week this way.

To remove the leaves from a head of lettuce, core the solid part (the heart), then hold the head upside down under cold running water. The force of the water running into the heart cavity will push the leaves apart.

If you don't have a wire basket for swinging lettuce dry (this is best done outside) wrap the leaves in a towel and dry them gently but thoroughly—wet greens will thin any salad dressing. You can also wash greens and wrap them in an absorbent towel, then refrigerate for crisping.

Tear salad greens into pieces instead of cutting them with a knife (unless it's stainless steel) because cutting sometimes causes the edges of lettuce leaves to turn dark.

If you have to cut a green of any kind into very fine pieces, wash it, shake dry, then gently blot with a dishtowel. If possible, hang to dry for ½ hour. Then you can successfully cut it into tiny bits which won't stick to a knife or cutting board.

You can get a salad started well ahead of time by tossing the well-drained and dried greens with a small amount of oil so that every leaf is lightly coated. Then refrigerate in a large plastic bag. The greens will stay very crisp. (It's not the oil in salad dressing which makes salad leaves limp, it's the vinegar or lemon juice.)

Dip the edges of lettuce leaves in paprika for an interesting look to a salad or garnish.

You can serve any salad green as a hot vegetable. Prepare as you would spinach, including sautéing or top of stove braising. Lettuce can usually stand a little extra flavoring such as celery seed, pepper, a little garlic, etc.

Salad greens are marvelous in soups. Add them to vegetable and cream soups. Watercress is particularly delicious minced and cooked in cream soups or clear bouillon.

Many wilted greens can be brought back to life if you soak them for a short time in very cold water, remove any brown parts, roll the greens in a dish towel, and stow in the refrigerator.

Serve a salad with your dinner every day. It's a great meal extender and marvelous as a method of using leftovers. One head of lettuce, properly prepared, can last for several meals. Remove

4 or 5 leaves each day, wash, dry, and tear them up. Add bits of anything else you have: cut-up celery, raw or cooked vegetables, perhaps a piece of tomato, some minced onion. A little goes a long way in a salad and the cost is low.

Pare broccoli stems, and slice the crisp interiors to use as a salad vegetable.

Very young dandelion greens, those found growing in early spring, are lovely when added raw to a leafy salad.

Who says you must have lettuce in every salad? You can make wonderful salads with no greens at all. Some possibilities to serve alone with a dressing—or two or three combined with either a dressing or plain lemon or lime juice—are: sliced tomatoes sprinkled with any kind of fresh herbs; drained and rinsed sauerkraut; grated raw turnip; orange sections; celery cut in crosswise slices; sliced onions, tamed by soaking in sweetened water; carrot slices, lightly poached, then chilled.

Before adding an egg to a Caesar salad, cook it in boiling water for 1 minute. Then break it over the salad greens and add the flavored salad oil. Add the bread cubes last. Toss well with two spoons.

If you're out of croutons to strew over a tossed salad, use dry cereals such as Rice Chex, Wheat Chex, shredded wheat bits, etc.

SALMON
See also *Fish, Poaching.*

To tell if a piece of salmon steak is cooked, lift the round center bone with the point of a knife. If you can raise it with none of the flesh clinging, the fish is done.

The bones in canned salmon are edible and especially rich in calcium.

SALSIFY: see OYSTER PLANT

SALT
See also *Low Salt Diet*

There's no need to add salt to the water in which you cook vegetables. In fact, salt toughens many vegetables in the cooking—this is particularly true of beans.

It probably wouldn't hurt many of us to cut down on the amount of salt we take in daily. We ought to stop deadening our tongues to the taste of salt by overusing it. You'll be surprised how you can taste the natural salt in most foods. Beef, for example, is naturally high in salt. If you get used to preparing it with very little—or no—salt, you'll discover that a beef roast can be adequately salty in its natural state.

A tablespoon of salt added to a quart of water is sufficient to keep certain fruits and vegetables (peaches, pears, apples, potatoes, avocados, etc.) from discoloring after you've peeled them.

A strong solution of salt water will remove fishy odors from a pot.

Use slightly more salt in a dish which you intend to serve cold than you'd use in one to be served hot. Heat more thoroughly releases all kinds of flavorings, including salt.

Don't add much salt to any liquid which has to be cooked down to a more concentrated form, since the proportion of salt to liquid will increase as the mixture continues to cook.

If you find you've added too much salt to any liquid you're cooking, add some slices of raw potato and cook until the potato is parboiled (begins to become translucent). The quantity of potato depends on the degree of excess saltiness. Remove the potato with a slotted spoon or a small strainer. (Don't let the potato cook too long or it will break and become hard to remove.)

You can often disguise a slight excess of salt in a dish if you add a small amount of sugar. If sugar won't go with the dish, try a little vinegar, or a teaspoon each of vinegar and sugar. Or add a teaspoon of brown sugar or molasses. Bring the pot to a simmer.

Salt helps to extract the juices from meat, so when you make meat or chicken soups, add it to the liquid early. But don't use salt during the initial cooking of roasts, chops or steaks, or their juices will be coaxed out. Add the salt shortly before serving time.

Salt toughens eggs, so add it to egg dishes after they're cooked.

If an egg cracks while it's boiling, quickly lower the flame and pour a large quantity of salt on the crack. This will often serve to seal the egg and keep much of the white from leaking into the water.

If you spill a raw egg where it's difficult to pick up, cover with salt and let set. Then pick it up easily with damp paper towels.

Use plain, not iodized, salt when you make pickles. Iodized salt gives the brine an unpleasant taste. Use coarse salt if you can.

Coarse (pickling) salt is also best for sprinkling on rolls.

Heated coarse salt is often used for bedding oysters and clams on the half-shell. Salt holds heat well, thus keeps the food piping hot during serving and eating. It also stabilizes the shellfish in the dish.

If juices from a pie boil over onto the oven floor, sprinkle salt over the drippings to prevent them from smoking.

Tie some coarse salt in a square of gauze and use this to remove egg remnants from an omelet pan. You won't have to use other abrasives which require water. (If you need some liquid, use oil.)

You can "sweeten" the drain of your kitchen sink (eliminate odors) if you moisten the drain, then pour ¼ cup of salt down it. Let stand until you use the sink again.

SANDWICHES

See also *Peanut Butter.*

1 cup of sandwich filling will usually make about 6 sandwiches.

1 pint of mayonnaise will cover 50 slices of bread.

1 stick of softened butter will cover 25 slices of bread.

Cream the butter to be used for sandwiches. It spreads more evenly and goes farther.

Very fresh bread is hard to slice for sandwiches. Expose the bread to air for a few hours or even half a day.

If you want extra-thin bread for sandwiches, freeze a loaf of unsliced bread and you'll be able to cut the frozen loaf into slices as thin as you want.

If you want to cut sandwiches into fancy shapes, you'll get more sandwiches from a loaf if you buy it unsliced, then cut it lengthwise into thin slices.

If you're making rolled sandwiches or canapés, you need very fresh bread. Cut off the crusts before rolling.

When you make sandwiches which you have to store, leave the crusts on. This helps prevent drying. Cut them off when you're ready to serve.

Don't prepare sandwiches with moist fillings in advance. The bread always becomes soggy.

Many kinds of prepared sandwiches or canapés can be kept for 24 hours in the refrigerator if they're very well wrapped, either in 2 thicknesses of very slightly moist dishtowels or in a plastic bag.

Meat and cheese sandwiches (without mayonnaise or lettuce) can be frozen for future use. If you remove them from the freezer in the morning, they'll be ready to eat at lunchtime.

If a sandwich filling is loose or very moist, be sure to first spread the bread with a thin layer of cream cheese or butter or margarine.

Make a basic sandwich spread with 1 part butter and 2 parts cream cheese. To this you can add anything that tastes good to you.

There's no reason that vegetables or meats must monopolize sandwich fillings. Consider using fruits. They're great chopped and mixed with cream cheese or cottage cheese, or chopped fine and combined with mayonnaise. (Fruits are good with lots of other cheeses, too.)

Use two different kinds of bread when you make a sandwich: one slice of white and one of whole wheat, for instance. And you don't have to rely on ordinary bread. Use slices of banana bread or other fruit bread, nut bread, cheese bread, etc. They taste good, and they're nutritious.

Slice white bread very thin, remove the crusts, butter the *outsides* of two slices, put a layer of finely ground sandwich filling between the slices, and brown in the waffle iron. This is a treat to the eye and to the taste.

Sandwiches made with cream cheese don't store well, even when wrapped and refrigerated. The cheese tends to dry out and yellow. Eat such sandwiches the same day they're made.

Put ketchup, mayonnaise, or mustard between the slices of meats, cheese, etc., instead of on the bread. This eliminates sogginess, especially if you make the sandwiches ahead of time.

Put leftovers in the blender with a little mayonnaise and jazz up the mixture with some seasoning. In no time—a sandwich spread.

SAUCES AND GRAVIES
See also *Egg Yolks, Panada, Roux, Thickeners.*

Use very little salt in the first stages of making a sauce, since any sauce becomes more concentrated as it cooks.

Most leftover fish, meats or vegetables can be puréed and used as a sauce or sauce base.

If you have a little leftover soup, run it through a blender or a vegetable mill or push it through a sieve. Then use this purée as a sauce base for meats, chicken, vegetables or fish.

Throw a can of any kind of soup into the blender and you have a base for a cream soup or bisque or a sauce for vegetables, meat, chicken or fish. Add herbs and garlic and anything else you think will add to the flavor. Wine is an excellent diluting agent for this kind of base as long as you heat the sauce long enough for the alcohol to evaporate.

A court bouillon (seasoned water in which fish has been poached) makes an excellent base for any sauce to be served over fish. Simmer the liquid until it's the desired strength. Season further if you think it needs it, then add a roux.

If you want to give a browner color to a sauce for meat or vegetables, add a few drops of caramel (burnt sugar). It doesn't take much.

You can make a quite passable pasta sauce out of the spaghetti sauce you buy in jars. Add a teaspoon or so of oregano (rubbed between your palms into the heating sauce) and either some garlic powder or sliced garlic cloves. Simmer for 10 minutes. You might also want to add some pepper and a tablespoon of olive oil.

339

When you're stirring a sauce on the stove, remove the pan from the heat frequently and stir to ensure that the sauce doesn't begin to scorch.

To keep a skin from forming on a sauce containing flour, mashed potato, or other starch, top the surface of the sauce with a little cream or melted butter before you refrigerate it. When you're ready to serve, stir well and heat.

When you remove a sauce containing eggs from the heat, stir rapidly to cool it. Sauce continues to cook when first taken from the heat and you don't want the inner part of the sauce to heat to the point where the yolks may curdle.

When cooking a sauce containing egg yolks in a double boiler, keep the water in the bottom pot at no more than a simmer. If you let the sauce become too hot because of the temperature of the water, the eggs will separate from the rest of the sauce. Play it safe, and lift the top pot out of the water every 10 seconds or so, whisking well as you do this.

Pour leftover sauce or gravy into a container and freeze it. You can always serve it over something else another day. And if you wish, you can add something new to change its character entirely.

Break up a few ginger snaps and add enough hot meat gravy to dissolve the pieces thoroughly. Add to the rest of the gravy, stir well, heat, and serve. You have a rich, pungent sauce for any meat dish.

Keep some chicken or meat broth in your freezer. When you cook chicken or meat requiring a sauce made from their cooking juices, heat the frozen broth to make the sauce, and it will be ready at the same time the chicken or meat is. This does away with the necessity of having to keep the chicken or meat hot while you make the sauce. And the juices from the chicken or meat you've just cooked can be poured into a container and stored in the freezer for use the next time.

Leftover sauce or gravy from any dish is a good base for spaghetti sauce. In fact, you can make a sauce for any kind of pasta out of almost anything edible. Honest. All that's required is that it have a good flavor and be moderately thick. This should be a challenge—and a great economy—for the imaginative cook.

A test for thickness when you're making your own sauce for pasta is to dip a spoon in the cooking sauce; if it coats the spoon, the sauce is thick enough.

Most spaghetti and other pasta sauces are delicious served over hot cooked vegetables such as broccoli, green beans, and asparagus.

Pesto sauce is an uncooked—heated—spaghetti (or other pasta) sauce made principally from fresh basil, olive oil, grated cheese, and crushed nuts (pignoli, walnuts, or hazelnuts). You can make this during the fresh basil season. The oil will rise to the top and the sauce will stay very well in the refrigerator for weeks. There should be about ¾ inch of oil on top. For longer storage, freeze small quantities of pesto sauce. It keeps excellently, and you can enjoy it all winter. Use pesto on everything: vegetables, potatoes, fish, and poultry. (Incidentally, if you're making the pesto sauce to freeze, omit the grated cheese. Mix this in after the sauce has thawed.)

Recipes for chicken, fish, meat, or vegetable sauces can be doubled, or even tripled. Refrigerate or freeze whatever's left to serve another day. Many sauces can be served not only hot but cold: for aspics and salads.

If you have to carry a container of hot liquid (coffee, tea, gravy, sauce, etc.) for a little distance, stick a spoon in it and it will be less likely to slurp over the rim of the container.

Sauces Made With Starches, Milk, Cream, and Eggs
If you want a sauce thickened but clear, use cornstarch, arrowroot or potato starch.

When you make a basic white sauce, make a white roux (by cooking butter and flour together slowly for several minutes), then add whatever hot liquid you're using. Using a roux, like a panada, eliminates the raw floury taste which uncooked flour gives to a sauce.

To make a thickener for a brown sauce, see *Roux*.

When you make a sauce by adding hot liquid to a flour-fat base or roux add all the liquid at once and beat vigorously with a whisk.

Cheese will melt smoothly in a milk sauce if you add the cheese to the cold milk and heat it slowly.

Cream sauces are easily scorched if cooked over direct heat. Make them in a double boiler over hot, not boiling, water.

When making most sauces, consider using 1 or 2 egg yolks instead of flour as a thickener. Egg yolks make a sauce velvety.

Beat egg yolks with a little cold liquid before you slowly add hot liquid to them and you'll never have to worry about curdling.

You mustn't boil any sauce containing mustard or eggs or it will curdle. Cook such a sauce in a double boiler over hot, but not boiling, water.

If a sauce containing eggs begins to curdle because of excess heat, try pouring it at once into a cold dish and beat it hard with a whisk. If this doesn't work, quickly beat in about 2 tablespoons of boiling water or the same amount of heavy sweet cream.

If a hollandaise sauce curdles, beat in 2 tablespoons of heavy sweet cream or 1 whipped egg yolk.

Hollandaise sauce should be served warm, not hot. Keep it warm on the stove over lukewarm water.

If you know ahead of time that you'll have to keep a hollandaise sauce warm for a considerable period, beat 1 teaspoonful of cornstarch into the egg when you make the sauce. This will hold it very well until you need it.

If you're making any sauce ahead of time, remember that any thickened mixture containing starch or egg yolks will develop a skin on cooling. You can prevent this if you float a little warm milk, stock or melted butter on top of the sauce or stir the mixture from time to time with a wire whisk as it cools. Then place plastic wrap or waxed paper flat on the surface.

Keep a sauce hot by putting it over hot water, never over a direct flame, no matter how low.

A little sherry floated on the surface of a sauce for meat, chicken or fish will keep it fresh in the refrigerator for 1 week if it's covered.

If you beat a sauce containing starch well before you serve it, it will have a nice gloss.

Swirl a pat of butter into a sauce just before serving and it will have a professional look and taste.

There's nothing like a blender for making white sauce swiftly and easily. Pour all the ingredients into the blender, and mix thoroughly, then pour the mixture into a rinsed pan and heat slowly, stirring with a whisk until the sauce is thickened. No worry about lumps, melting butter, stirring the flour in, etc. It works like magic and gives you a velvety sauce.

White sauce lends itself to a great variety of preparations. Here are some possibilities:

Use part bacon fat or rendered chicken fat for some of the butter called for. Or use some oil.

Substitute a cup of rich meat stock for an equal amount of milk.

Use white wine in place of part of the milk.

After you've made the sauce, mix in ½ cup of finely grated cheese of any kind.

Add finely chopped parsley and the cooked white of an egg, finely minced. Sprinkle the hard-cooked yolk over the surface when you serve it.

Make a caper sauce by adding ½ cup of mayonnaise to your basic sauce and half of a small bottle of drained capers. Heat lightly, don't boil. Great with fish.

To make white sauce into brown sauce, heat the flour in a dry pan over medium heat, mixing constantly until it's browned. And use some dark meat stock as part of the liquid.

Use a rich brown stock—instead of milk—and add some curry powder. Now you have a curry sauce.

Substitute ½ cup of white wine for ½ cup of milk, and add a teaspoon or more of prepared mustard.

If a white sauce is to go over a fish dish, use some fish stock or clam juice as part of your liquid.

To make a white sauce more delicate, substitute 1 egg yolk for 1 tablespoon of flour (or 2 yolks for 2 tablespoons of flour). But once you add yolks, remember not to boil the sauce—keep it at a low simmer, stirring until it thickens.

SAUERKRAUT

Sauerkraut is a neglected dish in American kitchens. Serve it hot, tossed with a little bacon fat or chopped crisp bacon. If you're serving it cold, toss in some ice-cold cranberries, cut in halves. You can also add some caraway seeds to it, served hot or cold.

If sauerkraut, especially canned sauerkraut, is too sour, you might try draining and soaking it in a large pot of cold water for 10 minutes, stirring now and then. Drain again and use in hot or cold dishes.

Toss a glass or so of cold white wine into well-drained sauerkraut. Mix well and let stand for at least 10 minutes, then drain. Sauerkraut treated this way is especially delicious in a hot dish such as *choucroute garni.*

SAUSAGES

Some sausages contain cereal as well as pork. Read the labels so you'll know what you're buying and how much value you're getting for your money.

Since sausages consist largely or wholly of pork, you have to cook them well. They must never be served with the inside bright pink.

Sausages won't burst or shrivel if you put 3 tablespoons of cold water in the pan before covering it, then cook slowly until the water has evaporated. Continue cooking without the cover until they're well browned.

Another good way to cook sausages and have them hold their shape without bursting is to parboil them for a few minutes, drain, roll them in flour, and then sauté.

Sausages will be less greasy if they're parboiled before frying, or put in a *cold* frying pan with no added fat. If they're put in a cold pan to cook they also become more tender.

SAUTÉING

Sautéing is cooking food in a low-sided pan on top of the stove, using as little fat as possible. You don't, for example, fry eggs—you sauté them. And when you talk about fried potatoes and mean "home fries," you are really referring to sautéed potatoes. (French-fried potatoes are "fried.")

When you sauté, use the smallest pan the food will fit in. You'll use less fat, and the food will cook more quickly.

Lightly heat a sautéing pan before adding the oil or solid shortening. Once added, continue heating until the oil or shortening begins to bubble. This will do away with the possibility of the food sticking to the pan. (You must be sure the oil or shortening is hot—not smoking—before you add the food.)

Another reason for not putting food in fat until it has reached the bubbling point is that food placed in tepid or cool fat absorbs a great deal of it while cooking.

Food to be sautéed should be at room temperature. If it is cold, the heat of the hot fat will become temporarily lowered and the food will not only absorb more fat, but also the contrast in temperature will cause the moisture in the food to condense quickly on the surface and make the food stick to the pan.

If food to be sautéed is wet, pat it thoroughly dry first; otherwise it will become partially steamed—and you may also get painful spattering.

The same is true if you're dipping food into batter, crumbs, or flour before sautéing. It won't cook to crispness unless you pat it dry before you dip it. (It can be downright soggy.)

While you're sautéing, shake the pan often so the contents move a little. Do this until the food develops a protective coating that will keep it from sticking to the pan.

Don't crowd food in the pan when you're sautéing. This makes it steamy and limp. If you have more food to sauté than one pan will hold, use two pans side by side. In this way everything will be done at the same time.

Some sautéed food can stay in a hot oven for a short time to be kept warm. But it's never as crisp as when you first lift it from the pan.

Sauté in a heavy frying pan or any heavy pan with low sides. If you try to sauté anything in a high-sided pan the food will become steamed before it cooks in the fat because the liquid in the food can't evaporate and escape quickly.

If you use oil for sautéing, add a little solid fat too. This will make browning faster and easier.

If you want food well browned, add a tiny bit of sugar to the fat in which you sauté it.

Large or tough vegetables should be lightly parboiled before you sauté them.

Never cover food which is being sautéed. It will steam and become limp.

SCALLIONS
Scallions are sometimes called green onions.

The white parts of scallions are a pretty good substitute for shallots.

Cut the green parts of scallions into string-like lengths and use these to tie stuffed cabbage or stuffed lettuce into "envelopes" which will hold their shape while cooking.

To keep scallions garden fresh for more than a week, stand them—bulb side down—in a glass or jar of cold water. Change the water daily.

SCALLOPS
See also *Shellfish.*

Scallops are almost always sold by the pound out of their shells.

Bay scallops are small, cream-colored and tender. They're sweeter, have a more delicate flavor and are also more expensive than sea scallops, which are larger, often whiter and very slightly tougher—but still very good eating.

After you wash scallops, sprinkle with lemon juice and let them stand for 20 minutes before you prepare them.

Don't cook scallops for too long; heat toughens them quickly—as it does all shellfish. Cooked at a high heat, scallops are done in 3 minutes or less.

SCISSORS
Keep a pair of sharp scissors in the kitchen only for cutting foods. They're handier than a knife for cutting fresh dill, chives or raw bacon.

SCORCHED FOOD
If you've only slightly scorched food, you can eliminate most of the burned flavor by immediately setting the scorched pan in a little cold water before you turn the contents (without scraping) into another pan.

SERVING DISHES
Heat in a low oven all dishes and platters on which hot foods are to be served. This will keep fried or sautéed foods from becoming soggy and will also keep food from losing its heat during serving.

Although this isn't usually a problem, you can prevent serving plates from cracking when you place them in an oven to warm if you spread brown paper over the oven surface on which you set them or place them on a wooden cutting board, such as a cheese board.

SHAD ROE
Shad roe is usually broiled or sautéed. It should be browned gently on both sides. You can tell when it's done by making a small incision with a knife. If it's no longer pink, it's ready to serve.

SHALLOTS
A shallot is a small bulbous herb which is midway between onion and garlic in taste. It's wonderful for soups, stews and salads.

If you can't find shallots in your neighborhood, try substituting the white parts of scallions or small white onions. They're not the same, but better than nothing.

Provided they're kept dry and exposed to air, shallots will keep for months in the bottom vegetable bin of your refrigerator or on the back of a refrigerator shelf.

Like garlic, shallots shouldn't be cooked long enough to brown in hot butter or fat or they'll give a bitter taste to the food to which they're added.

Shallots, like garlic and onions, are easy to peel if you wet them first. If you're peeling a lot of them, stand them in hot water for about 10 minutes.

SHELLFISH

See also *Clams, Crab, Lobster, Mussels, Oysters, Scallops, Shrimp.*

All shellfish are delicate. Avoid overcooking or they become rubbery.

1 dozen shucked oysters, with their liquid, equal about 1 cup.

1 pound of scallops equals about 2 cups.

Hard-shell clams, oysters, scallops—any bivalves you want to open raw—are a cinch to open if first placed in the freezer for 45 minutes to an hour.

When you make a seafood chowder, add a tablespoon or more of soy sauce, and maybe ¼ cup of sherry to the regular recipe. Simmer another 20 minutes.

A chicken lobster is a 1-pound lobster.

A stuffed, broiled live lobster can get very dry during cooking. To preserve moistness, cover the stuffing with large lettuce leaves, then cook the lobster 8 to 10 inches from the broiler for about 25 minutes. Remove the lettuce leaves. If the stuffing needs more browning, let it remain under the broiler for another minute or two. (Use lettuce leaves for the same purpose when you bake a stuffed lobster.)

A lobster plunged into several quarts of boiling water should cook no longer than 15 minutes, usually. By this time the intestinal vein will have turned bright red—this means the lobster is done.

348

Lobsters can be steamed as well as boiled. In fact, they'll lose less juice and flavor if you put them, live, in about 3 inches of briskly boiling salted water. Cover at once. Allow 18 to 20 minutes from the time the water boils again. Save the liquid to use as a marvelous soup or fish stock base. Boil it down a bit and freeze it.

To make lobster stew, let the butter and lobster meat cool somewhat before you very slowly add the milk. Then put the pot on low heat and stir constantly until the mixture turns a rich salmon color.

The secret for the finest lobster stew is to let the cooked dish stand a minimum of 5 hours (in the refrigerator, of course) before reheating and serving. Some Maine lobster catchers maintain that stew is at its best the day after it's made.

To stuff a shrimp (the larger size is best for this), shell it, remove the intestinal vein down the back, then slit lengthwise about halfway through along the vein side. Stuff with any mixture you like. Shrimp prepared in this way are best baked.

SHERBET: see ICES

SHERRY: see WINES

SHOPPING LIST
Buy a roll of adding machine paper and hang it on your kitchen wall with a pencil attached. Write down items as you need them, then tear off this portion each time you go on a shopping trip—nothing left out, nothing forgotten.

SHORTENING: see FATS AND OILS

SHRIMP
When you buy shrimp, look for those whose shells closely fit the bodies. Shrinkage is usually a sign of staleness. Raw shrimp are usually grayish green, although some shrimp from particular waters are slightly pink. (All cooked shrimp are pink.)

349

In general, small shrimp are better flavored and have a more delicate texture than larger ones.

Shrimp are easier to peel and devein when raw than when they're cooked.

If you have no shrimp peeler, you can shell shrimp by removing the legs and tails first, then lifting off the entire covering. You can also use scissors if you insert the small blade under the shell at the head and cut down to the tail, then peel off the shell.

To remove the intestinal vein (the gray or black line along the back of the shrimp after the shell has been removed), try using just your hands or the blunt end of a toothpick under cold running water.

If you're using canned shrimp, soak them for 5 minutes in cold water before cooking. This helps to eliminate much of the canned flavor.

You can bring out the flavor of shrimp beautifully if you add salt, peppercorns, thyme, a bay leaf and some parsley to the cooking liquid. A little white wine never hurts either.

If you're going to boil shrimp, first wash the shells you've removed, then put them in the water and bring to a boil. Let boil for a few minutes, strain and use this liquid to cook the shrimp. You'll get much more flavor.

Here's how to get very tender cooked shrimp: put raw, shelled shrimp in a pot, pour seasoned, or just salted, boiling water over them, mix, cover and let stand for 5 minutes (with no flame). The shrimp will be delicious, not like the white leather which results from overcooking these lovely fragile things.

Shrimp which is simmered (unpeeled) in beer has an interesting flavor, a little like lobster.

If you're going to serve shrimp cold, remove them from the water when they're cooked and let them cool gradually at room temperature. Don't refrigerate until they've cooled, otherwise they'll become tough.

SLICING
See also *Knives*.

The best thing for quick slicing of vegetables is a French chef's knife. By keeping the tip of the knife on the table and pumping the knife up and down as you slowly push the vegetable forward under the knife, you get uniform slices in no time at all.

If you have no chef's knife, you can get uniform thickness when slicing onions, bread, cabbage, cucumbers or tomatoes, if you rotate the food slightly after you've cut each slice. This method will decrease the tendency to end up slicing on the diagonal.

SOLE
See also *Fish.*

What's called sole in the United States isn't the same as the true English or Dover sole, but it's a delicious fish in its own right. Lemon sole comes from Florida, gray sole from Canada. These both have softer flesh than English sole.

Flounder is sometimes called sole in fish markets. It's much like sole in taste and texture and is even more tender. The underside of a flounder has white meat while the upper side is slightly gray. This is why a tray of flounder fillets at the fish market contains fillets of two different colors. There's no detectable difference in taste.

If you want to cook a whole sole or flounder (it will have more flavor than if you have it filleted), skin it on one side first, then raise the fillet on this side carefully along the backbone and break the backbone in 2 or 3 places. Flatten the fillet in place again. You'll find it much easier to remove the backbone after you've cooked it.

SOUFFLÉS
Unless you're already a good hand at making soufflés, practice on your family before you make one for guests.

Diluted evaporated milk is excellent as a substitute for fresh milk in soufflés. It actually improves the flavor.

The chief secret in attaining a high soufflé is that you beat the egg whites *absolutely* stiff before folding them into the other ingredients.

Add ¼ teaspoon cream of tartar or ½ teaspoon white vinegar to every 4 egg whites to help them hold their shape after they've been stiffly beaten.

When you fold whipped egg whites into a soufflé, whip in one-fourth the whites first, then *very lightly* fold in the remainder in a gentle over and over motion, so that the air remains in the whipped whites after they've been combined with the soufflé batter.

If you're making a cheese soufflé, use a dry, not too fatty, cheese like natural Cheddar, dry Swiss or Parmesan.

If your cheese is too oily to use in a soufflé you can dry it out by wrapping it in a piece of paper toweling and letting it stand at room temperature for a couple of days. Change the toweling from time to time as it absorbs the oil.

Dust a well-greased soufflé mold thoroughly with fine bread crumbs before you fill it. With some soufflés you can use finely grated cheese instead of bread crumbs.

Butter the mold for a dessert soufflé, then sprinkle it with sugar before you pour in the batter. The soufflé will come neatly from the mold and will have a fine sweet crust.

If the soufflé you're making calls for a high-sided mold (called a charlotte mold) and you don't have one, try this: make a cuff of waxed paper and tie it around the outside of your mold. The paper should extend upward several inches above the rim of the dish. Butter the inside of the paper well, as well as the rest of the mold—including the top rim. Then pour in the batter. When the soufflé rises during baking, the paper will keep it in shape.

If you're doubling a soufflé recipe remember, small soufflés usually come out better than large ones because they cook more thoroughly. Try making a few small ones rather than one large. A soufflé won't rise properly if the baking dish is too wide.

You can keep a soufflé from spilling over in the oven if you rub your finger around the top of the mold about ½ inch deep between the mold and the batter after you've poured the batter in.

If you put it where it will be protected from drafts, a soufflé ready for the oven will remain high and full as long as 45 minutes before you bake it.

You'll have better luck with a soufflé if you spoon the batter, instead of pouring it, from the mixing bowl into the baking dish. Be sure the dish has straight sides.

A soufflé will rise higher in the baking dish if you don't grease the side of the pan. (But do grease the bottom.)

Cooking

If you put a soufflé in the oven without an outer pan of hot water it will be light and crispy.

If you like a soft soufflé, put the filled mold in an outer pan of hot water, then set both carefully in the oven.

Sweet dessert soufflés made in a 3-cup mold usually bake in about 20 minutes. Those made in an 8-cup mold are done in about 45 minutes.

A chocolate soufflé usually takes about 10 minutes longer to bake than a regular dessert soufflé.

If you like a soufflé which has a soft center, cook it in a slightly hotter oven and for a shorter time than the recipe calls for. Remove it from the oven as soon as the top has browned.

If you like a firm soufflé, wait until the top has browned nicely, and then bake it 5 minutes more.

Since a soufflé always falls within a few minutes after you've removed it from the oven, time the baking so that you can serve it right away.

Dessert soufflés don't generally need a sauce—they have a naturally creamy center.

SOUPS

Note: Almost all the hints, suggestions and tips you'll find under *Stock* also apply to soups.

See *also Blenders, Bouillabaisse, Bouillon, Consommé, Fish Stock, Garnishes, Thickeners.*

Save all the juices from cooked or canned vegetables and mushrooms to use in soups. (They can be frozen until you're ready to use them.)

Never throw out bones from steak, roasts or chops or the bones and skin from chicken or other fowl carcasses until you've extracted all the good from them in the form of a soup or stock. If you don't feel like making soup out of the bones on hand, wrap well and put them in the freezer until you do feel like making soup.

Leg and knuckle bones are excellent for soup. Have your butcher cut or saw them into medium-sized pieces. You'll get more out of them.

Roast soup bones before you put them in liquid for soup. Salt them slightly and put in a pan in a 375° oven until they're brown and aromatic. Then put them in your soup liquid. This will vastly improve both the color and flavor of your soup.

Always put soup bones and meat in cold salted water to cook. This extracts the utmost flavor.

Any meat or vegetables first browned in a hot oven will give a soup or stock richer flavor and color.

Vegetables added to soup will make a much tastier dish if you sauté them first, preferably in a little butter.

You should add vegetables to soups toward the end of cooking so that they won't become mushy. (If you do leave them in, as in a permanent soup pot—pot au feu—they will disintegrate and contribute to the wonderful thickened consistency of these soups.)

If you want to add green color to a soup, pound some raw spinach leaves in a mortar and press the liquid through a fine sieve or tie the pounded leaves in cheesecloth and wring the juice into the soup 5 minutes before serving.

There's an enormous diversity of what you can put into soup, including leftover meats and vegetables. No matter how forlorn leftovers look in those little dishes on your refrigerator shelf, they're deliriously happy in the soup pot.

Mix a little flour with a little cold water to form a thin, smooth paste, then mix it into puréed soup. It will act as a binder and will keep the puréed vegetables from separating when the soup is standing.

Don't discard tough broccoli stems or the tougher parts of asparagus or hearts of cabbage. Cook them and purée in the blender. They can be a flavorful and nutritious basis for cream soup.

A little honey in tomato-based soup counteracts the acidity and improves the flavor.

Chop uncooked vegetables (onions, carrots, celery, garlic, green or red peppers, mushrooms, etc.), let them dry out thoroughly, then pulverize them in the blender. Bottle for use in soups and gravies. Or simmer them in water or stock for 10 minutes for a delicious, and practically instant, soup.

Add a tablespoon or more of soy sauce, and perhaps ¼ cup of sherry, to fish or seafood chowders containing tomatoes. Simmer 10 minutes before serving.

You can thicken soup by simmering peeled potatoes in it until they're soft. Then mash them in the liquid. Use a fork or potato masher, or dump the potatoes in the blender with some of the soup.

Another way to thicken soup is to add ¾ cup of finely grated raw potato to every quart of soup. Simmer for 15 minutes after you've added the potato.

Still another method of thickening soup is to pour some soup liquid into the blender, add a couple of tablespoons of flour and a teaspoon of butter or oil. Blend until everything is well mixed. Pour back into the soup pot and heat slowly, stirring, until the soup thickens. You can use cornstarch instead of flour to get a translucent soup, much in the style of Chinese soups.

Some cooks have a prejudice against using flour or cornstarch as a soup thickener. This is unreasonable. Starch is starch, whether its source is wheat, potato, rice, corn, or beans. The important thing is to *cook* the starch. Properly cooked, it need never taste floury. Only raw flour or cornstarch will.

Rice, lentils, beans, or peas of any variety will thicken soup. Yellow split peas are especially good for this. They'll cook to a

355

nice porridge consistency if you simmer them, covered, in liquid for an hour or so (much less if you soak them overnight first). You don't need to put them in the blender unless you want ultrasmooth soup.

Noodles, macaroni, and spaghetti broken into bits are marvelous soup thickeners.

To thicken soups put some cooked vegetables in the blender or through a sieve, then return the purée to the soup. Any cooked puréed, vegetable will thicken soup. Even cooked onion, when puréed, will thicken soup somewhat.

You can also deliciously thicken a soup by mixing ¼ cup of cornstarch with 3 tablespoons of sherry and adding some or all of this to your soup, depending on the desired amount of thickness and the total amount of soup.

Almost any good dry wine—in small quantities—will help a soup, especially a little sherry in consommé or some burgundy in borscht.

The most important part of an onion soup is the base. Never try to make a French onion soup without a good rich stock.

You can give a remarkable touch to clear chicken broth if you add a can or bottle of clam juice to the soup kettle.

Here's a way to use up the tail end of a pot of soup and at the same time make a new soup: Purée the last of the soup in the blender, add a little fresh or evaporated milk, spice it up a bit— nutmeg is good—heat, and serve.

The final step in soup-making has to do with seasonings. Use the following in various combinations (your choice will depend on the overall nature of the soup): salt, pepper, Worcestershire or Tabasco sauce, minced or powdered garlic, curry powder, chili powder, fresh or dried herbs, a hint of nutmeg, a bit of powdered mustard, a little tomato paste, ½ cup of wine, leftover gravy— the list is endless.

Cooking and Straining

The wider the pot you cook soup or stock in the faster the cooking liquid will evaporate. A heavy, deep, narrow pot with a heavy cover is best. If you use a wide pot, remember to check the water level now and then during cooking.

To cook soup, cover the ingredients with cold water and cook (never boil) for hours if possible, at low heat, skimming off any scum which rises to the top. (A small tea strainer is a good skimmer.) Because soup should simmer a long time, start it early in the day or, better yet, the day before.

Try keeping a pot of soup going on the stove, especially in cold weather. Boil it up once a day and simmer it covered for 10 minutes, adding more water or other liquids as necessary. Throw in leftovers from vegetable and meat dishes. This is enormously nutritious, and after the initial potful, costs very little to maintain. The flavor improves as the days pass. Throw a can of beans or other vegetables or a handful of macaroni or other pasta into the permanent soup pot from time to time.

If you have to strain a soup which contains large and small pieces, use two strainers at once, a coarse one set into a fine one. You'll avoid clogging the fine strainer with large pieces of food.

The best way to remove fat from a soup is to refrigerate the soup and remove the fat when it rises to the top and hardens.

If soup is sticking to the bottom of the pot while it's cooking, immediately remove the pot from the heat and let it cool. Only then stir with a wooden spoon, dislodging what's stuck at the bottom and mix well. Don't do this while the pot is hot because the solids won't come free. This hint isn't for soup that has *burned*. If, however, it has burned, pour the soup out of the pot into another pot without disturbing the burned portion at the bottom. You don't want burned solids in your soup.

If you have a soup pot going, use it as an adjunct to your other cooking. Instead of cooking whole carrots or potatoes in water to serve as a vegetable, toss them into the soup pot and simmer until done. Remove with a slotted spoon, season, and serve. They'll be a lot more flavorful than if you cooked them in water, and the soup pot will be enriched.

Cream Soup

Chicken stock or chicken consommé makes the best base for a cream soup.

You can give a richer consistency to a cream soup if you use undiluted evaporated milk as part of the liquid.

When you make a cream of tomato soup or any cream soup which is slightly acid, you can prevent curdling if you add the tomato or acidic ingredient to the milk rather than the other way around. Adding some cream or a little flour to the milk first will also prevent curdling.

If you can't serve a cream soup right away, keep it hot in the top of a double boiler. It will definitely scorch if put over a direct flame, no matter how low.

Cold (Jellied) Soup

A soup will jell naturally upon chilling if it has been made with bones (the best bones to use for this are cracked veal knuckles and chicken feet). All you have to do after the seasoning and cooking is strain and refrigerate. Remove the fat after it has congealed.

To jell a soup which hasn't been made with bones, add 1 tablespoon of unflavored gelatin for each 2 cups of liquid, then boil. (Soften the gelatin in a small amount of cold liquid first.)

A cold soup should always be thoroughly chilled—prepare and refrigerate it the day before if you can.

When serving a cold soup, especially a jellied one, chill the cups you're going to serve it in. The soup will remain cold longer and the gelatin won't begin to liquefy.

Any soup to be served cold must have every trace of fat removed from it. Congealed fat in a chilled soup is unpleasant in every way.

You can freeze broth in ice cube trays and store the cubes in plastic bags to use for seasoning vegetables.

SOUR CREAM

See also *Cream.*

To use yogurt to make your own sour cream—without the fillers so often found in commercial sour cream—mix a heaping tablespoon of yogurt into ½ pint of pure heavy cream (not "ultra-pasteurized"—this contains fillers). Be sure the yogurt contains active culture and is not pasteurized. Let the mixture stand a day or two in a warm place, lightly covered. When the cream is as sour as you want, refrigerate it.

Any cooked dish which contains sour cream will curdle if you cook it at too high a temperature. Keep the flame low when you're heating it. To discourage curdling, add a small amount of flour to the cream and mix it well with a whisk while heating.

To make a hot sour cream sauce, add the sour cream at the end, after the sauce is cooked.

Here are two fairly good substitutes for sour cream: 2 cups of buttermilk plus 3 tablespoons of melted shortening, whipped well, will give you the equivalent of 2 cups of sour cream; 1 cup of cold evaporated milk plus 1 tablespoon of clear white vinegar, whipped well, will make a good substitute for cooking although it will be a little thinner than sour cream. (To thicken chill the evaporated milk until ice crystals form before whipping.)

If you want to make a sour cream dressing but have no sour cream, add a little lemon juice or soft white vinegar to sweet cream or evaporated milk and beat well. Sweet cream will make a richer dressing than evaporated milk.

SPAGHETTI: see PASTA

SPICES: see HERBS AND SPICES

SPINACH
1 pound of fresh spinach, cooked, will serve 2 people.

1½ pounds of spinach, cooked, drained, and chopped, will give you 1 cup.

If fresh spinach begins to wilt, sauté it lightly with a very little bit of bacon fat and serve it hot. Or chill the spinach after you've sautéed it, add croutons, and serve as a salad.

If you buy spinach in plastic bags, remove the spinach as soon as you get it home and expose it to the air, then refrigerate it uncovered. Spinach spoils quickly if left in the bag.

Don't cook spinach in iron or aluminum pots. These give it a metallic taste (and don't serve it in a silver serving dish for the same reason).

You don't have to add extra water when you cook spinach—the water adhering to the washed leaves is enough.

Spinach cooks quickly. Cover and cook for about 6 minutes, but lift the cover a few times during cooking so it will stay a nice green.

You can cook spinach in a large quantity of boiling salted water if you cook it uncovered less than 5 minutes until barely tender, pour it all through a colander, splash with cold water and then squeeze out as much water as possible. Chop and serve any way you like.

Try adding a little fresh mint to spinach the next time you cook it.

Hard-boil some egg yolks and push them through a sieve with a wooden spoon over a dish of creamed spinach just before serving.

Add a little grated nutmeg to creamed spinach.

Tender baby leaves of raw spinach make a delicate salad green served alone or mixed with other greens.

SPONGE CAKE: see CAKE

SPOONS
The most useful spoons in the kitchen are a set of long-handled wooden ones. They come in 4 or more bowl-sizes and are much better than metal for all kinds of stirring and mixing where a whisk will not do—in pots on the stove, thick cake batters. . . . They have innumerable uses!

Keep a set of plastic measuring spoons on a ring in each of your flour, sugar and salt canisters. After you've used them, replace them in the canister until next time. No need to wash.

SQUASH

See also *Pumpkin, Zucchini.*

There are two main types of squash. The hard-fleshed winter squash such as butternut, acorn and Hubbard, of which only the flesh is generally eaten, are pumpkin-like in texture and color and can be served baked, boiled, mashed or in pies or cakes. The best winter squash is heavy for its size. Heft them before buying. The second type of squash is soft-skinned and soft-fleshed, like the yellow crook-necked summer squash and the green zucchini where the entire squash is eaten—seeds and skins included— mashed, sautéed, halved, stuffed or baked. Zucchini and yellow squash should have a shiny surface—a sign of freshness—and are at their best when they're 6 to 8 inches long. Larger squash are inclined to be dry and pithy inside. Again choose squash that are heavy for their size.

Winter squash has an affinity for ginger. Butternut squash is delicious served peeled, boiled and mashed with 1 heaping table-spoon of ginger marmalade mixed well into it (no butter needed). You can also try scrubbing acorn squash, cutting in half length-wise, seeding, then putting the halves in the oven with a teaspoon of ginger marmalade in the center of each and baking until the flesh is soft.

You can use pumpkin in place of squash in any recipe which calls for winter squash.

Try using winter squash as a substitute for carrots in carrot cake.

Acorn squash should have a dark-green rind—a sign of good quality.

Winter squash (acorn, butternut, Hubbard, etc.) are often hard to cut when raw. A small serrated meat saw does a better job than a knife and is safer because it's less likely to slip.

Winter varieties of squash are easily seeded and destringed at the same time if you use a serrated grapefruit spoon. An ice-cream scoop is also handy for removing the seeds quickly and neatly.

Use the flesh of any winter squash in place of pumpkin in a pie.

A little grated raw winter squash or pumpkin is a fine extender for meat loaf or hamburger.

You can pickle any type of winter squash or pumpkin just as you do watermelon rind. But in the case of squash and pumpkin, pare off the hard outer shell and pickle the flesh, in chunks. Use the same spices and technique as for watermelon rind, and heat the pieces in the pickling liquid until they become translucent.

STAINS

Salt combined with a little lemon juice or vinegar will usually remove burn stains from the outside of enamel-covered pots.

Stains can often be removed from a teapot spout if you pack the spout with salt, let stand overnight, and in the morning heat the teapot slightly and then pour boiling water through the spout. Or use a pipe cleaner, or two of them twisted together, to clean tannin stains and other deposits that accumulate in the spout of a teapot.

Yellow or gray stains in cups often are caused by the minerals in water, which, when combined with tea and coffee, leave deposits. You can get rid of the deposits by putting a teaspoon of baking soda in each cup, fill with very hot water, and let stand an hour or so. Wash well afterward.

Many mineral and tannin stains can be removed from the insides of cups by pouring in some salt, then rubbing well with your fingers moistened with water or vinegar.

STARCHES: see THICKENERS

STEAK
See *Meats*.

See *Beef Cuts* for the kinds, locations and properties of steaks and other cuts of beef.

You can tenderize tough steak by pounding it all over with the edge of a small metal pie plate or pot lid. (You can also pound flour into steak this way for braising.)

The secret of excellent Swiss steak is to pound as much well-seasoned flour into it as it will take. Wait 20 minutes, then pound more in. Repeat if possible.

Don't trim too much fat from a steak before broiling; the fat adds to the flavor and prevents drying (but pour off the melted fat from the broiler pan from time to time to prevent its catching fire).

If your steak has a border of fat, cut across the fat in several places and the steak will lie flat in the pan.

Put about ¾ cup of water in the bottom of your broiling pan when you broil steak. This lessens the possibility of the fat catching fire, and will also give you the base for a marvelous gravy.

You can learn to time a broiling steak properly and have it done to your taste if you always buy the same thickness. Make a note of the length of time you have to broil it to reach the degree of doneness you like. After an initial trial or two you won't ever over- or undercook a steak. (Of course you must always have the steak the same distance from the broiler flame.)

Thick cuts of meat should be placed farther from the flame than thin cuts, otherwise the center may still be raw when the outside is properly browned. A very thick steak (2½ to 3 inches) may be broiled until well browned on both sides and then transferred to the oven for further cooking.

To keep the juices from escaping when you turn a steak in the broiler or in a pan, use tongs instead of a fork.

If you're going to pan-broil a steak be sure it's thoroughly dry before you put it in the pan, otherwise it will never brown properly.

To pan-broil steak, preheat a heavy skillet which you've lightly but thoroughly wiped with fat or oil. Don't use any more fat. Sprinkle the pan generously with salt and pepper (optional) and put the steak in when the salt begins to turn dark.

Pan-broil a 1-inch steak at *very* high heat for 1 minute to sear and brown it well, then turn and do the same to the other side. Lower the heat and cook for 2 minutes more on each side. This will give you a rare steak.

A small steak to be pan-broiled can go straight from the freezer to the pan (though it won't brown as nicely as steak at room temperature). Use a low flame to start, and when both sides have been reasonably browned, cover the steak and finish cooking. With proper timing, a small frozen steak will remain pleasingly rare inside.

STEW

See also *Meats.*

If you want the gravy in a stew to have a lovely amber color, and the meat to taste twice as good, sprinkle a little sugar over the pieces of meat after the initial browning in the fat. (Use very little sugar.) Toss well over moderate heat for a few minutes until the sugar has caramelized.

Meat stew cooks even better in the oven (at about 325° F) than on top of the stove. The pot should have a heavy cover. Check now and then to see if a little liquid is needed.

Add a tablespoon of caraway seeds to the liquid of a meat stew, regardless of what kind of meat you use. Cook for at least 20 minutes after that.

The best stews are made from a combination of meats such as beef, pork, veal or lamb. The flavors blend magnificently and the gravy is as good as you can imagine. Don't worry about over-cooking, everything comes out fine.

When you brown pieces of meat for a stew, use a lowsided pan (a skillet is best) and put only a few pieces of meat in the browning pan at one time so that whatever steam forms in the pan can quickly escape before it steams the meat, spoiling its color and flavor.

For a superlative stew, brown scads of sliced garlic—6, 8 or even 10 cloves—with a little onion in some fat. Add this to your stew and cook for as long as you cook the stew. Your stew will taste delicious but not garlicky!

Vegetables in a stew taste better if you sauté them lightly in butter before adding them to the stew pot.

Since vegetables have different cooking times, combine them in a stew in the proper order so that the softer ones haven't cooked to mushiness by the time the tougher ones or the meats are done.

Don't add vegetables to a stew if you intend to freeze it. They usually become mushy when thawed. Make the stew omitting the vegetables and serve vegetables as a side dish, or add fresh vegetables to the stew after you've defrosted it and cook everything together just until the vegetables are done.

Don't put too much liquid in the stew pot, only enough to cover the contents. To avoid having it boil away too soon, cut a sheet of waxed paper a little larger than the size of the pot, make a tiny hole in the center, cover the pot with this and then cover with the pot lid. Cook over a slow flame.

Use beer in place of water or stock to make an excellent slow-cooking beef stew. This is how a *carbonnade* (Belgian beef stew) is made.

Always cook a stew at a gentle simmer, otherwise the meat is likely to fall apart.

All stews and thick soups taste better the day after they're made.

STOCK
See also *Fish Stock, Glaze, Soups.*

Keep a large container with a tight cover in your freezer and throw into it meat and chicken trimmings (including feet, gizzards, fat, skin, bones and whole carcasses), canned vegetable juices, vegetable parings and leavings, leftover gravies and more! When the container is full throw the contents into a heavy pot, add water and seasonings if necessary and cook the whole thing for a couple of hours. Strain, refrigerate, remove the fat, and you have a first-rate stock. (You'll discover you've been throwing away rubies.)

Don't use cabbage, cauliflower or turnips in stock—they give it too strong a flavor; and don't use starchy vegetables like potatoes, corn or rice in stock—they cloud it.

Save the water in which you soak dried mushrooms to make a fine stock for gravy bases and sauces.

When you're making meat stock from scratch, remember that the flesh of mature or old animals has more flavor than that of young ones.

Put beef bones cut into small pieces (the butcher will do this for you) in a shallow pan in a 375° oven, salt them if you like and roast until they're dark brown, stirring occasionally. Use these bones for your stock pot.

Always cook meats for stock in cold salted water. This extracts the utmost flavor from them.

You can make an excellent inexpensive chicken stock from chicken necks and backs simmered in water with any flavorings you like for a couple of hours. Strain, chill and remove the fat, then use or freeze for future use. You can also cook these in a pressure cooker.

Fish stock doesn't have to be made only from fish. Slip in a veal, a pork or even a beef bone when you begin to cook. The stock will be really lush.

Use veal bones, chicken skin and bones and unroasted vegetables to get a light-colored stock.

One way to give a brown color to a stock is to add a few drops of caramel. See *Caramel*.

Another way to give stock a rich brown color is to add a little tomato paste or a grilled sliced tomato. Boil it all well, then strain.

If you need a rich meat or chicken stock and don't have the time or the ingredients to make one, simmer some canned bouillon or canned chicken broth with carrots, celery, onions, herbs and a little wine for half an hour, then strain and use. This will be even better if you first brown the vegetables in a little butter.

To clarify 1 quart of stock, stir into it 1 egg white which has been beaten with 2 teaspoons of water plus the eggshell broken into small pieces. Boil for about 2 minutes, then strain the stock through several thicknesses of cheesecloth or a fine handkerchief draped over a large strainer.

To get a clear meat and vegetable stock with a minimum of straining, bring the stock to a boil, remove the scum which rises to the top and stir to bring up the rest of the scum, then remove this. When there is no more scum, cover the pot and simmer for hours without stirring. At the end of cooking turn off the flame and ladle out the clear soup carefully. Remove the meat, bones and vegetables with a slotted spoon, then *without stirring* add 1 cup of cold water to the hot liquid left in the pot. Let stand for about 10 minutes. The upper part of the liquid will be clear. Ladle this out.

Don't disturb the cake of fat which forms on meat stock after you've strained it boiling hot into a container and refrigerated it. It will preserve the stock in the refrigerator for 2 or 3 weeks.

You can boil stock down so that it will take up very little space in your refrigerator. When you're ready to use it, add enough water to make it the strength you want.

You can store stock in the refrigerator indefinitely if you take it out every 3 days and boil it briskly for 10 minutes, adding a little water or other liquid to replace what evaporates during boiling. Cover, cool and replace in the refrigerator.

Bring refrigerated stock to boiling point before you use it and it will have a good freshly made flavor.

Whenever a meat or chicken recipe calls for added water, add stock instead. The final dish will be much richer.

The liquid part of soup gives the fundamental goodness to the finished dish. Once you've got a thick and fragrant liquid, you can add almost anything to make first-class soup.

When you're using bones, chicken, or meat for soup stock, cut the pieces fairly small and cook them in cold water with a little salt added. This pulls out the flavor into the stock.

Never throw out the juices in which you cook vegetables (or the juices from canned vegetables, either). Save them in a closed jar in the refrigerator, or freeze them. Use for cooking vegetables. Soon this liquid will be so full-flavored that you can use it as the base of a soup.

It's not necessary to peel the vegetables that go into soup stock. Scrub well with a brush and water, then cut them up into the stock pot. (Vegetables with a wax coating are not generally used in stock, but if you use them, peel first.)

A namby-pamby stock will never make a decent soup. Stock is rarely too rich. If it is, all you have to do is dilute it.

Don't put too much water in your stock pot. You have to cook it too long to get rid of the excess liquid. If you think you have too much water, cook the stock without a cover so the excess water will evaporate and the flavors will be more concentrated.

To flavor stock of any kind, use a little wine or a bit of honey.

If you use canned chicken broth or beef broth as stock for soups or gravies, refrigerate the cans for a day before you open them. The fats will congeal and can be removed by pouring the broth through a fine strainer.

To make most stocks, cover the bones, meat, or chicken with liquid to a height of 1 inch above the surface of the solids.

You can make stock in a pressure cooker in about a third of the time it takes to cook it in a regular pot. Be sure *not* to fill the pot higher than the cooker directions tell you.

STORAGE TIPS

See also *Labels, Vegetables.*

There's nothing like a glass jar with a tight-fitting lid for storage. It keeps the insides fresh and prevents contamination of other foods. Keep spare jars and lids of all sizes. Attach a strip of white plastic tape across the top of each cover and pencil on this what each jar contains. The writing will erase easily and the tapes will survive many washings.

It's wise to store the following foods in the freezer to keep them from deteriorating: all whole grain flours, shelled nuts, cans or bags of coffee, jars of instant coffee, brown rice, cornmeal. If there's no room in the freezer for them, at least refrigerate them. Many contain natural oils that become rancid at room temperature if they stand for long. Yeast keeps longer in your freezer, too.

Try to store refrigerated (and other) foods in jars instead of plastic bags. Plastic releases gases, and it's possible these may affect the foods stored in them.

Anything stored in the refrigerator should be tightly covered not only to keep odors in, but also to keep moist foods from becoming dry. Frost-free refrigerators, especially, pull moisture out of the air and out of uncovered dishes.

If you have to store meat in the refrigerator a bit longer than you usually would, dust all the surfaces well with ground white or black pepper. Wipe it off with a damp cloth when you're ready to prepare the meat.

A sensible way to store granulated sugar is to pour it through a funnel into clean, dry, quart (or larger) bottles, such as pop bottles, with screw caps. When you need to measure out sugar or fill your sugar bowl, pour straight into the bowl or measuring cup. And *before* you pour, give the bottle a few hefty shakes to break up any small lumps. Sugar stored in a dry, narrow-necked bottle pours out like a dream, is easy to measure, and never cakes into a hard lump.

Some peanut butter comes in large jars that are a perfect shape to use for storage. They're wider at the top than at the bottom. Stored foods slide out easily from jars of this shape.

Quart milk containers are great for freezer storage. Wash and dry them thoroughly, and fill with either solids or liquids. Seal them well, label, and store. Once frozen, they can be stacked neatly in the freezer.

Wash, rinse, and save a few of the waxed containers milk comes in. They're excellent for stacking cookies that you have to carry somewhere. They're also handy for pouring waste fats in. You'll find your own uses for them.

Use the plastic tops of containers to set under jars and bottles kept in the refrigerator. They help keep the refrigerator shelves clean. Use for cupboard storage shelves, also. Set them under bottles of oil, syrup, or anything that tends to drip after you've used it.

If you nail the covers of screw-top jars to the undersides of cupboard shelves, you can fill the jars with herbs, spices, dried legumes, noodles, etc., and screw them into their tops. A handy, convenient place for storage.

Pasta, well wrapped and stored in a cool, dry place, will keep for about 1 year (6 months for pasta containing eggs).

The extra-large jars of instant coffee make excellent storage jars for spaghetti and macaroni. They're narrow and high and the contents are immediately visible. Break the strands in half and stuff them in. One of these tall jars holds an 8-ounce package of spaghetti, keeping it dry and safe.

The trays inside your kitchen drawers will stay in place and not slide back every time the drawers are opened if you stuff something behind the trays. The cardboard cylinders inside the rolls of paper towels or toilet paper are very good for this.

Slip the cardboard cylinder that's inside a roll of toilet paper over the spout of a delicate teapot when you're not using it. The cylinder will help keep the spout from getting chipped or broken.

S-hooks are handy items to hang things on in the kitchen. Slip them over a cupboard door or handle, or anywhere else they will fit.

Most foods, especially starches like bread and cracker crumbs, flour, beans, split peas and pasta products, deteriorate or lose their flavor and potency if kept on the shelf too long. Unless you bake a lot, buy smaller sizes of things like baking powder and flour.

When you buy starchy products to store on your pantry shelf, remove them from their boxes and wrappings and pour them into tightly capped containers, preferably ones with screw caps. This will keep out insects of all kinds, particularly those you wouldn't imagine could find their way into these foods.

It's hard to understand why this hasn't occurred to storage-jar manufacturers, but the only sensible jar for storage should be one that is larger at the top than at the bottom so that foods—especially those you freeze—can slide out easily. Some peanut butter comes in large jars that are this shape.

You can put most glass jars in the freezer if you don't overfill them, since solids and liquids expand when they freeze. Avoid a too-sudden change in temperature when you take glass out of the freezer. To quickly defrost foods which you've stored in glass jars, set the jars in *cold* water until the contents have loosened.

To store potentially large quantities of stock or soup in tiny jars, see *Glaze*.

If you have room, store potatoes in the refrigerator making sure you keep them dry. This will inhibit the growth of "eyes."

A little sherry floated on the surface of a sauce for meat or fish will keep it fresh for 1 week or more if the sauce is poured boiling hot into a jar and allowed to cool before being put in the refrigerator.

STRAINERS AND STRAINING
Try to buy stainless steel strainers. They're expensive but are stronger and last much longer than the more common varieties. You also won't get any food discoloration if you use stainless steel.

A wire strainer of any kind will last longer if you force foods through with a wooden spoon instead of a metal one.

If you need a very fine strainer, put a large handkerchief over a regular strainer and pour the liquid through this. A fine handkerchief is usually better than a double thickness of cheesecloth and you can wash and reuse it many times.

Be sure any receptacle you strain into is deep enough so that the bottom of the strainer is above the liquid you're straining.

When you pour boiling liquid through a strainer, try to do it at arm's length with your face averted.

If you have to strain the liquid from a large pot of mixed vegetables, meat and bones, the operation will be easier if you strain

371

it first through a coarse strainer to remove the larger solid parts. You can then pour the remaining liquid through a fine strainer.

Many soups and sauces call for the ingredients to be rubbed through a sieve. Put them in a blender first and the whole process will be easier.

Wash a strainer immediately after you use it so the holes won't get clogged. If you fail to do this and the holes *do* get clogged, soak the strainer to soften the food and then attack it with a soapy toothbrush.

Cut off the panty and feet ends of panty hose. Save the nylon stocking parts; they make good strainers.

Insert a wide-necked funnel into a piece of nylon stocking, draw the stocking tightly across the bottom opening of the funnel, and you have a fine strainer.

STRAWBERRIES: see BERRIES

STRINGBEANS: SEE BEANS

STUFFING
See also *Birds*.

Allow about ¾ cup of stuffing for each pound of bird.

If you plan to freeze a bird, cooked or uncooked, don't stuff it first. Stuffing tends to draw out the juices.

Gizzards and hearts are tough tissues and require long cooking. If you want to use them in a stuffing, first cook them well.

For a quick stuffing, soak large pieces of crusty French bread in very well-seasoned tomato juice until the crust is softened. Then pack this into the cavity of a chicken.

If you use cracker crumbs in a stuffing, fill the cavity of the bird only half full. Cracker crumbs swell more than other types of stuffing. Stuffings containing bread or rice also should be packed somewhat loosely. If necessary cook part of the stuffing in a separate pan.

Try using the heel of a loaf of bread to hold in the stuffing if the cavity opening is large.

You can neatly and easily close a stuffed bird by using large stainless steel safety pins.

You can also use uncolored toothpicks to pin the skin together after you've stuffed a small bird.

Roast a stuffed bird a little longer than an unstuffed one.

To make stuffing for a bird a couple of days ahead of time, mix all the wet ingredients and store them in a jar in the refrigerator. Mix the dry ingredients and set aside. When you're ready, combine them in a large bowl.

It's actually best to prepare and refrigerate stuffing you make for chicken or turkey a day ahead. The flavors mingle and ripen, and you'll also save time and bustle on the day you roast the bird.

To make a savory stuffing for chicken, use leftover bits of vegetables and meats. Mix with cubed bread, seasonings, and a little liquid.

Because stuffing expands during roasting, be sure you leave the skin around the stuffed cavity a little loose.

SUBSTITUTIONS
One test of good cooks is what they do with food that has to be used up soon. Make substitutions. For example, in creamed spinach soup use string beans instead. Use zucchini. Use broccoli. Make unusual spaghetti sauces with whatever you have at hand. Practically anything goes, if you just use imagination and good sense.

SUGAR
See also *Blender, Caramel, Honey, Storage Tips.*

Use a little sugar to sear meat to a beautiful brown color. Add 1 tablespoon of sugar to the heated fat, stir over a moderate to high flame until it browns, then add the meat. Cook, turning the meat on all sides until it's uniformly dark. The sugar will add no detectable sweetness to the meat, only color.

If you're cooking for a low salt diet, add a little sugar to the cooking water for vegetables and they'll be more palatable.

When you're making a dessert soufflé, sprinkle sugar over the surface of the buttered mold before you pour in the soufflé batter. This will give it a fine sweet crust.

Excess sweetness in a cooked dish can sometimes be disguised if you add a little mild vinegar while cooking.

Granulated Sugar

There are about 2¼ cups in 1 pound of granulated sugar.

If granulated sugar cakes and hardens, put it in a pan in a moderate preheated oven, turn off the heat and let stand until it softens.

When you sift sugar, use a fairly coarse strainer and push the sugar through with the side and bottom of a wooden spoon. (Don't use a flour sifter.)

Cakes will come out better if you use fine sugar instead of regular granulated. Either buy the super-fine (not confectioners') or put it in a blender for a short time before measuring.

You can turn regular granulated sugar into super-fine sugar, also known as castor sugar, if you put it in the blender for a short while.

Make vanilla-flavored sugar to use in cakes or puddings, by putting 8 or 10 whole vanilla pods (broken up if you like) in a quart jar with a tight screw cap. Fill the jar three-quarters full of sugar, screw the cap on tightly, shake, then store on your pantry shelf. You can omit vanilla extract when you use this sugar for cakes and they'll have old-fashioned vanilla flavor. Don't mind the little black specks of vanilla—they're supposed to be there. Replace the sugar in the jar as you use it. The vanilla pods last for well over a year.

Grate lemon or orange peel, or a combination of both, and mix the pieces into a small jar of sugar. Cap this and use the flavored sugar, without straining, in cakes, cookies, icings, puddings, and tea.

Use a clean, dry saltshaker when you need to sift sugar.

Confectioners' Sugar

1 pound of confectioners' or powdered sugar equals 3½ cups sifted.

You can make confectioners' sugar from granulated sugar if

you put the sugar in a blender and blend until you see it getting powdery. You may have to turn off the blender, stir the sugar well, then blend again for a little.

To dust cakes or puddings with confectioners' sugar, put the sugar in a strainer and turn the sugar around in it with a spoon, pressing gently.

If you want to dust a moist cake with confectioners' sugar, wait until just before serving. Confectioners' sugar turns a grayish color when it stands on a moist surface.

Before you add powdered sugar to a batter or icing, run the sugar in the blender to eliminate the lumps.

When a recipe calls for sifted confectioners' sugar, run the sugar in the blender for a few seconds instead of sifting.

Brown Sugar

1 pound of brown sugar equals 2¼ cups firmly packed.

When you measure light or dark brown sugar always pack it down. Recipes calling for a certain volume of brown sugar assume it's firmly packed.

A granulated form of brown sugar which is measured and handled like white granulated sugar can be bought in some stores but it's very expensive.

Keep brown sugar in a jar with a tight screw cap. If you leave it even slightly exposed to air it will harden.

If brown sugar does cake and harden, enclose half an apple with it in a jar, seal tightly and let stand 1 day, then remove the apple. The moisture will usually uncake the sugar.

If you use brown sugar to replace all or part of the white sugar in a cake recipe, use a little baking soda to counteract the acidity, otherwise the cake won't rise properly; ¾ teaspoon of soda to 1 cup of brown sugar is about right.

You can add a butterscotch flavor to cookies or brownies if you substitute brown for white sugar.

1 cup of brown sugar, well packed, weighs about 7½ ounces or 210 grams.

If you keep brown sugar well wrapped in the refrigerator, it rarely hardens or becomes lumpy.

If brown sugar *should* end up in one hard lump (because you didn't store it properly), you can always grate it, just as you do a piece of hard cheese. Or put it in the blender.

If you need brown sugar and don't have any, mix ½ cup of granulated sugar and 2 tablespoons of molasses with a whisk or wooden spoon. You'll get pretty much the equivalent of ½ cup of brown sugar.

SWEETBREADS

Sweetbreads are the thymus gland of young calves. Sometimes the term also includes the pancreas. Beef sweetbreads are generally tough.

Sweetbreads don't keep well. Use them within 1 day of buying.

Always parboil sweetbreads before cooking. Cover with cold salted water and a little lemon juice, bring to a boil and simmer for 10 minutes. Rinse with cold water. A second cooking (simmered in seasoned broth for another 10 minutes) before their final preparation will further tenderize and flavor them.

After you've finished with the initial parboiling (and perhaps second simmering) of sweetbreads, remove the membranes carefully and spread the sweetbreads flat on a plate (if they're large, first slice them lengthwise into 2 or 3 slices) and place a flat weight on them. Then put them in the refrigerator until you're ready to cook. They'll be flat and attractive-looking when they're prepared and served.

Sweetbreads become more and more tender with successive cookings, so heat and handle them gently.

SWEET POTATOES AND YAMS

1 pound of sweet potatoes or yams will serve 3 people.

Sweet potatoes don't keep as well as regular white potatoes, so don't buy them for long storage. And they must be kept dry. They deteriorate rapidly in a humid atmosphere.

Sweet potatoes won't turn dark after they're peeled if you

plunge them into salted water: 1 tablespoon of salt to 1 quart of water.

To make an interesting sweet potato flour, peel and slice raw sweet potatoes very thin. Dry them in the oven until they're as crisp as potato chips. Then grind into flour in the blender. Store in jars. Substitute for a portion of white or whole wheat flour for baking bread, muffins, etc.

You can remove the strings from cooked mashed sweet potatoes or yams if you beat them with an electric mixer. The strings will adhere to the beaters.

SWISS CHARD

Swiss chard is a form of beet whose large leaves and thick stalk can be eaten.

The only chard worth cooking and eating is young, fresh and crisp. Don't buy it if it's rubbery or wilted.

Like spinach, chard needs no cooking water except what clings to the leaves when they're washed. It does however need slightly longer cooking than spinach.

Avoid using salt in the water in which you cook Swiss chard—it tends to turn it dark.

SYRUPS

1 cup of syrup weighs 12 ounces.

The finest grade of maple syrup (which rarely reaches most markets) is very pale, almost waterlike, in color and has a mild maple flavor. This is Grade AA and is the product of the first sap flow in the spring. Later season runs, Grades A, B, and C, produce a progressively darker color and a more pronounced maple flavor. Read the labels on bottles or cans when you buy maple syrup—most "maple syrups" you buy in cans and bottles are a mixture of corn or cane and maple syrups. Almost all have artificial maple flavor and color added. For pancakes or waffles there's nothing quite like 100 percent maple syrup.

Store maple syrup in a cool dark place. Once you've opened

the bottle or can, keep it in the refrigerator to prevent fermentation. If fermentation does occur (you'll see bubbles and a grayish scum on top) strain the syrup into a pan, heat it to boiling and let it boil slowly for 1 minute. Then skim and strain it again into a clean hot jar. This will restore it almost to its former condition.

If you oil the inside of a cup or spoon before you measure syrup into it, the syrup will leave no residue after it's poured.

Always clean off the neck of a syrup bottle with a clean damp cloth before you replace the cover. This will make it easy to open the next time.

Don't overcook an icing which contains syrup. Heat it only until it will congeal into a malleable ball when a little is dribbled into a dish or cup of cold water, otherwise it will develop a fudgy consistency which is difficult to spread.

Collect and save the juices from canned fruits. Freeze them until you have a substantial amount, then gently boil them down to a syrup for pancakes and other dishes.

Syrup won't drip from a pitcher if you very lightly smear a bit of oil or butter across the inside of the pouring lip.

To make your own pancake and waffle syrups at a fraction of the cost of buying them, mix honey and molasses, a little vanilla extract and—if the mixture seems too thick—a tiny bit of water. Or thin it with a little frozen orange juice concentrate or any fruit juice for a fruit-flavored syrup. Heat gently, mix with a whisk, and pour into a bottle or small pitcher. (You can also add some broken nutmeats if you like.)

Corn syrup and honey can be used in interchangeable amounts in baking.

TABLECLOTHS

You can make beautiful tablecloths from new sheets. A couple of times a year, when stores have white sales, you often can buy attractively patterned, flat twin-bed sheets at very low prices. They come in many colors, are drip-dry, and it doesn't take long to cut them to size. You can even make round tablecloths out of them. Use a round vinyl cover for a pattern and hem the table-cloths when you have a little time on your hands. (Use the round vinyl cover underneath the tablecloth as a table protector.)

An old tablecloth is great to cool freshly baked cookies on. It's clean and porous.

TAPIOCA

Tapioca pudding gets sticky if you cook it too long.

TARRAGON: see HERBS AND SPICES

TEA

1 tea bag usually contains 1 teaspoonful of tea leaves, enough for one or two 6-ounce cups of tea, depending on the strength preferred.

¼ pound of tea makes about 60 cups.

Unlike coffee, tea doesn't deteriorate much with time. When you open a package of loose tea or tea bags, transfer the contents to a tight-capped jar or tin and store in a dark place. Tea must be stored airtight—it absorbs odors and moisture easily. It should last 6 months or more.

If you like teas with unusual flavors and don't want to pay a fortune for them, make your own. Pour loose tea in a jar and add small amounts of flavors that appeal to you in any combination: minced vanilla bean, whole cloves, cardamom seeds, anise, allspice, nutmeg, ginger, some cinnamon stick, etc. A piece of dried orange or lemon rind is also nice. Keep in an airtight jar.

For iced tea that will never cloud, pour cold water over the tea leaves, cover, and refrigerate for a day or two. Strain as you pour it over ice cubes. Strength varies according to taste, but begin with 3 teaspoons of tea leaves to every ¾ cup of cold water. If you find this too strong when you pour it over the ice, add some ice water.

To keep your teapot sweet-smelling and free of tea stains, rub the inside of the pot with a paste of baking soda and a little water, then wash and rinse well. (To clean the spout of a teapot, see *Stains*.)

Use a glazed pottery, glass or china teapot—not metal—when you make tea. Heat the pot first by filling it with boiling water, then rinse. Add the tea leaves, fill the pot with boiling water and let steep for about 5 minutes.

Use freshly boiled water when you make tea. And don't over-boil it, otherwise the water loses all the tiny oxygen bubbles it contains and the tea will have a rather flat taste.

Iced tea may become cloudy, but this doesn't affect the flavor.

You can also get a clear iced tea if you make strong tea by the hot water method, let it cool to room temperature and *then* pour it over ice cubes.

TEFLON-LINED PANS: see POTS AND PANS

TEMPERATURES

To convert Fahrenheit to Celsius temperatures, subtract 32, multiply by 5 and divide by 9.

To convert Celsius to Fahrenheit temperatures, multiply by 9, divide by 5 and add 32.

Here are some basic temperature equivalents.

	Fahrenheit	Celsius (Metric)
Freezing point of water	32	0
Boiling point of water	212	100
Low oven	250	121
Moderate oven	350	177
Hot oven	450	232
Broil	550	288

THICKENERS

See also *Egg Yolks, Panada, Roux, Soups.*

1 tablespoon of flour will thicken 1 cup of liquid to the consistency of medium cream, a thin sauce suitable for a soup base; 2 tablespoons of flour will thicken 1 cup of liquid to the consistency of a medium sauce. If you want a thick sauce, use 2½ to 3 tablespoons to each cup of liquid.

Flour makes soup or sauce opaque when you use it for thickening. Cornstarch will give a clear quality; 1 tablespoon of cornstarch equals 2 tablespoons of flour in thickening power.

Like cornstarch, arrowroot will thicken a mixture without making it cloudy. Use slightly less than you would of cornstarch.

Potato starch is another thickener which thickens without making a liquid opaque.

Flour and other powdered starches expand when they're dissolved in liquid and heated, hence their use as thickeners.

When you use flour to thicken gravies, soups, or anything else, cook it first for 1 or 2 minutes with a little hot melted fat. This helps the flour mix easily into the hot liquid and it will be less likely to have a floury taste.

If you must add flour without fat to a hot liquid, mix it first in a cup with enough cold water to make a smooth thin paste. Then add this slowly to the pot, mixing well.

For thickening some sauces you might prefer 1 or 2 egg yolks—the sauce will be more delicate and have no starchy taste. But be careful not to let the mixture approach boiling or it will curdle. Add the hot liquid 1 tablespoon at a time to the yolks, mixing well after each addition until you have a velvety cream. Add this slowly to the remainder of the hot liquid, whipping vigorously.

If you cook 1 cup or more of sliced okra with the vegetables in a soup, you'll have a good tasty thickener. Test, and vary the amount of okra to your taste.

Puréed onions or other vegetables are excellent as soup or sauce thickeners. They're less starchy and fattening than arrowroot, cornstarch or flour.

You can also use leftover cereal as a thickener for stews, soups and gravies if you put it in the blender first.

1 teaspoon of potato flour (also called potato starch) has the thickening power of 1 tablespoon of white flour.

Rice flour and barley flour, which give a more delicate taste and texture to a sauce than regular flour, are sometimes hard to find. You can make your own by putting ¼ cup of raw rice or barley in the blender at high speed until the flour is fine. You don't need much for most thickening purposes.

If you're using flour as a thickener in gravy, sauce, or soup, be sure you cook the dish—after the addition of the starch—for at least 2 full minutes, stirring occasionally. This breaks down the starch and eliminates any chalky taste.

Other thickeners for casseroles, stews, or soups are noodles, macaroni, or spaghetti broken into bits.

Cook any flour-thickened liquid that can't be simmered over direct heat in a double boiler over hot water. This is the secret for achieving a smooth, velvety sauce. Use a whisk for stirring and you'll avoid lumps.

If you want to thicken a pot of soup, scoop up 1 or 2 cupfuls with plenty of solids in it, and run in the blender. Then pour the mixture back into the soup pot, stir, heat, and serve. It's remarkable what this thickening technique does to a pot of soup—and without adding a single calorie.

TOMATOES
There are 4 or 5 medium tomatoes in 1 pound.

1 pound of tomatoes, peeled and seeded, will give about 1½ cups of tomato pulp.

If you want to parboil tomatoes to use whole in any dish or if you want to sauté, stuff or bake them, choose tomatoes which are heavy for their size. They have firmer flesh and will hold their shape better after being cooked.

Vine-ripened tomatoes are much more flavorful than those picked green and then ripened.

If you have green tomatoes, don't put them in the sun to ripen. Often they'll soften before they get red. Put them instead in a brown paper bag and set them in a dark spot (at room temperature) for 3 or 4 days, depending on how green they are.

Many tomatoes in the markets have been picked green, then gas-ripened. These are flavorless. Try to buy tomatoes that are marked "vine-ripened."

Cherry or plum tomatoes taste more like tomatoes than the large ones you see nowadays in most markets.

Tomatoes are like wine in one regard—their flavor is impaired if they're refrigerated for more than 1 or 2 hours. Keep tomatoes at room temperature if you can. If you have more tomatoes than you can use immediately, keep them in a moderately cold spot, but don't put them in the refrigerator. They'll be a dozen times more delicious.

If you want to peel a firm tomato, rub the skin gently all over with the side of a knife handle, then split the skin carefully and peel.

You can also peel a tomato by impaling it on a fork and holding it over a gas flame, turning it until the skin begins to shrivel.

If you have several tomatoes to peel, the simplest thing to do is to bring a pot of water to the boiling point, turn off the flame and place the tomatoes in the water. Remove them with a slotted spoon after 1 or 2 minutes. Pierce the center top of each with a sharp pointed knife and peel the skin down in strips. It will come off easily.

To remove the seeds from a tomato, cut it in half crosswise and hold the cut side under cold running water, using your fingers to help push out the seeds.

If you cut a tomato lengthwise instead of crosswise, you'll release less juice. Tomatoes cut in lengthwise sections are better for salads.

If you add tomatoes to a dressed salad, do it just before serving, otherwise the juices may dilute the dressing or make the salad soggy.

Before you stuff tomatoes, peel, seed and salt and pepper them, then turn them cut-side down on a plate. Chill well. This will remove all excess water and make them easier to handle.

2 smallish tomatoes, coarsely chopped, equal 1 cup.

Use plum tomatoes to make homemade tomato sauce or tomato paste. They have more flesh and less moisture.

A cracked tomato won't keep; use it right away. Spoilage starts at the crack.

The sharpest knives may have a tough time cutting through the skin of a tomato. To slice it neatly, without squashing or losing juice, make a small incision with the point of the knife at each spot where you want to slice.

You can freeze tomatoes to use in the future for stews, soups, sauces, etc. Cut the tomatoes in quarters or eighths and set them on a cookie sheet in the freezer. When the pieces are frozen, put them in a plastic bag and store in the freezer. No need to peel them first; the skins peel off like a breeze when the pieces begin to thaw.

TOMATO PASTE, PURÉE AND SAUCE
A 6-ounce can of tomato paste equals ⅔ cup.

Tomato paste is puréed tomato with a great deal of the water removed. It's usually seasoned with salt, although it's available salt-free.

Tomato purée is the strained pulp of tomatoes which have been peeled, seeded and boiled.

Tomato sauce is tomato purée seasoned with salt, pepper and spices. It contains a little more water than tomato purée.

A 15-ounce can of tomato sauce equals about 2 cups.

You can make tomato purée, tomato sauce and even tomato juice from small or large cans of tomato paste. A 6-ounce can of tomato paste, 3 cans of cold water, and 1 teaspoon of salt, all well mixed, will give you a very nice tomato juice. You can add pepper, garlic powder, sugar and a little lemon juice for a pleasant tomato juice cocktail. To make tomato sauce from tomato paste, add 2 cans of water; for tomato purée, 1 can. Add seasonings to taste. Keep cans of tomato paste on your shelf. They're easier to store and carry and less expensive than tomato juice, purée or sauce.

TONGUE

Adding 1 tablespoon of vinegar to the last water in which you cook tongue will make peeling easier.

You can cook a smoked beef or steer tongue quickly without lengthy soaking if you pressure-cook it 3 times for 20 minutes (60 minutes total), each time pouring off the water in which it was cooked and covering it with fresh cold water. You'll have a very tender and not too salty tongue.

Always peel a tongue while it's still hot from cooking. Do this under cold running water so that you won't burn yourself.

Fresh beef tongue makes marvelous stew. Parboil it for 15 minutes, then cut into pieces and treat it exactly as you would raw stewing beef.

TOOLS

See also *Knives*.

When you buy kitchen tools, avoid those with painted wooden handles. The paint will eventually peel off, flaking into the food you're preparing.

When you wash wooden-handled tools, don't let them stand in water. Wash at once, dry and put them away.

TRUSSING: see BIRDS

TUNA

Weight for weight, tuna is one of the cheapest sources of animal protein there is.

You can buy canned tuna in flake, chunk and solid pack forms. The solid pack is a continuous piece or slice of the fish, more expensive than the other two. But flake or chunk are fine for salads or any dish calling for tuna mixed with other ingredients.

Solid pack tuna comes in three grades: white, light and dark meat. The white is favored for its flavor and looks and is the most expensive, but the light and dark are excellent in any tuna dish.

Bonito is a variety of tuna which comes canned in both flaked and solid pack forms. It's much, much cheaper than and every bit as good as other kinds of tuna.

You can substitute white tuna for chicken in salads and curried dishes. In fact if you buy the solid pack form and prepare it properly, it's very hard to tell from chicken. To use white tuna for this purpose, drain, soak it in cold water for 10 minutes, then drain well again. Treat it like cooked chicken.

You can flake the more expensive tuna. A 6½- or 7-ounce can, after flaking, will give you over 1 cup.

Canned tuna comes packed in oil, broth, or water. If you're on a weight-reducing diet, read the labels on tuna cans. You'll save calories.

TURKEY

See also *Birds, Stuffing.*

An ideal turkey for roasting is about 10 pounds. This will serve 12 people.

A fresh turkey is always better than a frozen one. Just remember to order it from your butcher a few days ahead of time.

When you buy a freshly killed turkey, make sure that the breastbone and joints are flexible. This means it's a young bird. If it still has the feet on, they should be blackish in color. (A medium-aged turkey has pink feet and an old turkey has gray feet.)

Buy a fresh or frozen turkey out of holiday season when the

demand is less and they're often cheaper. You can divide it, then freeze in sections for separate meals. If you've bought a frozen bird, let it thaw in the refrigerator until you're able to cut it into pieces, even though it's partially frozen. Wrap each piece properly and put it in the freezer.

Turkeys should be well oiled or larded with fat, particularly on the breast, because they tend to become dry in the oven. Baste a turkey often.

Stuff a turkey lightly. Use the heel of a loaf of bread to hold in stuffing if the cavity opening is large.

Use dental floss instead of thread to sew up a stuffed turkey—it won't tear the skin and holds better.

Heavier turkeys generally cost less per pound than lighter, smaller ones, and there's a larger proportion of meat to bone on the bigger ones.

For an amazingly good stuffing, use nothing but apples. Peel, core, and stuff the bird with them. After the turkey is cooked, remove the apple stuffing and mix with gravy.

It takes 2 to 3 days, depending on size, for a frozen turkey to defrost in the refrigerator. (It's preferable to defrost a turkey in the refrigerator because it will lose less of its juices.)

Because turkey wing tips often burn when a turkey is being roasted, cut them off before you put the turkey in the oven and throw them into your stockpot. Or freeze them with other odds and ends you're saving for the stockpot.

Cooking

A 10- to 13-pound turkey should roast at 325° for about 20 minutes per pound or until the drumstick moves easily or even breaks from the carcass when you move it gently. Another test for doneness is to pierce the thickest part of the thigh with a fork. If the juice runs clear, the turkey is done.

Try laying a stuffed turkey on its side in the oven until the top side begins to brown. Then turn it on the other side. Put it on its back to let the breast brown for ½ hour before you remove it from the oven. If you roast a turkey this way it will be evenly cooked, down to the last bit of stuffing.

You can broil a very young turkey just as you would a chicken. Since a turkey has less fat on it than any other domestic bird, oil it well and baste frequently. Use a medium flame. Add a few tablespoons of water to the broiler pan after you've turned the turkey. This will help keep the meat from scorching.

You can also sauté a young turkey just as you would a chicken. Remember that it takes longer and you must use more fat or oil.

Use rubber household gloves to pick up or turn a turkey in the roasting pan.

To carve a turkey, remove the wing on each side where it joins the body. Disjoint each leg and thigh. Separate the lower legs (drumsticks) from the thighs. Carve the breast meat into slices. Turn the turkey over and remove the meaty little "oyster" from each side of the backbone. This is the prize meat of the turkey.

You can make a most delicious curry with leftover turkey. Use lots of onions.

Save all the turkey bones after the bird is eaten to use in making soup or stock.

TURNIPS

Turnips are undeservedly a much-neglected vegetable. They can be boiled, mashed with butter and nutmeg or cubed and served with or without cubed carrots. They're great in stew and delicious sautéed with a little onion.

The yellow turnip is also known as rutabaga. You can cook it in most of the ways you would white turnips except that it requires slightly longer cooking.

Boiled turnips are sweeter if you don't skin them before cooking.

Turnips with a strong flavor can be made milder if you parboil them in salted water for about 4 minutes, then drain and continue as your recipe directs.

A little sherry added to mashed turnips just before serving gives a fine touch to the dish.

Turnips and pork go together beautifully. Add some turnips to the pot 45 minutes before a pork roast is done, cover and continue roasting.

1 pound of yellow or white turnips, diced, will give you about 4 cups.

To reduce the odor when you cook turnips, add a little sugar to the cooking water.

Mashed turnips are delicious, but if you find their consistency a trifle thin, mash in one boiled potato.

VANILLA

For a pure vanilla flavor in your puddings, sauces, etc., split an inch of vanilla bean and cook it with the other ingredients. Remove it when the cooking is finished. For cakes and cookies, open an inch of bean and scrape the insides well into the batter.

Vanilla will give a lovely odor to your refrigerator. Put a drop or two on a piece of folded paper towel or a bit of cotton and set it inside.

To make vanilla sugar, see *Sugar*.

Use 2 teaspoons or even 1 tablespoon of vanilla instead of the usual 1 teaspoon called for in most recipes so that you can taste the vanilla flavor. Vanilla extract seems rather weak these days.

VEAL

See also *Larding, Liver, Meat, Roasts, Stew.*

The meat from very young veal is mother-of-pearl white in color because the animals are milk fed. Every cut of milk-fed veal is tender.

When you buy veal scallops (the best cuts are from the upper part of the hind legs) be sure you get milk-fed veal.

As calves get older and begin eating grass, the flesh becomes pink, then reddish. Don't buy rosy veal if you want a tender, sweet taste to the meat.

Veal contains much less fat than beef and therefore dries more easily in cooking. Regardless of how you cook veal, place some thin strips of fat across the top to baste it during cooking. Lard it also (see *Larding*).

If you're using ground veal in a dish, grind some fat in with the meat or add some cooking oil, otherwise it will become very dry in cooking.

After you bread veal chops, refrigerate them for an hour or more before cooking so that the breading will adhere better.

Before you broil veal chops, make slashes about 1 inch apart on the fat surrounding the meat. This will keep the edges from curling.

Spread floured veal chops with a little melted butter before you put them in the broiler. They'll taste better and have a beautiful golden color.

You can give veal chops a nice butter flavor without burning the butter if you sauté them with oil or other fat as you normally would, but add a small amount of butter to the pan before the chops are done. Turn once after you've added the butter.

When veal is boiled, it releases more scum into the water than any other meat. If you're going to add veal or veal bones to a pot for stock, parboil them first for 5 minutes, starting with cold water. Drain them, throw this water away and rinse the meat and bones well under cold water, scrubbing until all the scum which the boiling has brought out is washed away. Scrub the inside of the pot too and then start to cook your stock with the clean meat and bones.

A veal bone (shank or knuckle) gives a marvelous flavor to a gravy base or soup stock. Ask your butcher to split the bones.

Because veal is so delicately flavored, don't serve strongly flavored vegetables with it.

VEGETABLES
See also names of individual vegetables.

Try to buy your vegetables from a market where you can pick them individually. If you buy vegetables like potatoes, onions or tomatoes in ready-packed bags you run a good risk of finding some of them partially spoiled, of a size you don't want or not ripe enough.

With very few exceptions, small younger vegetables are preferable to large mature ones. Tender vegetables, no matter how you prepare them, have twice the flavor of tough ones.

Always cut the leafy green tops from root vegetables (beets, carrots and turnips) before you store them, otherwise their juices continue to be drawn from the roots into the stems and leaves.

To store fresh vegetables which you intend to use within 3 days, wash and wrap them in paper toweling and put them in the vegetable compartment of your refrigerator. There'll be just enough moisture adhering to them to keep them fresh.

Leafy vegetables are likely to harbor insects, so soak them in well-salted cold water for about ½ hour before using. Do this with broccoli, Brussels sprouts, artichokes and curled leaf lettuce. Rinse in clear cold water afterward to remove the salt.

Potatoes, eggplant and every vegetable which tends to darken after you've peeled it should be dropped in water the moment it leaves your hands.

You can slice a round vegetable easily (without its slipping) if you first cut a thin lengthwise slice and hold this cutside down against the cutting board as you slice.

When a recipe calls for a very finely chopped vegetable, try grating it.

Any fresh vegetables which you can buy dehydrated at fancy prices you can also dry yourself to use in soups and stews. Cut in thin rings or finely dice them. Dry them on a paper towel spread on a cookie sheet in a *very* low oven, stirring from time to time. When they're dried to paper-like consistency with absolutely no moisture left, pack them in covered jars and store with your herbs and spices.

Before you use store-bought or homemade dehydrated vegetable flakes, soak them for about 10 minutes in a very small amount of water to bring out the flavor. When you cook them they'll cook more quickly and uniformly.

If you're going to serve vegetables raw, first soak them in ice water for about 20 minutes.

If you want to serve delicate vegetables braised or sautéed (zucchini, summer squash, tomatoes, etc.) in slices, cook them in your widest pan so they'll keep their shape.

When you're selecting onions or potatoes or carrots to use whole, as in a stew, be sure to choose all the vegetables of each kind as close to the same size as possible so they'll cook uniformly.

Withered vegetables often can be brought back to life if you let them stand for an hour or so in cold salted water.

Dehydrate vegetable bits by placing them in a large strainer and set the strainer over a heat register or radiator. Bottle them when they're dry and papery.

Use the leg of a nylon stocking for dehydrating vegetables or mushrooms. Knot one end and pop in the pieces of vegetables. Then knot the other end and hang up until the pieces are thoroughly dry. (There's no better place to hang it than an attic, but the kitchen does fine if it's not too humid.) Then bottle the pieces and keep them beside the stove. They come in handy when you need to add a little flavor to a dish.

Never throw out the liquid in which you cook vegetables (or the juices from canned vegetables, either). Store the liquid in a closed jar in the refrigerator or freezer. Use it to cook other vegetables in. Soon it will be so full-flavored that you can use it as the base of a soup.

Use in place of the water generally called for in bread recipes, the water you've cooked vegetables in. It will add marvelous flavor to the bread and will also add to the bread's nutritive value.

You can make dehydrated vegetable powders in the blender (onion, garlic, celery, carrots, green and red pepper, mushroom, etc.) to use in soups and gravies.

Leftover cooked or canned vegetables (green or yellow string beans, pimientos, red or green peppers, black olives, etc.) can have their refrigerator storage life extended if you first pour enough plain cooking oil over them to cover.

Any parts of vegetables that seem too tough or coarse to be served as a vegetable can be cooked, then puréed in the blender. They become a flavorful, nutritious base for a cream soup.

Cooking

If you double a vegetable recipe, increase the liquids, herbs and spices by less than one-half.

Cooking vegetables in salted water tends to draw the vitamins out of the vegetables into the water. Add salt just before serving.

All vegetables keep their vitamin content better in a slightly acid solution, so add a little lemon juice to their cooking liquid.

A little lemon juice added to the cooking water also helps green vegetables stay green.

Cook green vegetables uncovered and they won't be as likely to lose their color.

Vegetables which discolor easily (artichoke hearts and bottoms and oyster plants) should be blanched in 1 quart of water into which ¼ cup of flour and 2 tablespoons of lemon juice have been beaten.

Vegetables like wax and string beans, broccoli, Brussels sprouts, cauliflower, peas, spinach and turnips will be more delicious and keep their color better if you blanch them before cooking. Drop them into a large quantity of boiling water for about 4 minutes, then drain quickly and cover with a lot of cold water to stop their cooking. When they've cooled, cook them according to the recipe you're following, but slightly shorten the cooking time.

Most vegetables can be cooked either in a lot or in a tiny amount of water and be equally delicious. The chief things to remember is to have the water boiling before you add the vegetables and then not to overcook them.

If your vegetables are tough and your recipe calls for cooking them in water, simmer them in milk instead. It doesn't matter if the milk curdles slightly.

When you prepare creamed vegetables, use evaporated milk instead of fresh milk and you'll get a richer flavor in the cream sauce.

Try cooking vegetables in well-flavored soup stock instead of water. They'll be superb. (This also further enriches the stock.)

Heat canned vegetables only to the simmering point before serving.

If you intend to sauté vegetables and you have only tough, mature ones to work with, try parboiling them before sautéing.

When you sauté vegetables, keep your eye on the pan. Sautéing can be the most delicious way to cook vegetables, but not if you let them get mushy.

One Chinese method of cooking vegetables is to sauté quickly in a small amount of hot oil, then finish cooking with a little added hot liquid, removing them from the pan while they're still slightly crisp. These are good!

Add leftover vegetables to the soup pot or freeze them for use in future soups if you don't have a soup pot going at the moment.

Save all vegetable parings and leaves to add to water for soup stock. Strain and use for soup or cook them in a little water and add them to dog food. They're very nutritious and most dogs love them.

You don't really need a steamer to steam vegetables. Put ¼ inch of water into a heavy saucepan (1 inch of water if the pan is a thin one), bring to a boil, then put in the vegetables and cover the pan tightly. Peek in to see if the water has returned to a boil. When it does, lower the heat so that the water bubbles slowly. Cover again. Keep peeking. Don't overcook vegetables.

VINEGAR
See also *Garlic, Salad Dressing.*

Cider vinegar and distilled vinegar are harsh tasting white vinegars. Try not to use them in cooking. Buy white wine vinegars. Among these rice wine vinegar is one of the softest and most pleasant—particularly delicious in a salad dressing. You can get it in Oriental food stores and in the foreign food departments of most supermarkets.

If you want to make red or white wine into wine vinegar, you must introduce some "mother of vinegar" into the wine. You can do this by pouring a little actively fermenting wine vinegar (not distilled vinegar) into the wine. You'll recognize the right kind of vinegar by the slight sediment (the "mother") on the bottom of the bottle. Cover the jars with gauze or cheesecloth. Fermentation will take place only if there's plenty of oxygen present. You'll have wine vinegar in a few weeks.

If you have a bottle of red wine which is beginning to turn sour set it aside to complete the turning. It will give you a very nice red wine vinegar.

Add leftover wine to undistilled vinegar and you'll have a new supply of wine vinegar.

Use red or white wine vinegar for marinating.

Beat 1 teaspoon of white vinegar into 4 or more egg whites and they will hold their shape when you've whipped them to stiffness.

Add a little vinegar to the water in which you cook beets and it will keep them from fading.

Add ¼ teaspoon of salt to your vinegar cruet and the vinegar will stay clear.

To make herbed vinegar, heat the vinegar to quite hot, but not boiling, before you pour it over the herbs. This will speed up the flavoring process.

Why not make fruit-flavored wine vinegar? Add preserves or jams to a jar of red or white wine vinegar and let stand for a few days. Use in salad dressings or add a little cream to it to make a sauce for meat or chicken.

WAFFLES

To get a new waffle iron ready to bake waffles, heat it, then brush the upper and lower grids with plenty of vegetable oil. Unplug it and let stand until cool. Wipe off some of the excess oil with paper towels. Plug the iron in again until it gets hot and unplug it once more, letting it cool. Again wipe off the excess oil. Make the first waffle and throw it away. Then you're in business. (When you've finished baking waffles, put a piece of waxed paper across the bottom grid, close the iron and let it cool. Store until you need it again.)

Waffle batter should be quite thin. Don't overload it with flour.

If you're using a new waffle iron for the first time, put a little extra shortening in the batter to help temper the iron.

Use buttermilk in place of regular milk in waffle batter (add a pinch of baking soda too) and you'll have very soft and delicate waffles.

If you like your waffles soft, add a little sugar to the waffle batter. If you like them crisp, omit sugar from the batter.

For a delicate waffle crust, separate the eggs and add the beaten whites last, folding them into the batter just before using.

For a really crisp crust, use pale olive oil instead of melted butter in the batter.

The less batter in the waffle iron, the thinner and crisper the waffle will be.

To tell when a waffle iron has reached the right temperature to use, heat it, put in 1 teaspoonful of water, then close. When the steaming stops, the iron is ready.

Use the same size measuring cup each time you take batter from the bowl to pour on the waffle iron and you'll have waffles of uniform thickness.

405

A waffle is done when the upper lid of the waffle iron is slightly raised, the side of the waffle which you can see is lightly tanned and—most important—the steaming has stopped for about 10 seconds.

Don't open the lid of a waffle iron before the waffle is done. The result is often a catastrophe.

If catastrophe occurs and you have messed-up a non-Teflon waffle iron, dig out as much batter as you can, apply oil to the grids with a pastry brush, then scrub with a wire brush.

If you find you've mixed more batter than you need, make the waffles, let them cool, then wrap and freeze them. You can take them out and put them in the toaster without thawing when you want them.

Dip bread slices in leftover waffle batter, sauté as you would French toast. Marvelous with cinnamon and sugar, jam, preserves, or syrup.

WALNUTS: see NUTS

WATER
A pot of water can be brought to a boil much faster if you cover it. But be careful—it can boil over.

WATERCRESS: see SALADS AND SALAD GREENS

WATERMELON: see MELONS

WAXED PAPER
Some waxed paper manufactured today is waxed on one side only. You may need to know which is the waxed side before using.

If you like to roll pie dough out on waxed paper, put the paper on a wet surface and it won't slip.

Put a piece of waxed paper under anything you put in the freezer and the container won't stick to the freezer floor. Do this with anything that has a moist bottom, such as an ice cube tray.

Waxed paper makes an excellent seal on pots for top of stove or oven cooking. Cut a circle slightly larger than the pot size, put it over the pot, make a small hole in the center, then put the pot lid on top of the paper.

Cookies which tend to harden will stay softer longer if they are individually wrapped in waxed paper before storing.

If you're wrapping dough in waxed paper for temporary refrigerator storage, be sure to use *heavy* waxed paper—the kind that's waxed on both sides. Some bargain waxed paper is so flimsy that doughs stick to it and it's a major chore to remove.

WHIPPED CREAM: see CREAM

WINE
If you've discovered a wine you like, consider buying a case of it from your dealer. It's almost always cheaper by the case, and you can generally count on it remaining good for at least a year.

Keep wines in a moderately cool place with the bottles lying on their sides so that the corks stay wet and expanded on the inside, not allowing air to get in. Air inside a wine bottle will quickly ruin it.

Cool a dry white or rosé wine for a short time before serving. Refrigerate it for about 2 hours—not much more, or the flavor will be impaired. Red wines are generally served at room temperature except in hot weather, when they should be slightly chilled.

Be gentle with a wine bottle before you open it. Be especially careful not to stir up any dregs which may be at the bottom.

Stand a good red wine upright for 24 hours before serving. Open it and let it stand uncorked for 1 hour before drinking.

Dry white wines with their light flavors are usually served with fish, seafood, poultry and light meats; pink rosé wine can be served with all types of food; and more robust red wines are usually served with red meat and game. But chicken is often cooked with red wine and beef with white, and if you like to drink white wine with beef or red wine with chicken or fish, go ahead. Drink what tastes best to you.

Cooking

Cooking concentrates the flavor of wine, so any wine you cook with should be pleasant to drink. Don't use any wine in cooking which you wouldn't also enjoy drinking. A poor wine will give its flavor to the food.

Alcohol evaporates at well below the boiling point of water. Using wine in cooking doesn't add alcohol to food; it adds flavor.

Use certain wines such as Madeira, Marsala, port, sherry and vermouth in moderation when you cook with them. You only need a little of these to flavor your food.

Any dish or sauce which contains wine should be simmered uncovered until the alcohol has boiled off. If you smell alcohol, cook slowly a little longer.

If there's any food which calls for wine in the cooking, it's fish.

Use a little sherry when you cook shellfish or when you're making a cocktail sauce for shellfish. (You can also use sherry in creamed dishes and consommé.)

Dry vermouth, a full-flavored wine, is marvelous for chicken. You need very little other seasoning. Vermouth contains many roots and herbs and is more potent than any other dry white wine.

If you intend to cook meats in wine, it's generally better if you brown them first in hot fat. Searing keeps them from becoming wine soaked. Wine-soaked meats (except for the special tenderizing process rendered by wine marinades) usually do not taste good.

The time to add wine to a stew is after the meat and vegetables have all been browned in fat or oil. Add the wine and allow it to boil down to a near syrup. Then add the stock and let the stew simmer.

When you use a particularly tart red wine for a sauce, it's often a good idea to add a pinch or so of sugar while cooking to correct the acidity. You can also add a few slices of carrot to the cooking pot. Remove these before serving.

Add a little white wine, Marsala or sherry to uncooked rice into which you've stirred some melted butter in a skillet. Then add your liquid and cook. Superb rice.

Crumble dry leftover cake and add some sherry to the crumbs. Use this as a topping for dessert soufflés and cream desserts.

An opened bottle of dry cooking wine will keep better if you carefully drip in a little olive oil which will spread to cover the surface and seal the wine from air.

If you have an opened bottle of wine, pour it into a jar or bottle with a tight cover. It will keep well for cooking if you use it within 3 weeks after opening. Don't refrigerate it or the taste will change.

If wine begins to sour, don't try to use it in cooking. Let it go all the way and become wine vinegar. Wine which begins to sour is no longer wine.

Add leftover wine to a bottle of vinegar and you'll have a new supply of wine vinegar.

A tablespoon of sherry does wonders for scrambled eggs and omelets. Beat it into the eggs before you cook them.

A rather tough chicken can be very much tenderized if you marinate it overnight in the refrigerator with seasoned white wine or dry vermouth.

Use red wine for basting a beef roast after it's halfway roasted. Burgundy is first-rate for this.

Substitute white or red wine for cream to pour over berries when serving them as a dessert.

It's a good idea, just before you serve a sauce or a soup made with wine, to add a tablespoon or so of the wine after the pot is taken off the heat.

Pour a little port wine over baked apples just before you take them from the oven.

When you sauté any food, add a little wine to the pan to braise the contents. Be sure you lower the heat first and add the wine a little at a time, otherwise the wine and fat mixture will spatter.

409

If you're poaching fish for no more than 4 people, use white wine and seasonings instead of water. (Poaching for more than 4 will require at least 2 bottles.) And don't throw the poaching liquid out afterward—use it as the base of a fish sauce, or a fish or seafood chowder. You can freeze it.

Substitute wine (white, red, or rosé) for the liquid called for in your meat loaf recipe.

YAMS: see SWEET POTATOES AND YAMS

YEAST AND YEAST DOUGH

See *Bread*.

1 level tablespoon of dry granulated yeast equals 1 cake of compressed yeast.

Fresh compressed yeast is a light grayish-tan color. If it's dark and brownish, it is old and may not be fully viable.

1 envelope of active dry yeast (sold dated) can be used interchangeably with a cake of compressed baker's yeast, but you should set it to soften according to the directions on the package. Compressed yeast isn't often found these days, though you can sometimes buy some from your local bakery shop. It has a shorter shelf life and is active for about 1 month after you buy it. Both kinds of yeast should be refrigerated.

If you have any doubt about how good your yeast is, "proof" it. Dissolve 1 teaspoonful in a little tepid water with a bit of sugar. If it foams lightly in 5 minutes, it's alive.

Brewer's yeast has no leavening power and you can't use it in baking.

Frozen yeast will last as long as most frozen foods.

Remove yeast from the refrigerator about 1 hour before using. It's less active when it's cold.

You can bring any yeast quickly to a light foam by adding ¼ teaspoon of sugar to the water in which you dissolve the yeast. A pinch of ginger also speeds yeast action.

Most yeast doughs refrigerate well for 2 or 3 days. You can make the dough one day and bake it a day or two later. Just be sure to let it come to room temperature again before you handle it. And it should be allowed to rise once, at least, before baking.

413

Sweet raised yeast dough needs less kneading than regular bread dough.

Yeast stored well wrapped in the freezer will stay in good condition for about 6 months.

Too much yeast in yeast dough will make bread grow stale more quickly.

Many bread recipes call for more yeast than is necessary. For every 3 cups of flour, 1 level teaspoon of yeast granules is enough. If you double the amount of flour, add only ½ teaspoon more of yeast.

Don't let yeast dough stand too long during the final rising just before it goes into the oven, otherwise it is likely to fall during baking. The dough should rise until it's doubled in volume, no longer.

YOGURT

See also *Sour Cream.*

Many of the flavored yogurts you buy in stores contain imitation flavoring and coloring. Why not buy plain yogurt and do the flavoring yourself? Add any fruits or berries you like, as well as honey, jam, syrups, etc. Yogurt is good mixed with salad vegetables, too.

You can freeze yogurt and make a delightful dessert. First mix the yogurt with chopped fruit or nuts or both, then pour into a loaf pan and wrap well. Freeze. Serve it sliced with or without a sweet sauce.

Yogurt contains less fat and is more nutritious than sour cream. Substitute it for sour cream in baking as well as in custards, salad dressings, and sauces.

Mix plain yogurt with mayonnaise, other salad dressings or your own oil and vinegar mixture for a zippy salad dressing.

Try using a cup of yogurt in place of a cup of water in a gelatin dessert.

ZUCCHINI

See also *Squash and Pumpkins*.

4 medium zucchini weigh about 1½ pounds and, unpared and thinly sliced, will give you about 5 cups.

1 pound of zucchini will serve 4 people generously.

Don't buy zucchini that are soft or wrinkled. They won't have a good texture or much taste.

Zucchini are done as soon as the skin gives easily when pressed. Don't overcook.

Cut well-scrubbed raw zucchini into almost paper-thin slices to use with other greens in a salad. The best zucchini for this are very young, slender ones.

You can substitute zucchini in practically any recipe calling for cucumbers. It makes marvelous relish, too. Use any cucumber relish recipe.

Notes

Notes

Notes

Notes

Notes